BARRON'S BUSINESS LIBRARY

Writing a Convincing Business Plan

Arthur R. DeThomas, Ph.D.

and William B. Fredenberger, Ph.D.

All inquiries should be addressed to:
Barron's Educational Series, Inc.
250 Wireless Boulevard
Hauppauge, New York 11788

Library of Congress Catalog Card No. 95-7940

International Standard Book No. 0-8120-9091-8

Library of Congress Cataloging-in-Publication Data

DeThomas, Arthur R.
    Writing a convincing business plan / Arthur R. DeThomas,
William B. Fredenberger.
        p.   cm. — (Barron's business library)
    ISBN 0-8120-9091-8
    1. Business planning.   I. Fredenberger, William B.
II. Title.   III. Series.
HD30.28.D477 1995
658.4'012—dc20   95-7940
                                                        CIP

PRINTED IN ITALY
5678   9929   987654321

Contents

Preface

During the many years your authors have worked with and studied small- and medium-sized businesses, we have found that the most troublesome issue for entrepreneurs is finding an answer to the nagging question: What can be done to increase the chances of success for my new business venture or improve the performance of my existing business?

While the business environment has changed in many respects over this time span, the answer to the question has not. In fact, what we have recommended is even more critical to entrepreneurial success today than in the past. What is this time-tested advice? It is simply to:

■ Carefully research the firm's existing or intended industry, market, and competition; identify the factors that do or will account for its success or its failure; and make an informed, educated estimate of the chances for success.

■ Develop a detailed plan for favorably influencing the factors that determine success; for operating the business; and for acquiring and managing the human, physical, and financial resources that are needed to operate it profitably.

In short, what has been suggested is the need to prepare a business plan, or, as it is occasionally referred to, a feasibility study. There will be more discussion of what is meant by "feasibility study" in the pages that follow. It is an important theme of this book and, hopefully, for the business plan that is prepared.

Given the importance we attach to the business plan, the reader may wonder why the planning process and preparation of a formal plan are so important. The answer is simple: Gathering the information and data needed to prepare a complete business plan minimizes the possibility of failure and maximizes the likelihood of success. This is as true for an existing business as for a new venture. Preparing a business plan converts pipe dreams into realities by forcing the entrepreneur to:

■ Think carefully about each phase of the business, the details of its operation, and how the various details and parts must fit together to form a viable, ongoing business entity.

■ Gather the information needed to make an informed estimate of the firm's probability of success and the degree of risk to which it will be exposed.

■ Crystallize his or her thoughts and submit them to paper so they can be evaluated personally and by an informed outsider.

■ Examine the strengths and weaknesses of the firm relative to its industry, its market, its competition, and its customers.

■ Evaluate the feasibility of his or her business concept and identify the specific factors that determine or will determine the firm's success or failure.

■ Think about realistic, attainable goals that can serve as guidelines for making day-to-day operating decisions as well as standards for measuring the firm's progress.

■ Do what business managers are supposed to do: maintain an ongoing process of investigating, gathering and evaluating information, identifying needed resources, setting goals, and preparing a road map for achieving them.

These analyses are important to the effective operation of any business but are especially crucial to the entrepreneur seeking financing. The prevailing attitude among financiers is skepticism. Before the typical financier will consider making a loan to, or an investment in, a business firm, the entrepreneur must demonstrate:

■ A clearly defined business concept.

■ A working knowledge of the major functions of the business: production, marketing, sales, finance, and human resource management.

■ A clear understanding of the industry, market, and competitive environment in which the firm or new venture operates or will operate, and a detailed plan for capturing the opportunities they present.

■ A true picture of the current financial position of the firm or new venture and its expected financial needs.

■ Supporting documentation and convincing arguments for why and how the business will succeed.

A well-researched, carefully prepared business plan conveys this information. It is unmistakable evidence of the entrepreneur's ability to plan his or her business operation. It is also the type of evidence for which the intended reader of the business plan will be carefully searching.

It is equally important that the entrepreneur demonstrate personal knowledge of the contents of the business plan. It is not enough to simply present a business plan and then respond to questions posed by the financier with answers such as: "I have a sales manager and leave all marketing matters in her hands," or "I leave financial details to my accountant." Financiers want assurances that the dollars they may commit to a business will be managed by an informed, competent manager. Demonstrating personal knowledge of the information contained in a first-rate business plan goes a long way toward providing these assurances.

Business Plan Specifics

Not surprisingly, when our approach to maximizing the chances for business success is explained, entrepreneurs usually respond with questions such as the following:

- "Exactly what is a business plan?"
- "Is a business plan hard to prepare, and can someone like me do it?"
- "Exactly what is included in a business plan?"

The answers to these questions are straightforward. First, a business plan is exactly what its name implies. It is a blueprint, prepared by the entrepreneur with or without professional assistance, detailing what the business or business concept is, what is expected for the business, how management intends to get the firm to that point, and, of greatest importance, *the specific reasons why it is expected to succeed.* This last point is crucial whether the business plan is used to attract the interest of a prospective financier or is used internally as the master plan for operating the business.

Providing convincing and verifiable reasons why a business concept or action plan for an existing business is feasible is the ultimate test of how well the business plan has been prepared. A business plan without valid justification and supporting evidence for the entrepreneur's contention of success is nothing more than an exercise in wishful thinking. To be effective, the business plan must detail what is possible for the business, how it will be done, and the reasons it will be successful. In short, our definition of a business plan is *a good feasibility study.*

The response to concerns about preparing a business plan is positive: Preparing a business plan requires time and effort, but the task is certainly not beyond the reach of the typical entrepreneur. It involves performing the same activities that successful managers perform as a standard part of managing and operating a business. Planning is one of the important administrative functions performed by effective business managers.

The answer to the question on the content of a business plan is also straightforward. An effective business plan contains the same fundamental information that is needed to effectively manage an existing business or to evaluate the merits of a new business venture. Included are specifics on the firm's product or service, its industry, the markets and customers it serves, how its product or service is marketed, how operations are conducted, and what resources are required to do so. This is the same information that practicing managers use for planning, developing business strategies, and decision-making.

About This Book

Writing a Convincing Business Plan is a how-to book for practitioners. It is designed and written as a comprehensive tutorial for understanding how business planning is done, what information is needed to do it, where this information is found, and how it is organized and written. As such, the book addresses the needs of both the new entrepreneur and the veteran manager faced with the prospect of preparing a complete business plan or any of its parts.

A number of attractive features combine to make *Writing a Convincing Business Plan* an easy-to-read authoritative guide to the how and why of business plan preparation. Included among these helpful features are:

■ Real-world examples of prepared business plan components.

■ Detailed illustrations of business plan tools and techniques.

■ A comprehensive, annotated bibliography of the major sources of industry, market, and competitive information as well as explanations of how they are used.

■ Guideline questions for each business plan component that help identify the factors that should be gathered to prepare the business plan.

■ A glossary of definitions and explanations of key business terms and concepts.

Before delving into *Writing a Convincing Business Plan*, the reader should note that the sequence in which its chapters appear is neither the order in which business plan information is gathered nor the order in which a business plan is written. The rule of thumb for researching and writing a business plan is to begin with the critical components and end with the easier summary components. In general, this means starting with the industry and market analysis components and ending with the business plan summary. The chapter sequence of the book, however, reflects the order in which a complete business plan would typically be arranged for presentation to an outside reader.

Arthur R. DeThomas
William B. Fredenberger

SUPPORTING DOCUMENTS FOR THE PRESENTATION PACKAGE

Packaging the Business Plan

THE IMPORTANCE OF GOOD PACKAGING

Among its many important uses, a business plan is a calling card. It is the entrepreneur's best opportunity to introduce the business and himself or herself to the intended reader in their most favorable light. While a prospective financier or investor will ultimately make a decision based on the business merits of the plan, appearances are important. An attractively packaged business plan helps promote a favorable first impression. It sends an implied message about the care and diligence used in preparing the plan and managing the business. On the other hand, a carelessly prepared or inadequate presentation package has the opposite effect. It runs the risk of having the entrepreneur and the business plan regarded lightly, or worse, not at all.

After studying the material in this chapter, you will:

■ Understand the importance of having an appealing presentation package.

■ Know which supplements should be included with the presentation package.

■ Know how to prepare the supplements to the business plan.

WHAT SHOULD ACCOMPANY THE BUSINESS PLAN?

When prepared for a reader outside the firm, three important embellishments to the business plan should be included in the presentation package: a cover letter, a title page, and a table of contents. Equally important, the entire package should be enclosed in a conservatively attractive folder or binder. If the package is large, it may be necessary to have the binding done commercially. These additions, while seemingly trivial, are the enhancements that give the presentation package a professional appearance.

The Cover Letter

A cover letter, or letter of transmittal, is the vehicle that introduces the entrepreneur and the business plan to the intended reader. As such, it should identify the entrepreneur, the reason the business plan is being presented, and the documents included in the presentation package. Equally important, the letter should be brief, to the point, and written in clear, concise language. A busy financier or investor should not have to read several pages of text to determine the nature and purpose of the communication. A sample cover letter appears below as Figure 1-1. It should be noted that this document:

- Identifies the entrepreneur and the firm.
- Is brief and to the point.
- Immediately identifies the nature and purpose of the presentation package.
- Identifies enclosures and their purpose.
- Conveys a positive but not presumptuous introductory message.

The Title Page

The title page is both a formal mantle for the documents that follow and a convenient location for descriptive information. It should identify:

- The content of the package, which is normally the business plan.
- The name, address, and telephone number of the firm.
- The name(s) and position(s), for example, president or chairman of the board, of the principal(s) in the business.
- The contact person in the firm, if he or she is different from the listed owner(s).
- The current date.

If the business plan contains confidential or sensitive information, such as the description of a new product or the explanation of a strategic advantage, the chances of this information remaining private are improved if a "confidentiality statement" is included on the title page. One example of a confidentiality statement is shown below on the sample title page of The Ideal Growth Company business plan (see Figure 1-2).

There is no one correct format for a title page. The rule of thumb is to arrange the information in an appealing yet conservative format. One such arrangement is illustrated on The Ideal Growth Company title page.

Table of Contents

The table of contents should identify the documents included in the presentation package and the pages on which they first appear. This addition to the package not only enhances its appearance but also eliminates the reader's need to search through the business plan to find specific topics. The location of the table of contents should be immediately after the title page of the business plan.

FIGURE 1-1 *Sample Cover Letter*

[*Date*]

Jeremy M. Davis
Commercial Loan Officer
Unionville State Bank
Lawrence, GA 30011

Dear Mr. Davis:

As agreed during our meeting on June 5, I am providing the enclosed business plan to support the $100,000 loan request for my firm, The Ideal Growth Company. Details of the request are contained in the loan proposal accompanying this plan. As indicated in the proposal, the $100,000 loan would be divided into a $30,000 line of credit to be repaid in ten months and a $70,000 term loan repayable in quarterly installments over three years.

The key points discussed in the abbreviated business plan are the firm's anticipated market conditions, the sales forecast, and an operating and financial plan for the next three years. It represents the concerted effort of my management team and the confidence we share in the firm's future.

Thank you for your consideration. I eagerly await your reply and look forward to the prospect of a mutually successful, long-term relationship with your bank.

Sincerely,

Elizabeth George, President
The Ideal Growth Company
500 Industrial Park Rd.
Unionville, GA 30012

Enclosures (2)

FIGURE 1-2 *Sample Title Page*

The Business Plan
of
The Ideal Growth Company
500 Industrial Park Rd.
Unionville, GA 30012
(492) 247-1000

Presented By:
Elizabeth George, President
[*Date*]

The content of this report is confidential and is the sole property of The Ideal Growth Company. Its use is strictly limited to those readers authorized by the Company. Any reproduction or divulgence of the content of this report without the written consent of the Company is prohibited.

FIGURE 1-3 *Example Table of Contents*

Again, there is no one correct arrangement for a table of contents. A commonly used format displays the content items at the left margin and corresponding page numbers at the right margin. The sample table of contents that appears below uses this format (see Figure 1-3).

TIPS FOR PREPARING AND PACKAGING THE BUSINESS PLAN

■ **Appearance is important.** Since the reader forms first impressions about the entrepreneur, his or her business habits, and the business or business concept from the presentation package, it is important that the package have an attractive, professional appearance. To ensure this result, the following minimum guidelines should be observed:

1. The package should be neatly prepared.
2. The pages should be clean and free of marks from type-overs or erasures.
3. The content should be free of spelling and grammatical errors.
4. The content should be typed or, preferably, prepared with a PC and word processing or desktop publishing program.
5. The material should either be printed using a quality printer or should be prepared by a commercial printer.

■ **Write a good business plan.** While appearance is important, the business plan is the critical component of the package. In order to stimulate interest, it must effectively address the intended reader's concerns. In general, this means the business plan should be written as a good feasibility study. Each component of the plan should emphasize *what* is feasible, the reasons *why* the business or business concept is or will be successful, and *how* success will be achieved.

■ **Content will vary.** Although this book covers every aspect of a business plan, not every business plan will necessarily contain this amount of detail. The content of a particular business plan should be governed by its intended use and the targeted reader. For example, if the plan were to be used only as a guide to internal management, its content would typically focus on a general plan of action rather than descriptive detail. What's more, such components as the cover letter, financing proposal, executive summary, and business description would not be included. On the other hand, if the plan were written for presentation to a venture capitalist, it would have to contain descriptive detail to be effective.

■ **Use business language.** The business plan and accompanying documents should be written in conservative business language. Business and financial terms should be used wherever possible, and superlatives or exaggerated claims should be avoided. Any reader experienced in business or finance will recoginize hyperbole for what it is, and its presence will detract from the merits of the business plan.

■ **Clearly identify supporting information.** If the intended reader is expected to take the business plan seriously, its assumptions, forecasts, and projections *must* be clearly stated and supported with convincing rationale and creditable evidence. Doing so provides the "why it will succeed" explanations that are critical to writing the business plan as a good feasibility study. Financiers, investors, and other experienced businesspeople are accustomed to dealing with facts and informed judgments, and to basing decisions on the merits of underlying assumptions, justifications, and supporting evidence. If this information is missing, the reader will regard the business plan as nothing more than wishful thinking.

■ **Highlight key numerical values.** Discussions involving numerical values such as cost figures, sales quantities, and cash-flow projections can often be enhanced through the use of tables and graphs. These tools highlight key points that may be overlooked or unappreciated if confined to text material. Tables and graphs should, however, be used judiciously. A financier or other experienced businessperson reading the business plan will focus on finding answers to the implicit questions of *what*, *why*, and *how*. Overuse of tables and graphs may suggest that the plan lacks substance and the entrepreneur is attempting to disguise this weakness with meaningless glitz.

■ **Know the reader.** There is an old adage for writers and public speakers that states: To be effective, write or speak to the level of your audience. This advice applies to the preparation of a business plan as well. If the business plan is to attract and hold the reader's interest, it must be written with the reader's concerns in mind. To do so effectively, it is necessary to understand the reader's business and the nature of his or her potential financial involvement with the firm. Or, put another way, it is important not only that the entrepreneur understand what constitutes a good business plan, but that he or she also understand what the intended reader thinks constitutes a good plan. For example, the emphasis in a business plan that is used to support a loan request from a commercial bank should be different from what is stressed in a venture-capital proposal. When written as part of a loan request, the business plan should highlight the firm's ability to generate the cash flow necessary to repay the loan and the availability of suitable collateral. In the case of a venture-capital proposal, emphasis should be on such considerations as the existence of a market opportunity that promises heavy sales volume and large profit potential and on a timetable for the liquidation of the venture capitalist's interest in the business.

━ **Pretest the business plan.** Before the final version of the plan is prepared, the draft should be proofread by capable individuals. The first reader should be proficient in English and should check the plan for grammatical flaws. The second should be capable of rendering an informed judgment on the business merits of the plan.

CHAPTER PERSPECTIVE

Since opinions are often formed on first impressions, it is important that the business plan be well prepared and attractively packaged. Three important supplements add to the professional appearance of the presentation package: the cover letter, title page, and table of contents. The business plan and supplements should be intelligently written using appropriate business language, neat and free from typographical errors and erasure marks, and enclosed in a conservative but attractive binder.

The Executive Summary

WHAT IS AN EXECUTIVE SUMMARY?

An executive summary is a thumbnail sketch of the business or proposed venture. The primary purposes of this supporting document are to give the intended reader advance information about the financing proposal and business plan that follow and to supply the information the reader needs to quickly determine whether continued reading is warranted.

The executive summary is typically the first document in the presentation package that an experienced reader will seek. Whether he or she continues reading beyond this critical juncture depends on both the content and the quality of the writing. If the summary does not spark the reader's interest, it may be the only document that is read.

After studying the material in this chapter, you will:

- Understand the role of the executive summary.
- Know what information to include in the executive summary.
- Understand the two formats used to prepare an executive summary.
- Know when to include an executive summary.

INFORMATION NEEDED TO PREPARE THE EXECUTIVE SUMMARY

The executive summary is a synopsis of the key issues in the business plan that are of primary interest to the intended reader. Normally, these include a concise description of the following:

- The firm's basic business.
- How business is or will be conducted.
- The intended market for the firm's products or services and the sales potential of this market.
- How and why the firm can penetrate this market.
- The competitive or marketing advantage the firm has over its competition.
- The resources and amount of financing needed to implement the business plan.

WHEN TO INCLUDE AN EXECUTIVE SUMMARY IN THE PACKAGE

An executive summary should be included in the presentation package when a complete or essentially complete business plan is presented to the intended reader. Since documents such as legal briefs, overviews, abstracts, or summaries typically accompany lengthy documents, the intended reader will expect an executive summary to be included in the presentation package. For example, a busy venture capitalist normally looks to the summary and then the business description (discussed in Chapter 4) to decide whether the business concept has merit and whether it is consistent with his or her investment interests.

If only selected portions of the business plan will be presented to an outside reader, an executive summary would normally not be included in the package. For example, if the entrepreneur is making a routine loan request from a banker familiar with the business, the presentation package may consist of only a cover letter, a detailed loan proposal, and update information from the firm's internal marketing and financial plans. For situations such as this, there is no need to summarize an already limited package.

CHOOSING THE APPROPRIATE FORMAT

The summary should be written using either of two styles: topical or narrative. The most straightforward and least difficult to prepare is the *topical format*. In this format, the executive summary consists of the essential points or conclusions distilled from the most important topical components of the business plan. For example, the operating plan (see Chapter 8) describes how management intends to conduct business and the resources needed to do so. If the firm's operations are crucial to the success of the business, a synopsis should be included in the executive summary. It should be written as answers to the implied questions of *how* operations are conducted and *why* this method of operation contributes to the success of the firm. The contribution can result from any of a number of factors, such as greater cost efficiency, better technology, superior product quality, or most attractive store location.

As noted above, the alternative to the topical format is the *narrative format*. The narrative style, as illustrated in Figure 2-1 at the end of this chapter, uses descriptive prose to tell a story about the business or business concept. This approach is most effective when used to describe a start-up firm, a planned venture, or an existing business that has developed a unique competitive advantage such as revolutionary cost-saving technology or an exciting new product or service. If done well, the narrative style conveys the entrepreneur's message more effectively and offers a better chance of stimulating the reader's interest than its topical counterpart. The key to success with this narrative style is to write provocative prose and yet avoid hyperbole or misrepresentation.

TIPS FOR PREPARING AN EXECUTIVE SUMMARY

■ **Write it last.** Whether the topical or narrative format is used, the summary should be prepared after the entire business plan has been written. It is difficult, if not impossible, to identify and effectively summarize key points about the business and its planned operation until these issues have been completely fleshed out.

■ **Keep the main theme in mind.** It cannot be overemphasized that a professional reader of the business plan will be most concerned with *why* and *how* the business or business concept is expected to succeed, and *what* factors will account for this success. Since the summary is normally read first, a clear and convincing case for the *why* and *how* of success must be made in this document.

■ **More risk means more proof.** To a business or financial professional, a new business or an untried business concept represents more risk than an established firm or a proven method of doing business. This fact of business life makes the intended reader an unyielding skeptic about claims for success. Consequently, the summary written for a new business or an untried business concept must make a stronger case for commercial and economic success than one written for an existing business. The supporting documentation must be carefully detailed in the body of the business plan and more convincingly articulated in the summary.

■ **Avoid hype.** Although the executive summary must be convincing, the temptation to make exaggerated claims or to misrepresent facts must be avoided. A sophisticated reader will immediately recognize hype for what it is and will sooner or later disprove misrepresented facts. When either occurs, the entrepreneur and the business plan lose credibility along with the chance to stimulate the reader's interest.

■ **Topical versus narrative summaries.** As a general rule, it is easier to write an acceptable topical summary than a stimulating narrative summary. The topical summary simply condenses key points or conclusions contained in the business plan. A tantalizing narrative summary, however, requires creativity and a higher level of writing ability.

■ **Length is important.** Regardless of the format used, the executive plan summary must clearly convey the entrepreneur's message but, at the same time, be brief and to the point. Although there is no hard-and-fast rule governing length, a summary is customarily no longer than two pages and may be as short as one page.

■ **Know the target audience.** The executive summary should be written with the intended reader in mind. This is accomplished by having a prior understanding of the reader's particular business or profession and the standards that govern it. As discussed in Chapter 11, this includes considerations such as the type of financing offered and the nature and degree of risk the reader is willing to assume. Without this understanding, it is virtually impossible to tailor the writing to the reader's interests.

A SAMPLE EXECUTIVE SUMMARY

Figure 2-1, a sample executive summary for the Real McCoy Antique Shop, uses the narrative style to tell a brief story about the firm's successful past and the owner's plans for introducing a business concept unique to the retail antique industry. In writing the summary, the McCoys were able to blend into the narrative *how* and *why* success for the new business concept can be expected. For example, it is made clear that:

■ The owners' management and marketing skills are a major reason for the success of the business.

■ Expectations for future success are based on sound reasoning, including the success of the existing business, the entrepreneurial skills of its owners, indicated evidence of continued growth in the retail antique industry and local economy, a unique marketing concept that shows evidence of business potential, and a prime location for the business.

■ Revenues from the signed tenant leases are sufficient to exceed the breakeven point.

■ The entrepreneurs are openly enthusiastic and have made a sizable commitment of equity funds in support of the venture.

CHAPTER PERSPECTIVE

It is common practice to summarize the key issues from the business plan in a separate document known as the executive summary. The summary is a convenience the intended reader expects to find in the presentation package. It can be written in either a topical or narrative style. Regardless of which format is chosen, it is important that the summary pique the reader's interest by clearly articulating why the plan is feasible and how it will lead to the success of the firm.

FIGURE 2-1 *Sample Executive Summary for The Real McCoy Antique Shop*

The Real McCoy Antique Shop was established by Ian and Meggin McCoy in 1983 and has been in operation since that time. The success of the Shop, as reflected by its average annual sales and profit growth rate of 15%, is attributed to the management and marketing skills of its owners, the growth in the retail antique industry, the increased size of the Shop's target customer group, and the economic growth in the six-county area the shop serves. This success, coupled with the prospects for continued growth in both the antique industry and local economy, suggests that our local market is ripe for a new concept in the retail marketing of antiques: an antique mall housing the Real McCoy Antique Shop and 11 other retail antique shop tenants.

The mall will be located on Exit 3 of Interstate 75 on the corner opposite the highly successful outlet-store mall. This centralized location, along with the mall's unique, single-showroom marketing concept, offers shoppers convenience, variety, and shopping opportunities that cannot be gained elsewhere. The Exit 3 location also allows the tenant merchants to capture the marketing benefits of heavy auto-traffic flow during the entire year, easy off-road access, a well-known outlet-store mall with over 40 retail establishments, a variety of eating and sleeping accommodations, and heavy pedestrian traffic. The retail customer mix already attracted to this location by the outlet-store mall includes residents of approximately six adjoining counties; southbound Florida vacationers from all areas of the Southeast and the eastern seaboard, including Canada; and northbound Floridians.

Revenues from the mall will be derived from a combination of the Real McCoy Shop sales and rental fees paid by tenant retail shops. There has been considerable interest in the mall concept shown by antique shops in our local, six-county market area. To date, we have signed lease agreements, contingent upon financing for the venture, with six retail tenants. These advance signings place the mall in the enviable position of being profitable from opening day. As shown in the Financial Plan component of the enclosed Business Plan, cash-flow projections indicate that slightly over five tenants, or a remarkably low 45% occupancy rate, are needed to break even. Based on the six signed leases, the cash-flow projections indicate an

FIGURE 2-1 *(continued)*

estimated free-cash-flow figure of approximately $5,000 per month. Each new tenant beyond the original six leases is expected to increase monthly free cash flow by $6,000. If the more normal 80% tenant occupancy rate is maintained, the combined Real McCoy Shop profits and net profits from tenant leases after estimated debt costs will generate an estimated annual return on investment of 12%. When the loan is repaid, the estimated annual return on investment (ROI) at the 80% occupancy rate increases to 20%.

As discussed in our Loan Proposal and Financial Plan, an estimated $2,750,000 of total financing is needed to buy the land, construct the mall, and maintain working capital. Toward this amount, we have invested $100,000 to obtain the purchase option on the land, and we are prepared to invest an additional $175,000 of equity capital toward the project. We propose that the remaining $2,475,000 of required financing be in the form of debt capital. A suggested maturity and repayment schedule for the proposed debt financing are detailed in the Loan Proposal and Financial Plan.

The Financing Proposal

WHAT IS A FINANCING PROPOSAL?

A financing proposal, like its counterpart the executive summary, is a supporting document for the business plan and an integral part of most presentation packages. As its name implies, the proposal is a formal request for financial backing. It is an effective summary of the key issues in the financial plan.

The financing proposal makes two important contributions toward an effective presentation package. First, if the business plan is prepared to support a financing request, the financier expects a financing proposal to be included in the presentation package. It provides him or her with the information needed to determine whether the proposed financing request is of interest. Failure to provide a busy financier with the summary information found in the financing proposal may be ample reason for an out-of-hand rejection of the business plan.

Second, a well-prepared financing proposal is unmistakable evidence of the entrepreneur's financial savvy and his or her ability to do the type of investigation and planning that is characteristic of effective managers. This is often the inducement needed for the financier to read the complete business plan.

After studying the material in this chapter, you will:

■ Understand the role of a financing proposal.
■ Know what information is needed to prepare a financing proposal.
■ Know the steps to preparing a financing proposal.

INFORMATION NEEDED TO PREPARE THE FINANCING PROPOSAL

Since the financing proposal is essentially a summary of the financial plan, the information needed to prepare it comes directly from that document and other business plan components. For example,

■ An analysis of the financing required to support working-capital needs such as inventory or the purchase of fixed assets such as equipment or buildings should be contained in the financial plan.

■ A description and justification of the land and buildings needed to support expansion plans should be contained in the operating plan.
■ An explanation of the amount of financing needed to implement management's promotion and advertising strategy should be contained in the marketing plan.

As illustrated in the sample loan proposal at the end of this chapter (see Figure 3-1), when the discussion involves points summarized from other components of the business plan, it is advisable to reference those components and the pages on which the information appears. These cites afford the reader an opportunity to quickly locate desired background information.

WHEN TO INCLUDE THE FINANCING PROPOSAL WITH THE PACKAGE

As a general rule, a financing proposal should be included in the presentation package whenever the business plan has been prepared to support a financing request. In some cases, an expanded financing proposal *may* serve as a substitute for a complete financial plan. This is true when the necessary financial information can be included in the proposal without making it inordinately large, or when a detailed financial plan is unnecessary. For example, when working-capital financing is sought from a a banker familiar with the firm and its management, only the proposal, a cash-flow projection (cash budget), and the most recent set of financial statements are usually needed.

STEPS TO PREPARING THE FINANCING PROPOSAL

As is true of each component of the business plan, the key to preparing the financing proposal is to first divide the task into a series of small, manageable steps, and then complete each step before undertaking the next. The seven steps identified and discussed below offer a logical sequence for gathering information from the financial plan and preparing the proposal. However, because financing needs differ for different businesses, each step need not be included in every proposal. Some steps may be omitted because they are inappropriate, some may be combined under one title for clarity or convenience, and some may have titles or headings different from what is suggested in here to better fit the situation.

1. **Identify the amount needed.** The exact dollar amount of the financing requested should be clearly indicated and, as discussed below, tied directly to the intended use(s) of the funds. The temptation to state a broad dollar range rather than a specific amount should be resisted. Expressing financial needs as a range implies the absence of careful investigation and planning.

2. **Explain how the financing will be used.** A prospective

financier is as concerned about the intended use(s) of the financing as he or she is about the amount requested. Before a financial commitment is made, the financier must be satisfied that the funds will be used wisely and that the expected returns for both parties are commensurate with the level of risk involved. These considerations should be explicitly addressed in the proposal.

For example, if financing is needed to support seasonal upswings in normal operations, commonly referred to as working-capital needs, each component of working capital to be financed should be identified. Or, if financing is needed to purchase fixed (plant) assets, a detailed description of the asset(s) should be provided. In each case, it is important to explain *how* and *why* the planned uses for the funds will contribute to the success of the business.

3. **Specify the type of financing needed.** The proposal should stipulate whether borrowed funds (debt) or owner's invested capital (equity) are needed. As explained in greater detail in Chapter 10, debt financing is money borrowed under a contractual agreement. This contract legally obligates the borrower for repayment of interest and principal and for compliance with all other provisions stipulated in the agreement. Failure to meet debt obligations constitutes a breach of contract, and possible resulting litigation could mean bankruptcy for the firm. On the other hand, equity financing is owner's capital. Raising ownership funds avoids the burden of mandatory debt payments but forces the entrepreneur to relinquish some portion of his or her interest in the business.

4. **Specify the maturity of the financing needed.** The financing proposal should also specify whether short-term, intermediate-term, or long-term financing is needed. A prospective financier will be concerned that the intended uses of funds will be properly matched with an appropriate maturity period for the financing. In general, short-term debt financing is used to meet temporary or seasonal working-capital needs. This financing should be repaid within the firm's normal working-capital cycle as inventory and customer accounts (accounts receivable) are converted to cash.

Intermediate-term financing typically takes the form of an installment loan with periodic payments that amortize interest and principal over a maturity of two to ten years. This financing is usually used to acquire assets with a life span approximately equivalent to the maturity of the loan. Fixed assets such as vehicles, machinery, or electronic data processing equipment are common purchases made with intermediate-term credit.

Long-term financing represents the more permanent component of the firm's financial structure. In general, financiers expect equity financing to constitute the largest percentage of these dollars. A solid equity base is the cushion that protects the financial commitment of creditors and increases the firm's likelihood of surviving a business downturn. Lenders often use the size and strength of the firm's equity base as an indicator of the maximum amount of debt financing the firm should carry. For example, a long-established rule of thumb among bankers is the 50%-50% financial structure. According to this rough guideline, the amount of debt financing used should not exceed 50% of the firm's total financing.

5. **Suggest a payment schedule.** The proposal should *suggest* a timetable of when and in what amounts the financier will be repaid or remunerated. In this way, the entrepreneur sends a clear message that he or she understands the financier's major concerns. A financier wants assurances that the entrepreneur recognizes the importance of:

- The legal and/or moral repayment obligation associated with the financing received.
- Generating cash flows sufficient to support operating plans and to meet financial obligations.
- A repayment or remuneration plan that is consistent with the needs of the financier and the cash-flow pattern of the firm.
- Sound financial management principles to the successful operation of the firm.

Unless the financing proposal and financial plan provide these assurances, financing will not be forthcoming.

If debt financing is sought, a *proposed* repayment schedule covering interest and principle should be offered. If equity financing is needed, a schedule of the amount and timing of expected cash flows, profits, and owner's withdrawals (dividends if the firm is incorporated) should be provided.

In the case of venture-capital financing, the proposal should also identify dates or milestone events that indicate the firm's progress toward a specified liquidation date of the venture capitalist's interests in the business. Contrary to common belief, the typical venture capitalist is not interested in owning or operating the business. Most venture capitalists are high-risk investors who provide financing by buying an ownership interest in the business. They expect to earn a return on their equity investment that adequately compensates for the degree of risk assumed, and to liquidate this investment at some definite date through a public offering of the firm's stock or a planned buyout agreement.

6. **Identify available collateral.** If debt financing is sought, the proposal should contain a detailed description of the type and market value of assets that can be pledged as collateral, if required, to secure the

loan. The existence of collateral reduces the risk of loss for the lender in the event the borrower is unable to make the required loan payments.

For an established, profitable firm with a proven credit record, the pledge of collateral may not be a prerequisite to obtaining a loan. On the other hand, if the firm is new or has unproven or questionable credit standing, pledging collateral may be the only means of obtaining debt financing. This is true even when the loan is sound and the prospects for repayment are strong. The reverse, however, is not true. Since the return on a loan is limited to the interest received, a creditor must limit default-risk exposure. Rarely, if ever, will a creditor accept collateral as a substitute for poor repayment prospects. Bankers frequently use an old banking adage to describe this situation: "Good collateral does not make a bad loan good."

7. **Indicate the owners' investment.** If the firm is a new venture, or if additional equity financing is sought for an existing firm, the financing proposal should also provide a detailed description of the amount invested by each existing owner and the percentage of total equity financing each investment represents. If the firm is incorporated, the proposal should indicate the number of shares of common stock held by each major stockholder and the percentage of the total number of shares outstanding that each holding represents.

TIPS FOR PREPARING THE FINANCING PROPOSAL

━━ **Write the proposal last.** Although the financing proposal should be located immediately after the executive summary in the presentation package, it should be one of the last components written. The information needed to write the proposal comes from the financial plan and possibly other relevant business plan components. These documents must, therefore, be completed before an effective summary can be written.

━━ **Do not rewrite the financial plan.** While the financing proposal identifies the key elements of the financing request, it should be written as a supporting *summary* document. A lengthy rehash of the financial plan should be avoided. As a general rule, the proposal should not exceed approximately two pages in length.

━━ **Appreciate the importance of this component.** Since financing is critical to the question of feasibility, the information provided in the proposal will be carefully evaluated by the prospective financier. It is important, therefore, that this writing address the implicit questions of *how* and *why* the financing will contribute to the success of the venture. One aid to accomplishing this end is writing the proposal from the financier's perspective. To do so, the proposal must convince the financier that the financing provided will both produce the cash flows necessary to recapture the financier's investment and generate a rate of return that fairly compensates both parties for the risk assumed.

▬ **Know the intended reader.** As is true of the business plan, a good financing proposal is one the intended financier thinks is good. In order to write such a proposal, the entrepreneur must understand the financier's business and his or her perspective on risk and return. Financial institutions are not homogenous. They differ in the type of financing offered and in the amount of risk that can be assumed. It is important, therefore, to make sure that the financing request fits the parameters governing the intended financier's business. For example, requesting a short-term working-capital loan from a venture capitalist would be as foolish as approaching a bank for a long-term equity investment. An overview of financial institutions and sources of financing is provided in Chapter 11.

▬ **Heed basic financial principles.** As explained in the "Tips For Preparing A Financial Plan" section of Chapter 10, the financing proposal should leave no doubt in the reader's mind that the entrepreneur understands basic financial management principles. Particular attention should be given to such points as the prudent use of debt financing, having an adequate equity base, and using cash-flow projections to support the financing request.

SAMPLE LOAN PROPOSAL

Figure 3-1 is a financing proposal for the hypothetical firm used in Chapter 1, The Ideal Growth Company. In this case, the proposal is identified as a loan proposal rather than a financing proposal because Ms. George is seeking only conventional debt financing.

FIGURE 3-1 *A Loan Proposal For The Ideal Growth Company*

Amount and Type of Financing Needed

Our loan request, in the amount of $100,000, is structured as follows:

1. A Line Of Credit. A $30,000 line of credit is needed to support the increase in seasonal working capital (see the Financial Plan, pp. 24–26) that will accompany the anticipated 10% growth in sales and profits over the next 12 months (see the Marketing Plan, pp. 14–16).

2. Three-Year Term Loan. A three-year installment loan in the amount of $70,000 is needed to purchase additional delivery equipment and the maintenance contracts on this equipment.

Use of Proposed Financing

The line of credit will be used to finance the estimated $15,000 increase in accounts receivable, the $12,000 increase in inventory, and the additional operating-cash needs of $3,000 that will accompany the anticipated sales growth next year.

The equipment to be purchased with the term loan is needed to accommodate the increase in customer deliveries that will result from the anticipated 10% growth rate in sales and profits for each of the next three years. The equipment to be purchased at the indicated prices includes:

1. A new flatbed truck purchased from Union Motors, Inc., at a delivered price of $48,000.
2. Delivery equipment, in the form of a large-capacity hydraulic hoist and a self-powered conveyer belt system, purchased from Griner Equipment at a price of $22,000.

Complete sets of manufacturer's specifications for the truck and the delivery equipment, along with a copy of the maintenance plan for each, are contained in the Appendix to the Business Plan (not shown).

Proposed Repayment Schedule

As shown by our cash budget (see the Financial Plan, p. 21), Cash Flow from Operations will be more than sufficient to repay the $30,000 line of credit within the required 10-month period.

The cash budget also clearly indicates the seasonal nature of the firm's cash flows. The recurring quarterly pattern suggests that quarterly payments on the three-year term loan are in the best interest of both the Bank and Ideal.

Available Collateral

The following assets are available to collateralize the $100,000 of proposed debt financing.

1. All accounts receivable and inventory are available for collateral on the $30,000 line of credit.
2. The new truck and delivery equipment to be purchased with the term loan are available for collateral.
3. A personal guarantee of both notes by Ideal's president, Elizabeth George.

CHAPTER PERSPECTIVE

A financing proposal is a supporting document included in the presentation package whenever the business plan has been prepared to justify a financing request. It should be written as a concise summary of the amount of financing needed and of other key points discussed in the financial plan. In some cases, the financing proposal *may* serve as a substitute for the financial plan. The proposal should summarize the amount, type, and maturity of the required financing; describe the intended uses of the funds received; suggest a repayment or remunerations schedule; identify the proportion of owner's funds invested in the business when equity capital is sought; and identify available collateral when debt financing is sought.

The Business Description

CHAPTER

4

WHAT IS A BUSINESS DESCRIPTION?

As its name suggests, this component of the business plan describes
the basic nature and purpose of the business. A well-written business
description explains who and what the business is, what it does, how
it is done, who gets it done, where it has been, and where it is
expected to go in the future. By so doing, the business description
anticipates and provides answers to questions that are initially of foremost concern to the intended reader. These are:

- What is the exact business of the firm or venture?
- What product or service does it sell?
- Where is the market for this product or service?
- To what target market (specific customer group) will the product
or service appeal?
- What important events have brought the firm to the current stage
of its life cycle?
- How is the business operated?
- Who will manage and lead the business?
- What is the firm's past and/or current financial position?
- Why will it be successful?

A business description that effectively answers these questions
meets two important goals. First, it serves as a gauge by which the
entrepreneur measures his or her understanding of the business and
the factors that lead to its success or cause its failure. An inability to
formulate clear, convincing answers to key questions about the firm is
strong evidence that the entrepreneur does not fully understand the
business and the factors that affect it. This happens when an entrepreneur becomes so involved with the day-to-day operations of an existing business that he or she loses an overall perspective; or it occurs
when the entrepreneur fails to thoroughly research the new venture.

An effective business description also meets the expectations of
the intended reader. A busy professional usually does not have the
time or inclination to read an entire business plan to determine

whether there is sufficient interest to warrant further consideration. He or she expects the business description to provide the information needed to make this judgement. If this information is missing, the entrepreneur runs the risk of not having the business plan read.

After studying the material in this chapter, you will:
- Understand the role of the business description.
- Know what information is needed to prepare the business description.
- Know the steps to preparing the business description.
- Understand the business life-cycle concept.
- Become familiar with the Standard Industrial Classification (SIC) coding system.

INFORMATION NEEDED TO PREPARE THE BUSINESS DESCRIPTION

The business description should be the easiest component of the business plan to prepare. Since, as suggested in the "Tips" section of this chapter, the business description should be the last component of the business plan that the entrepreneur prepares, its content is drawn directly from existing material. For example, the summary description of the firm's market and target customer group or its financial profile uses information taken from the market analysis and financial plan components of the business plan.

WHEN TO USE A BUSINESS DESCRIPTION

A business description is normally included with the presentation package when a complete, or essentially complete, business plan is prepared. In some cases, an expanded business description *may* serve as a substitute for a complete business plan. This is true if the description contains sufficient information to adequately answer the essential question of feasibility, and if:
- The plan is written for a business that is small and uses a conventional method of operation.
- The plan is written for a business whose industry, market, and target market are already familiar to the reader.
- The amount of information needed to adequately expand the description does not make it inordinately large.

STEPS TO PREPARING THE BUSINESS DESCRIPTION

The seven steps identified and discussed below offer a logical sequence for gathering information and preparing the business description. As suggested in the last chapter, the recommended approach is to treat each section as a separate task, and then to complete it before moving to the next. As an additional aid to preparation, guideline questions are included where appropriate to indicate the type of information that should be gathered. Also, a sample business description for a hypothetical retailer is included at the end of this chapter (see Figure 4-1).

1. **Identify the firm and location.** The first section of the business description normally consists of the information needed by the reader to identify the firm and the appropriate contact person. This includes:

- The business name of the firm.
- The legal name of the firm if it is different from the business name.
- The address, or addresses if there are multiple locations, of the firm.
- The person to contact and his or her office or personal telephone and fax numbers.

Identifying information, especially that of the contact person, is essential if the entrepreneur is unknown to the intended reader, or if the business plan is not delivered by the entrepreneur. This would be the case, for example, if presentation packages were mailed to a number of prospective financiers.

2. **Trace the firm's history.** If the business description is written for an existing firm, this section should contain a thumbnail sketch of the significant events, episodes, or major milestones through which the firm has passed. This historical perspective should indicate *why* the firm has been successful to this point or the major obstacles that management has overcome. Significant events or milestones might include:

- The firm's date of origin and the founder(s) name(s).
- The firm's legal ownership form and the date established.
- A profile of the major stages of the life cycle through which the firm has passed.
- The major episodes in the firm's financial history.
- A brief description of significant changes the business has undergone.
- A brief description of a major crisis the firm has encountered and the strategy management used to successfully overcome the problem.

If the description is written for a new venture, this section should explain the stages of development through which the firm has passed, what has been accomplished to date, and what remains to be accomplished before the business is operational.

3. **Identify the business mission statement.** This section should explain the firm's primary purpose or reason for existence, the

direction the entrepreneur expects to take the firm, and what he or she expects the firm to accomplish. The expected accomplishments are normally expressed as broad, strategic goals. For example, strategic marketing goals may be set in terms of sales growth or share of the market, and strategic financial goals may be expressed as profit growth or cost-reduction targets.

The following guideline questions are designed to help the entrepreneur focus on the issues that should be considered in formulating the firm's mission statement.

- What broad expression defines the primary business of the firm? For example, if Hallmark limited its business solely to greeting cards, its stores would carry only a very limited line of merchandise. Rather, the stated business of this company is "social expression," which suggests that a wide range of products can be included in its product line.
- What is the basic purpose of the business? For example, Kmart Corporation identifies itself as a general merchandise retailer that profitably distributes a wide range of merchandise through a chain of discount department stores.
- Where is the firm expected to be next year, three years from now, and five years from now as measured by growth indicators such as profits, assets, sales, share of the market, etc.?
- What basic business strategy will be used to move the firm toward these targets?
- What are the firm's goals in regard to its owner(s), customers, employees, suppliers, and the general public?

The mission statement should *not* exclude the profit motive. Earning a compensatory return for the firm's owners is the primary reason for starting a business and a necessary condition for staying in business. Failure to express this objective in the mission statement would cause the intended reader to wonder whether the entrepreneur understands how the capitalistic system functions. On the other hand, mission statements that border on the ridiculous should be avoided. For example, the reason for starting a restaurant should not be expressed as a fondness for cooking. Rather, the reason should be tied to the profit motive with a statement such as "a potentially profitable market niche that is not being filled."

4. **Define the firm's industry and market description.** This section should contain a synopsis of the firm's industry, the geographical location of its market(s), and the target market to which it appeals. These external factors are important determinants of the firm's commercial success or failure. The term *industry* refers to the group of businesses that produce or supply related products or

services. *Market location* is the geographic trade area that the firm serves, and *target market* is the distinct segment or group of customers the firm is attempting to reach.

The summary of the firm's industry should consist of information such as the following:

- The Standard Industrial Classification System (as explained later in this chapter) number and name.
- The primary product or service provided by the industry.
- The major firms in the industry.
- The industry's major competitors.
- The current stage of the industry's life cycle.
- The outlook for sales and revenue growth.

Often, the most effective approach to summarizing the firm's market and target market focuses on geographic, demographic, and psychographic characteristics.

- *Geographic* refers to the area, region, country, or continent in which the firm's target market is located. The term is also used to describe the climate conditions that are important to sales of the firm's product or service. For example, the moderate to semi-tropical climate of the sunbelt states.
- *Demographic* means the specific features that profile either a geographic market area or target customer group. For example, geographic markets are often described using characteristics such as the Standard Metropolitian Statistical Area designation (see Chapter 6), population, number of households, or number of people in a given age group. Likewise, a target market may be distinguished from other customer groups by such demographic characteristics as occupation, income level, race, or sex.
- *Psychographic* refers to the psychological makeup of the target market and includes such considerations as needs, motives for buying, lifestyle, tastes, values, beliefs, and interests.

It is important that the industry and market summary address the issue of commercial feasibility. This issue will be the intended reader's first major concern. If the firm's target market cannot produce a satisfactory volume of sales, then the firm cannot succeed, and nothing else in the business plan matters.

The following questions should serve as helpful guidelines for preparing the industry and market section. Complete discussions of industry analysis, market analysis and sales forecasting, and the marketing plan are provided in Chapters 5, 6, and 7 respectively.

- Is the firm's industry growing or declining relative to competing industries or to broad economic indicators such as gross domestic product (GDP)?

- What strategic opportunity is available in this industry?
- How does the firm's product or service differ from that of competitors?
- Where is the firm's market, and who constitutes its target market?
- What specific characteristics of the firm's geographic market make it attractive?
- What specific feature of the firm's product or service makes it attractive to the target market; or, alternatively, why should this customer group buy from the firm rather than from its competitors?
- Does the target market have sufficient purchasing power to provide the business with a profitable level of sales?
- What is the sales estimate for next year, the next three years, and the next five years?
- What evidence is there to support these sales estimates?

5. **Description of operations.** In a business firm, the system or the set of procedures, processes, and methods that is used to convert resource inputs (such as raw materials, labor, or an advantageous business location) into a valuable output is known as operations. The summary description of this key function should focus on the flow of activities that identify what the business does and how it gets done. For example, if the business plan is written for a manufacturing firm, the description provides a thumbnail sketch of the product, the work flow that produces this product, and any competitive advantage or contribution to success offered by this particular method of operation. If the firm is a service business, this section consists of a summary of the activities required to perform the service and a brief explanation of the advantage or contribution it provides.

The following guideline questions should help the entrepreneur focus on the important issues to be summarized in this section of the business description. A complete discussion of the operating plan is provided in Chapter 8.

- What product or service does the firm produce or provide, or what product or product line does it merchandise?
- What competitive advantage or contribution does the firm's location offer?
- If the firm is a manufacturer, what are the major steps in the production process?
- What are the keys to success for the production process?
- What competitive advantage or contribution does the production process provide?
- What is the gross profit margin (sales less cost of goods sold)

or contribution margin (sales less variable costs) on the major product(s) produced?

- If the firm is a service business, what steps are required to provide that service?
- What competitive advantage or contribution do these operating procedures provide?
- What is the gross profit margin or contribution margin on the service offered?
- To which merchandising category does the business belong and what is its major product or product line?
- What competitive advantage or contribution does this product or product line provide?
- What selling strategy is employed?
- What advantage or contribution is offered by the firm's physical facilities and/or layout?
- What advantage or contribution is offered by the firm's purchasing procedures?
- What advantage or contribution does the firm's inventory management system offer?
- What advantage or contribution do the firm's quality control and customer service system offer?

6. **Develop profiles of top management and other key personnel.** This section should identify the key positions in the firm and summarize the job qualifications and contributions of the individuals that hold them. If the addition of key personnel is part of the long-term plan, a brief description of these positions should be provided as well.

While writing this section of the business description, it is important to keep in mind that the intended reader will be keenly interested in the job qualifications of key personnel and how these people contribute to the success of the firm. He or she knows that an organization is only as effective as its employees and the management team that leads them.

The following guideline questions should help the entrepreneur focus on the important organizational issues to be summarized. A complete discussion of the organization plan is provided in Chapter 9.

- What are the top-level management and staff positions in the firm?
- What are the primary duties and responsibilities associated with the top-level management and staff positions?
- Who holds each management and staff position?
- What are the job qualifications of each position-holder?
- What professional or job-related successes has each position-holder enjoyed?

- What unique contribution does each position-holder make to the success of the firm?
- What salary is paid each position-holder?
- What bonus or incentive plan is provided each position-holder?
- What key positions are planned for the future?
- Why are these positions needed, and what contribution will they make to the success of the firm?

7. **Develop a financial profile.** The financial profile should summarize the important points made in the firm's financial plan. Normally this includes information such as the following:

- If the firm is an existing business, a brief review of the firm's past financial performance, as measured by the growth in cash flow and profit, and current financial position.
- The financial goals that have been established for the firm's planning period.
- The financing needed to support planned operations.
- The type and maturity of the needed financing.
- The expected sources of this financing.
- The existing proportions of debt and owner's equity capital used to finance the firm.
- The proportions of debt and equity capital that will exist after the proposed financing.
- Projected cash flow and profit levels or growth rates.
- Any considerations or planned actions that have major financial consequences such as the liability on a pending lawsuit, a change in financial strategy, or the intention to take the firm public.

If a financing proposal is included with the presentation package, summaries of anticipated financing needs should be omitted from this section of the business description. In this case, only summary information on financial performance, financial condition, financing mix, and other important financial considerations should be included.

The following questions should serve as helpful guidelines for preparing the financial profile section of the business description. A complete discussion of the financial plan is provided in Chapter 10.

- What attainable financial goals have been established for the upcoming planning period?
- If the firm is an existing business, what has been its financial performance for the past three years as measured by the trend in key ratio values such as the growth rate of cash flow and profit, or return on investment?
- If the firm is an existing business, what is its current financial

position as measured by key indicators such as cash flow from operations, profit margins, and the debt ratio?

- As shown by the cumulative financing figure on the cash budget, what amount of seasonal working-capital financing is needed during the first year of the planning period?
- As shown by the pro forma balance sheet plug figure, how much external financing must be raised to support anticipated growth during the planning period?
- Given the current stage of the firm's development, what category of financing should be used?
- In what form, debt or equity capital, will this financing be raised?
- Given the degree of risk to which the business is exposed, what is the maximum percentage of debt financing that should be used?
- If debt financing is contemplated, would the proportion of debt existing after the financing violate the maximum percentage?

THE LIFE-CYCLE CONCEPT

The life-cycle concept is widely used in business to describe the state of development of a business firm, a product, or an entire industry. The business life cycle analogous to that of living organisms, is assumed to have four distinct phases: Birth, growth, maturity, and death. These periods are generally referred to as the development stage, the growth stage, the maturity stage, and the decline stage.

The Development Stage

This stage covers the period from the formulation of the business concept to start-up. It is characterized as the period when market acceptance has not yet been established. For entrepreneurs able to develop a new product or service or to get in on the ground floor of a new industry, this stage often offers the opportunity for large-scale profits. Unfortunately, this profit potential is accompanied by high risk. Since there is no hard evidence at this time of wide-scale consumer acceptance, there is no accurate gauge for measuring success.

As applied to the individual business, the effort required to move the venture from birth to actual operation will test the mettle of the most determined entrepreneur. This stage of the firm's life cycle is fraught with frustrations that range from searching for qualified employees to dealing with unsympathetic, recalcitrant financiers.

The Growth Stage

This phase of the life cycle refers to the period of accelerating market acceptance and the corresponding rapid expansion of sales and profits. As is true of the development stage, the growth phase may offer excellent profit opportunities for the alert entrepreneur. Equally important, the risk exposure at this time is less than during the developmental stage.

The growth phase of a typical business can also be a mixture of satisfaction and frustration for the entrepreneur. The profits that replace start-up losses are rewards for the time, effort, and financing invested in the business. Unfortunately, growth usually creates its own brand of management problems, such as inadequate staffing, production bottlenecks, inadequate cost control, or the chronic need for financing.

The Maturity Stage

This stage of the life cycle refers to the period of successful stability for the firm, a product or service, or an industry. Weaker firms or less competitive products or services have been eliminated by competition, and growth has declined to levels that leave industry or market survivors profitable and financially secure. A product in the maturity stage of its life cycle is usually in the enviable position of a cash cow. Sales are strong and profit margins are healthy because fixed overhead costs, such as R&D (research and development) expenditures, have usually been recaptured by this time.

When applied to the individual firm, the maturity stage usually means the time when the entrepreneur is able to enjoy the fruits of his or her labor. Cash flow and profits from the business are rewarding, and the disruptive problems encountered in the earlier stages of the firm's existence are only vague memories.

The Decline Stage

This last stage in the life cycle refers to the period during which disruptive changes have reduced product/service demand to a point where profit and cash flow of the industry or firm are declining. Unless a strategic overhaul is possible, this stage signals the ultimate demise for the product/service or the industry. This same prognosis holds for the individual firm in the decline stage of its life cycle. To counteract the forces of decline and avoid liquidation of the firm, a new strategy that rekindles consumer demand or creates a new direction for the business must be devised.

THE SIC CODING SYSTEM

The most descriptive characteristic of an industry is its primary product or product feature, and the most widely used method for coding industry characteristics is the Standard Industrial Classification (SIC) system. The SIC is a uniform number-coding and verbal-description system created by the federal government to classify business firms according to the specific business activities in which they engage. The system was developed as a response to the need for an organized framework for identifying, classifying, and reporting the vast amount of business and economic data collected and used by the federal government. The SIC coding system is explained and detailed in the *Standard Industrial Classification Manual* (Washington, D.C.: U.S. Government Printing Office, 1987). An excerpt from this manual is reproduced at Table 4-1.

TABLE 4-1
Standard Industrial Classification Coding System

Industrial Division	Industry Name	Major Groups
A	Agriculture, forestry, fishing	01–09
B	Mining	10–14
C	Construction	15–17
D	Manufacturing	20–39
E	Transportation, communications, electric, gas, and sanitary services	40–49
F	Wholesale trade—durable goods	50–51
G	Retail trade	52–59
H	Finance, insurance, and real estate	60–69
I	Services	70–89
J	Public administration	91–97
K	Non-classifiable establishments	99

The major industry groups shown on Table 4-1 are identified by two-digit code numbers such as 01–09 and 15–17. These groups are further subdivided into three- and four-digit industry sub-groups. For example, Industrial Division G, Retail Trade, has eight major groups coded 52–59. Group 57 is titled Home Furniture, Furnishings, and Equipment Stores. Included in this classification is sub-group 571, which is Home Furniture and Furnishings Stores. Industry sub-group 571 consists of additional sub-groups such as segment 5712, which is the designation for Retail Furniture Stores; 5713, Floor Covering Stores; or 5719, which is all other Miscellaneous Home Furnishings Stores not previously identified. See Table 4-2.

TABLE 4-2
An SIC Four-Digit Industry Sub-Group

Major Group 57
Home Furniture, Furnishings, and Equipment Stores

This major group includes retail stores selling goods used for furnishing the home, such as furniture, floor coverings, draperies, glass and china-ware, domestic stoves, refrigerators, and other household electrical and gas appliances. Establishments selling electrical and gas appliances are included in this group only if the major part of their sales consists of arti-cles for home use.

Industry Group 571—Home Furniture and Furnishing Stores

Industry Number

5712—Furniture Stores

> Establishments primarily engaged in the retail sale of household furniture. These stores may also sell homefurnishings, major appliances, and floor coverings.

5713—Floor Covering Stores

> Establishments primarily engaged in the retail sale of floor cover-ings. Establishments included in this industry may incidentally perform installation, but contractors primarily engaged in installing floor coverings for others are classified in Construction, Industry 1752.

5714—Drapery, Curtain, and Upholstery Stores

> Establishments primarily engaged in the retail sale of draperies, curtains, and upholstery materials. Establishments primarily engaged in reupholstering or repairing furniture are classified in Services, Industry 7641.

5719—Miscellaneous Homefurnishings Stores

> Establishments primarily engaged in the retail sale of miscella-neous homefurnishings, such as china, glassware, and metalware for kitchen and table use; bedding and linen; brooms and brushes; lamps and shades; mirrors and pictures; venetian blinds; and window shades. Establishments primarily engaged in the retail sale of miscel-laneous homefurnishings by house-to-house canvass or by party-plan merchandising are classified in Industry 5963.

Many of the four-digit sub-groups have been further subdivided into five-digit, or five-digit with an alphabetic character, by many of the government and private agencies that use the system. This has been done, where needed, to better detail the vast number of specialized industries and markets that exist in the U.S. economy.

Because the SIC system is widely used by agencies that publish industry and market data, it is an excellent tool for gathering information needed for industry and market research. Information sources using this system are often available in the public library of larger cities and are virtually always available in the reference or government documents section of college and university libraries. An annotated list of such sources, along with a discussion of how they are used, is provided in Chapter 5. Examples illustrating the use of SIC-coded information sources are provided in Chapters 7 and 8.

TIPS FOR PREPARING THE BUSINESS DESCRIPTION

▬ **Draft it first.** It is a good idea to attempt a rough draft of the business description before writing the business plan. Doing so provides an indication of the entrepreneur's understanding of the business and the adequacy of his or her research and planning effort. An inability to draft a summary of the critical issues surrounding commercial and financial feasibility is an indication of gaps in the entrepreneur's understanding of the business and the factors that affect it.

▬ **Write it last.** Since the business description is a synopsis of the entire business plan, the final version of this document should be written after the business plan has been completed. Doing so ensures that important issues are addressed and that the content of both documents is consistent.

▬ **Keep it brief.** The business description also serves as a convenience for the intended reader and should, therefore, be brief and to the point. The intended reader will expect no more information than is necessary to understand the business or business concept and to summarize the crucial points made in the business plan.

▬ **Stress commercial and financial success.** The first concern of the reader will be the sales potential of the firm or venture. It is important, therefore, that the business description identify the intended target market for the firm's product/service, why this customer group should buy it, and what level of sales can reasonably be expected as a result. The reader's next concern will be financial success. In this case, the description should focus on key financial indicators such as expected return on investment or profit and cash flow potential.

▬ **Experienced management is important.** Another major concern of the reader will be the quality of the management and staff team that leads the firm. The job qualifications and abilities of the entrepreneur and other key personnel should be stressed. If the firm has administrative weaknesses, the description should also indicate the existence of a plan for correcting them.

━━ **Be accurate.** Do not diminish the quality of the business description or alienate the reader with hype, misrepresentations, or fabrications. A sophisticated reader is interested in facts, solid evidence, and sound reasoning. He or she will recognize anything else for what it is and the entrepreneur and the business plan will immediately lose credibility.

SAMPLE BUSINESS DESCRIPTION

The following business description (Figure 4-1) is for a hypothetical retailer of women's clothing, Alain's Fashions for Women. The business was started as a women's clothier in 1897 and housed in rented space in the same building it now occupies. The building was purchased in 1947, and the mortgage was retired in 1967. The building has undergone three major renovations in the past 45 years. The most recent was completed in 1986.

Since its inception, ownership and management of the business have essentially remained in the Alain family. Mr. C. C. Alain, the firm's current CEO, took full control of the business from his retiring father in 1978. He is totally responsible for designing and implementing the major changes in marketing and operating strategies that took place in the middle 1980s.

Prior to 1986, Alain's sold low- to middle-quality lines of women's clothing using a traditional retailing strategy. The new operating and selling strategies, which have been highly successful over the past nine years, changed the firm to an upscale retailer catering primarily to middle- and high-income professional females. Alain's now operates as a full-markup retailer specializing in top-of-the-line apparel, and its selling strategy emphasizes a high level of service and complete customer satisfaction.

An important part of Alain's strategy is the exclusive territorial rights it holds to the entire product line of the two foremost apparel houses in the industry. To complement its product lines, Alain's offers plush surroundings and a variety of amenities such as an in-house cosmetics and fashion consultant, an in-house seamstress who does same-day alterations, a trained sales staff that prides itself on product knowledge and fashion trends, delivery service, a 90-day interest-free charge policy, and a no-questions-asked merchandise return policy.

FIGURE 4-1 *Business Description of Alain's Fashions for Women*

Business Name and Location

Business Name: Alain's Fashions for Women
Legal Name: Alain's Incorporated
Location: 10 Azalea Avenue
Azalea City, Georgia 30000
Telephone: (100) 555-0000
Fax: (100) 555-0101
Contact Person: Mr. C. C. Alain

Business History

Alain's, a family-owned, top-of-the-line retailer of women's clothing, has been in business since 1897. The firm was legally incorporated in 1953 and currently has S Corporation tax status. It is operated by its major stockholder, C. C. Alain. Mr. Alain is responsible for the extensive renovation and major change in marketing and operating strategies that took place in 1986. These changes moved the firm from a modestly profitable retailer of low-to-medium priced women's apparel, to a highly profitable, top-of-the-line, retailer.

Business Concept and Mission Statement

Alain's business strength and profitability stems from its rigid adherence to its goal of maintaining the image of a unique, customer-oriented, top-of-the-line retailer of quality women's clothing. The firm's basic philosophy is to profitably meet the needs of the discriminating customer by providing a quality product, tasteful fashions, meticulous personal service, and total shopping satisfaction.

Alain's management realizes that, in order to maintain the 17% growth in sales and 10% profits the firm has enjoyed over the past nine years, management must be sensitive to new opportunities and to changing customer needs, attitudes, and preferences. It is the ongoing goal of Alain's management and employees to continually search for new profit opportunities and for ways in which the firm can better meet the needs of its customers.

Market and Target Customer Group

Alain's serves a four-county area located in south-central Georgia and northern Florida. Over the past ten years, the population in

FIGURE 4-1 *(continued)*

this region has increased at a 4% compound annual rate of growth, and disposable income has increased at a 6% growth rate. The two market areas in which new store openings are planned have similar growth patterns.

Alain's target market consists of middle- and upper-income professionals. As detailed in the market analysis section of the business plan, the firm's target market makes up approximately 18% of the total adult population in its current and planned market areas. While approximately 80% of Alain's existing sales are to females in this customer group, about 20% are to males who patronize Alain's for gift purchases. In general, this target market is brand- and image-conscious, attentive to style and fashion trends, and has the purchasing power to be discriminating consumers.

Description of Operations

A combination of somewhat unique, but highly successful, marketing and operating strategies have been crucial to Alain's growth. The most important among these is the decision to carry only high-quality product lines. Alain's has secured exclusive territorial rights to the industry's two prestige brand names, and its management and employees work diligently to maintain the standards of quality and service needed to preserve these agreements.

Alain's sales policy complements its product line. The firm has well-trained sales personnel who pay particular attention to product knowledge, fashion and style trends, and the the individual needs of its customers. Alain's also provides a no-questions-asked merchandise return policy, a delivery service, free same-day alterations, and a 90-day interest-free charge policy.

An important part of Alain's sales strategy is maintaining a store atmosphere that supports its upscale image. Alain's maintains plush surroundings and a variety of amenities, which not only add to the firm's image but make shopping a comfortable social outing for its customers.

Management Profile and Needs Assessment

Alain's management team consists of the CEO, Mr. C. C. Alain, the Store Manager, Mrs. Elizabeth Gray, and the Buyer,

Mrs. Lisa Marie. Mr. Alain holds a B.S. degree in Marketing from Valdosta State University and an M.B.A. from Indiana University. He has 19 years experience in retailing and women's apparel. Mr. Alain owns 87% of the firm's outstanding shares.

Mrs. Marie holds a B.S. degree in Marketing and Retailing from the University of Georgia, has successfully completed numerous administrative seminars and workshops, and has 11 years of experience with Alain's. During this time she has held positions as junior buyer, senior buyer, and buying manager. Mrs. Gray has 10 years of experience with Alain's and has also successfully completed numerous administrative seminars and workshops. She has also held positions as part-time summer employee, full-time sales trainee, and sales representative with Alain's. Mrs. Gray has held the sales manager position for the past 4 years.

The planned opening of two new stores during the next three years will create the need for additional management and staff personnel. Included are a controller, a vice president of sales and operations, a personnel director, and two store managers.

Financial Profile

Since the implementation of Alain's current marketing and operating strategies in 1986, sales have grown at an average annual compounded rate of 17%, profits at a 10% rate of growth, and cash flow from operations at a 13% growth rate. It is estimated that new store openings will cause sales, cash flow, and profits to quadruple over the next six years.

Alain's owns all its assets, and there currently is no long-term debt outstanding. There are short-term working-capital loans outstanding in the amount of $187,000. These loans are drawn against the $500,000 line of credit granted by First National Bank of Azalea City. As required by bank policy, outstanding loans against the line will be repaid by the end of November of this year.

The new store openings will create the need for approximately $500,000 in new capital. Management feels this amount can be raised through debt financing in the form of a five-year term loan.

CHAPTER PERSPECTIVE

The business description is a summary of the key points or conclusions contained in the business plan. It is included in the presentation package when a complete plan has been prepared for the intended reader. The sections typically included in the business description are the firm name and location, business history, mission statement, industry and market description, description of operations, management and key personnel profile, and financial profile. Since the intended reader will look to the business description to determine whether further reading is warranted, it is important that this document pique his or her interest. To do so, the focus of this writing should be commercial and financial feasibility.

PREPARING OPERATING PLANS

The Industry Analysis

WHAT IS AN INDUSTRY ANALYSIS?

In order to effectively plan, forecast, and project success for an existing business or new venture, the entrepreneur must first identify those factors in the firm's external and internal environment that determine its ability to generate sales (commercial success) and positive cash flows (financial success). The *internal environment* refers to those activities in the business, such as production or cash-flow management, that are under management's direct control. On the other hand, the *external environment* refers to the variables that affect the firm's performance but are outside the direct control of management. Included in this category are such influences as:

- The industry, market, and competitive environment.
- The economic environment.
- The technological environment.
- The social, legal, and political environment.
- The demographic environment.

While all these factors affect the firm, the performance of the firm's industry is one of the stronger influences. An *industry* is defined as a group of businesses producing or supplying related products or services and the complementary firms that support them. Complementary firms include indirectly related businesses such as industry suppliers and distributors. An *industry analysis*, then, is a study of the set of characteristics that define and influence a group of primary and secondary businesses supplying a related product or service. When prepared for a business plan, an effective industry analysis provides the following information:

- A discussion of the characteristics that define the industry, including information on the products or services provided, the scope and geography of its markets, the major competitors in the industry, and the demographics of the industry's major customers.
- A description of the economic, competitive, social, legal, and political factors that drive the industry, and those from this set that directly impact the firm's performance.

▬ An indication of the historical trends of sales and profits in the industry, an explanation of the factors responsible for this performance, the outlook for future industry sales and profits, and the reasons these projections should materialize.

▬ A description of the strategic opportunity that exists for the firm in this industry, why this opportunity exists, how the firm plans to exploit it, and why this opportunity should result in success for the firm.

After studying the material in this chapter, you will:

▬ Understand the role of the industry analysis.

▬ Know the information needed to prepare an industry analysis.

▬ Know the major sources of information available for performing an industry analysis.

▬ Know the steps to performing the industry analysis.

WHEN TO USE AN INDUSTRY ANALYSIS

The information provided by the industry analysis is usually required in any well-prepared business plan. This is true whether the business plan is used internally, whether the presentation package is limited to a loan proposal and summary updates from selected business plan components, or whether a complete business plan is presented to the intended reader.

The industry analysis provides the entrepreneur with the understanding and insights needed to begin formulating informed responses to the questions of *why* commercial success for the firm can be achieved and *how* this success will come about. An analysis of the firm's industry also provides essential information for the internal planning process. Realistic operating, marketing, and financial strategies cannot be developed without an understanding of the industry factors that directly affect the firm.

THE INFORMATION NEEDED TO PREPARE AN INDUSTRY ANALYSIS

The information collected for the industry analysis should consist of what is necessary to describe the product or service the industry provides, its most important customers and suppliers, the dominant firms in the industry, its major competitors, and its past performance and future outlook. These information needs are described in the guideline questions listed below and in the following sections of this chapter.

The chapter also contains an annotated bibliography of the principal sources of published information used in industry and market analyses. A sample industry analysis at the end of this chapter illustrates how Standard Industrial Classification (SIC) codes can be used in conjunction with these published sources to gather industry and market information. The sample market analysis in Chapter 6 contains an example of how published information sources are used to prepare a market analysis and a sales forecast for a proposed new venture.

The entrepreneur faced with the task of preparing an industry analysis for the first time is often faced with the questions, how do I get started and how do I know when the process is complete? Using the sequence of steps discussed above should provide the guidance needed to start and progress through the information gathering process. The process is essentially complete when answers to the following guideline questions can be supplied.

■ What is the economic sector and sector classification for this industry?

■ What is the SIC code number and name for this industry?

■ What are the primary products or services supplied by this industry?

■ Which products or services compete directly and indirectly with those of the industry?

■ Who are the major firms in the industry and which firms compete directly with the entrepreneur's business or new venture?

■ How many new firms have entered this industry in the past three years?

■ What new products/services or innovations have been introduced in this industry in the past three years?

■ What is the average rate of technological obsolescence for products in this industry?

■ What major technological changes have taken place in this industry in the past three years?

■ Who are the industry's primary suppliers, and how reliable are these supply lines?

■ What are the primary distribution channels used to move the industry's product to its consumers?

■ What is the scope of the market for the industry's products or services?

■ Who are the industry's primary customers, and what common buying characteristics do they share?

■ What factors influence the purchases of the these customers?

■ What are the major economic, competitive, and demographic factors that drive this industry?

■ What are the trends and outlooks for these key factors?

■ Is there any evidence that the key industry factors are changing?

■ What are the growth trends of industry sales, profits, and other key indicators of industry performance over the past three to five years?

■ How do these trends relate to those of broad-based indicators of the economy and to those of competing industries?

━━ What is the outlook for industry sales and profits over the next three to five years?

━━ What key assumptions underlie these forecasts?

━━ Why should these forecasts materialize?

━━ What strategic opportunity exists in this industry for the business or new venture?

━━ Why should this strategic opportunity be successful for the business or new venture?

━━ What are the major threats to the industry?

━━ What strategies do the major firms in the industry use to protect against these threats?

━━ What strategies would the firm use to protect against these threats?

STEPS TO PREPARING AN INDUSTRY ANALYSIS

While preparation of an industry analysis may appear daunting when viewed in its entirety, it is not difficult if properly approached. The key is to divide the analysis into a series of small, sequential tasks, each of which are completed before the next is undertaken. The order in which the following information requirements are presented provides one logical approach for doing so.

1. **Industry analysis summary.** This optional section *may* be used when the analysis is prepared for outside presentation. The summary is a convenience for the reader and should be no longer than what is needed for him or her to gain a basic understanding of the industry and the major factors that affect it. This can usually be accomplished in one paragraph.

2. **Industry description.** A discussion of the firm's industry should begin with an identification of the economic sector and industry classification or segment to which it belongs. The term *economic sector* refers to a primary business area such as manufacturing, merchandising, service, transportation, or construction. An *industry classification* identifies the various segments into which an economic sector is divided. For example, retailing is one classification under the merchandising sector, and industrial chemicals is a segment of the manufacturing sector. Industry classifications are further divided into a wide variety of subcomponents. For example, the classification for retailing contains myriad subcomponents such as sporting goods, women's apparel, and hardware. As indicated in Chapter 4, the most widely used system for classifying industries is the SIC system.

The industry description should further identify the geographical boundaries of the industry and the products or services supplied to its markets. For example, basic steel manufacturers operate primarily in the national market supplying such products as steel plate, cold-rolled sheet steel, and tin plate. Commercial banks, on the other hand, tend to confine their various financial service operations to either regional markets (e.g., the Southeast) or local markets (e.g., Atlanta).

3. **Industry suppliers, customers, and distributors.** The industry characteristics that should be described next are those relating to the primary suppliers of the industry, the products or services they supply, the major customers of the industry's product or service, and the channels of distribution used by the industry to move the product or service from producer to ultimate consumer. Each description should include a discussion of the factors that materially affect them. For example, the key concerns regarding suppliers are normally the cost of the product or service they provide, the extent to which it is available when needed, and the reliability for on-time delivery. If access to industry supplies or suppliers is limited or unreliable or supply costs are prohibitive, it will be difficult, if not impossible, to convince a knowledgeable reader that a strategic opportunity exists for the firm in this industry.

The discussion of the industry's major customers should include considerations such as why they buy the industry's product or service; why, as a member of this industry, the firm is able to reach them; whether the customer base is stable or changing; and what future industry changes are anticipated. Likewise, the discussion of distribution channels should include key considerations such as whether existing channels maximize customer exposure, whether they are cost-effective, and how the firm will be able to use or modify them to its advantage.

4. **Competition.** Since commercial feasibility is critical to the success of any business, the intended reader of a business plan will be keenly interested in the extent to which sales of the industry's product or service are exposed to both direct and indirect competition. *Direct competition* refers to products or services that consumers treat as acceptable alternatives, such as McDonalds and Burger King, Kmart and Walmart, and plastic and aluminum. *Indirect competition* refers to products or services that can be easily substituted for one another, such as automobile travel for air travel, video movie rentals for attendance at a movie theater, and yogurt for ice cream.

In writing this section, the entrepreneur should avoid statements or suggestions indicating an absence of competition for the industry's product or service. A knowledgeable reader would, upon encountering this statement, immediately conclude that the entrepreneur is either naive about the business world, does not understand the meaning and significance of competition, or has not done his or her homework. Unless the industry has an absolute monopoly on a life-essential item such as water or insulin, varying degrees of alternatives or substitutes are always available. For example, the local electric utility may have a monopoly on the sale of electricity in a particular city, but residents can, given the right incentives, resort to generating their own electric power. Or, while the prospects of being without an automobile may be troublesome, other means of transportation are available.

Strategic opportunity or competitive advantage does not exist because of the absence of competition. It results from having a product or service that is, in the mind of the consumer, a better choice than available alternatives or substitutes. The industry analysis must, therefore, make a convincing case for why the product or service represents a *better choice*.

5. **Historical performance.** This section of the industry analysis should use both prose and graphics to sketch a picture of industry performance to date. Typical performance indicators are sales revenue, units shipped, operating profits, workers employed, and the number of customers served. In order to highlight trends, industry performance data should be compared to the same data series for competing industries or to indicators of aggregate economic activity such as gross domestic product (GDP) or personal disposable income (PDI).

The discussion of industry performance should include reference to the cyclical and seasonal patterns, if any, evidenced in the data. *Cyclical patterns* are those recurring swings in business activity that move production, sales, cash flow, profits, and employment through a recessionary phase to the peak of an upswing. Industry cycles should be compared to those of the overall economy as measured by key indicators of activity such as GDP. These comparisons indicate the extent to which industry sales and profits are sensitive to economic change. For example, sales and profits of consumer durables such as autos and appliances are highly sensitive to changes in PDI. When the economy is in a general recession, sales of consumer durables decline as the level of PDI declines. Other industries, such as health care, are more recession-proof.

Seasonal patterns refer to pronounced changes in activity within a calendar year. Most industries evidence some intra-year pattern in sales, cash flows, and profits. For example, the retail apparel industry normally does a large percentage of its business during the fall holiday season. On the other hand, the largest portion of the winter holiday season output of toy manufacturers is produced and shipped by the preceding August. Seasonal peaks and troughs affect a number of business variables such as cash flows, working capital build-up, and financing needs.

An essential component of this section is an explanation of the factors that determine and drive industry performance. For example, the widespread acceptance and use of personal computers in business, government, education, and the home are an important reason for the existence of a large-scale software industry. By identifying factors responsible for industry performance and relating these to the performance of the firm, the entrepreneur effectively addresses the implicit question of *why* success is anticipated.

6. **Future outlook.** The outlook for industry growth is an important indicator of both the extent to which strategic opportunities exist and the degree of risk associated with entry into the industry. For example, because developing industries have not gained wide-scale product/service acceptance, they typically offer the opportunity for large-scale profits, represent the least competition, and have the highest risk of failure. On the other hand, industries in the rapid-growth stage have gained product/service acceptance, enjoy a rapidly expanding customer base, experience increasing sales and profits, represent lower investment risk, but experience more formidable competition.

Again, it is essential that the discussion of growth prospects include a convincing explanation of *why* expectations should materialize. A forecast or projection is meaningless unless its underlying assumptions are clearly identified and convincingly supported. Without justification, a forecast is nothing more than a guess, which will be quickly dismissed by an experienced reader.

7. **Strategic opportunity.** The primary reason for preparing the industry analysis is to determine whether a commercially and financially successful industry niche exists. Fortunately, there is no one formula that defines a successful strategic opportunity. A successful strategic opportunity may be achieved in a variety of ways, including:

- Creating a marketable new product or innovative service.
- Finding a market niche in a rapidly growing industry.
- Meeting an unfilled need or unsatisfied market demand.
- Developing or accessing a new or untapped market for an existing product.
- Developing a lower-cost method of doing business.
- Providing better service than what is currently available.

Regardless of the opportunity envisioned, a convincing case must be made for *why* the firm can capitalize on it. The factors that should lead to success must be identified and the reasons the firm is or will be in position to take advantage of them must be carefully explained. It is also advisable to include in this section a discussion of the pitfalls that can result in failure and, to the extent possible, the entrepreneur's plans for protecting against them.

An informed reader of the business plan knows there are risks associated with any business opportunity. It is as important, therefore, to identify what can go wrong and what precautions will be taken to minimize risk as it is to explain what leads to success. By so doing, the entrepreneur goes a long way toward convincing the reader that he or she has the management savvy to guide the business in bad times as well as good. If the entrepreneur fails to address this issue, the reader may conclude the analysis is unreliable.

SOURCES OF INDUSTRY INFORMATION

The information needed to conduct a diligent industry analysis may come from primary sources, secondary sources, or some combination of the two. The former term refers to the use of research tools to gather information directly from original data sources. For example, the entrepreneur may make direct contact with firms in the industry to gather information, or interviews may be conducted with consumers to identify buying habits. Most original industry research is done by specialized data gathering agencies. Groups such as the federal government, state governments, industry trade associations, specialized research agencies, security analysts, and financial investment services routinely gather both numerical data and qualitative industry information. Much of this information is published and made available through secondary sources.

Secondary information refers to published sources such as those shown in Table 5-1. This annotated bibliography identifies the most widely used government and privately published sources of secondary information for conducting industry and market analyses. Many of these sources are available in city libraries, and virtually all are available in college and university libraries. This latter group of institutions often devotes an entire section of the library to federal government publications alone.

The sample industry analysis at the end of this chapter explains how the SIC system can be used to identify and obtain industry information from secondary sources. In addition, the sample market analysis in Chapter 6 illustrates how secondary sources can be used to do a market analysis and sales forecast for a new venture. Because of the large number of secondary sources available, finding information for the industry and market analysis components of the business plan is not a problem. Rather, the job is one of becoming familiar with available sources and then narrowing down the choices to those that are most relevant to the needs of the particular analysis.

TABLE 5-1
Industry and Market Information Sources

Federal Government Sources

American Statistics Index (ASI), (Published by the Congressional Information Service).

The ASI is a comprehensive index of U.S. government statistical publications. Accompanying the index is an abstract volume which contains descriptions of the content and format of each publication.

Census of Population: General Population Characteristics: U.S. Summary, (Published by the U.S. Department of Commerce, Bureau of Census).

The U.S. population census, which is taken every ten years, provides a wealth of comprehensive demographic data. These data are organized by Metropolitan Statistical Area (MSA) and include key demographic characteristics such as age and income distributions, number of households, and ethnic group concentrations. Business firms use these data in a variety of applications. For example, market analysis, sales forecasting and numerous business decisions such as where to locate the business, mapping sales territories, and choosing advertising and promotion strategies require demographic information.

County Business Patterns (Published by the U.S. Department of Commerce, Bureau of Census).

This annual publication provides data on employment, total payroll, and number of business establishments classified by employment size, by county, and by two-, three-, and four-digit SIC codes.

Current Population Reports (Published by the U.S. Department of Commerce, Bureau of Census).

The *Reports* are published monthly and include information on eight demographic subject areas.

Economic Census (Published by the U.S. Department of Commerce, Bureau of Census).

The Census Bureau conducts an economic census every five years and publishes the statistical information that has been gathered. The data, which are organized by industry classification, appear in the following Bureau publications: *Census of Construction Businesses, Census of Manufactures, Census of Mineral Industries, Census of Minority-Owned Businesses, Census of Retail Trade, Census of Selected Service Industries, Census of Transportation Businesses,* and *Census of Women-Owned Businesses.*

TABLE 5-1 *(continued)*

Federal Reserve Bulletin (Published by the Board of Governors of the U.S. Federal Reserve System).

This monthly publication contains a wealth of economic, business, and financial quantitative data as well as analyses and discussions of current economic trends and events.

Monthly Catalog of U.S. Government Publications (Published by the U.S. Government Printing Office).

The *Catalog* is is a comprehensive index of available government documents. It can be accessed by subject, author, or title and contains a current list of publications issued by departments and bureaus of the U.S. government.

SIC Manual (Published by the U.S. Government Printing Office).

This publication provides the three- and four-digit classification codes for U.S. industries.

Statistical Reference Index (SRI) (Published by the Congressional Information Service).

The SRI is a convenient, comprehensive index to statistical information published by U.S. associations, institutes, businesses, state governments, independent research organizations, commercial publishers, and university research centers. As true of the ASI, the SRI also has an "Abstracts" volume.

Subject Bibliography: Small Business (Published by the U.S. Government Printing Office).

This partially annotated bibliography provides a list of U.S. government publications dealing with small business.

U.S. Industrial Outlook (Published by the U.S. Department of Commerce).

This annual publication provides data and explanations of historical trends and future growth prospects for a wide variety of U.S. industries.

Printed government publications can be obtained from:

Superintendent of Documents
U.S. Government Printing Office
Washington, D.C. 20402
(202) 783-3238

U.S. government data can also be obtained in computer-readable form. To inquire about obtaining this information, contact:

Data User Services Division
Bureau of Census
Washington, D.C. 20233
(202) 763-4100

State And Local Sources

City Directories (Published by The R. L. Polk Company).

R. L. Polk is the largest publisher of city directories in the United States. Polk's directory format is similar to that of other city directories and includes an alphabetical listing of people and companies, a street index, a telephone number index, and a classified business directory. The most useful sections for industry and market analyses are the street index, which lists occupants by address, and the telephone number index, which lists telephone numbers by subscriber name.

Area Industrial Information (Published by county and city planning commissions and industrial authorities).

Various municipal agencies responsible for the promotion of new business and economic growth in their areas typically publish information on businesses by industry classification and by individual plant or office location. While publication dates for these sources vary, most are published annually or biannually.

State Industrial Directories (Published by state agencies).

All state industrial agencies publish, either annually or semi-annually, some form of state business or industrial directory. While these directories vary in scope and content, they usually provide information on company names and addresses, employment size, product or industry classification, and names of key executives. Some states do, however, limit their data and listings to manufacturing firms in the state.

Private Sources

The Almanac of Business and Industrial Financial Ratios (Published by Prentice-Hall, Inc.).

This annual publication contains financial statement data and selected financial ratios for a large sample of businesses. The data are organized by SIC industry classification and asset-size categories and are especially useful for sales forecasting and for preparing pro forma financial statements for a new business.

Census of American Business (Published by Dun & Bradstreet, Inc.).

This annual publication provides information on business firms by type of business, sales volume, employee size, and location.

A Guide to Consumer Markets (Published by The Conference Board).

This annual publication provides a wealth of demographic and economic data classified by Standard Metropolitan Statistical Area.

TABLE 5-1 *(continued)*

Million Dollar Directory (Published by Dun & Bradstreet, Inc.).

This four-volume directory, which is published annually, lists 160,000 businesses alphabetically by name, geographically by name, and by SIC number and name. It also contains such information as business address, telephone number, line of business, number of employees, names of company officers, and annual sales.

Predicasts Forecasts (Published by Predicasts, Inc.).

This two-volume publication provides a comprehensive index of published articles from a wide variety of secondary information sources. These sources include business and trade association magazines, newspapers, financial publications, and special reports that provide industry and market analysis information. The publication is divided into the "Industries and Products" issue and the "Companies" issue.

Robert Morris Associates Annual Statement Studies (Published by Robert Morris Associates).

This annual publication contains financial statement data and selected financial ratios organized by firm size and SIC industry classification for a large sample of businesses. These data are especially useful for sales forecasting and for preparing pro forma financial statements for a new business.

Standard & Poor's Industry Surveys (Published by Standard & Poor's Investor Services).

This valuable resource provides historical data, qualitative information, and predictions for a wide variety of industries. It is particularly useful for the novice analyst because each analysis is essentially a tutorial on how to perform an industry analysis.

Sales & Marketing Management's "Survey of Buying Power" and "Survey of Industrial & Commercial Buying Power" (Published by Bill's Communications, Inc.).

Sales & Marketing Management is a monthly periodical that provides feature articles and pertinent news about marketing topics. The "Survey of Buying Power" and the "Survey of Industrial & Commercial Buying Power" are two of four special annual issues that provide valuable information for industry and market analysis. The former title provides regional, state, metropolitan, county, and city data for selected population characteristics, household income distribution, and retail sales by store group. The latter title provides data on industrial and commercial activity by state and county.

Thomas Register of American Manufacturers (Published by Thomas Publishing Company).

The *Register* is divided into four volumes. The Products and Services volume provides names of companies classified under 50,000 different product and service categories excluding food and food-related products. This latter category is contained in the volume entitled *Thomas Grocery Register*. The *Company Profiles* volume provides addresses, phone numbers, asset ratings, sales office locations, and product lines of some 135,000 manufacturers. *Thomcat* is a detailed catalog of product information for over 12,000 firms. The information includes particulars such as drawings, photos, specifications, and performance data.

Trade and Industry Journals (Published by various trade and industry associations).

There are a large number of associations representing various industry and trade groups that publish periodicals containing industry data, qualitative information, descriptions of trends and analyses, and growth expectations. An excellent reference for identifying national and international trade associations is *Gale's Encyclopedia of Associations* published by Gale Research. *Gale's Encyclopedia* is carried by most public, college, and university libraries. An excellent reference to trade association information such as trade and industry publications, trade shows, venture capitalists, and consultants is the *Small Business Sourcebook*, also published by Gale Research.

A frequently overlooked source of data and information on industries and markets located within state boundaries are various research bureaus and academic departments housed in schools of business administration of state colleges and universities. Business research bureaus typically gather and evaluate industry and market data and publish periodicals or newsletters containing updates of economic data series and forecasts of activity in state and local industries and markets. Various academic departments within schools of business have highly qualified faculty that often do research and consulting in specialized areas that directly or indirectly involve industry and market analysis.

TIPS FOR PREPARING AN INDUSTRY ANALYSIS

■ **Don't slight this component.** Given the importance of the industry analysis component to the overall business plan, the intended reader will carefully evaluate its content. He or she will first become familiar with the nature and scope of the industry as provided in the description section of the industry analysis. Next, the data on historical performance, industry growth prospects, and strategic opportunity will be examined. Then the assumptions underlying all projections and conclusions will be evaluated. Last, the documentation used to support the assumptions, projections, and conclusions will be assessed. It is important, therefore, that this information is both present and convincing.

━ **Do the necessary homework.** Preparing an industry analysis capable of satisfying both the concerns of a knowledgeable reader as well as the needs of the entrepreneur is a valuable learning experience. The required effort forces the entrepreneur to develop industry expertise and to identify and evaluate those factors critical to the success of the business. Equally important, doing the necessary research wards off the dangers of the "fuzzy thinking" syndrome. This is a malady caused by inadequate effort and insufficient information. It reveals itself in the industry analysis as fanciful assumptions, unrealistic expectations, and unsupported projections and conclusions. Evidence of this ailment usually spells disaster for the business plan.

━ **Reference the life-cycle stage where appropriate.** The industry analysis is often more effective when presented within the context of the current stage of the industry's life cycle (see Chapter 4). For example, the description of the industry's historical performance is more effective when incorporated within a discussion of its development and growth stages. Or, the arguments for strategic opportunity are usually more persuasive when coupled with a description of the factors responsible for rapid industry growth. Explicit reference to the life-cycle stage of an industry is often found in secondary information sources.

━ **Emphasize opportunity.** Since strategic opportunity is critical to the success of any business, it is important that the industry analysis leave no doubt in the reader's mind about the existence of a commercially and financially attractive opportunity.

━ **The first step for a new venture.** Before time and energy are committed to planning a new venture, the entrepreneur should do a preliminary feasibility study to investigate and evaluate the merits of the proposed business concept. This entails research into the commercial and financial potential of the venture. The logical starting point for this effort is an evaluation of the proposed industry and its market(s).

━ **Use graphics.** Some portion of the industry analysis will necessarily deal with quantitative data such as sales revenue, units shipped, and growth rates. The message in these data is delivered more effectively when verbal explanations are judiciously accompanied by tables, graphs, and charts.

■ **Take advantage of available help.** The small-firm entrepreneur should be aware of consulting assistance that is available at no cost. There are two major sources of this help: state Small Business Development Centers (SBDC) and the U.S. Small Business Administration (SBA). Both agencies offer management education programs, business management literature, and consulting assistance. The SBDC is a state-sponsored agency. It is structured as a statewide network of satellite centers that serve local small-firm entrepreneurs. The SBA has regional offices located throughout the country. Both agencies offer consulting assistance at no charge to the small-business entrepreneur and management education programs and literature at nominal prices.

■ **Don't be intimidated.** There is a natural tendency, especially for those unfamiliar with using library references or collecting data, to be apprehensive about performing an industry or market analysis. Don't be! The task can be done effectively by the typical entrepreneur willing to put forth the necessary effort. As previously discussed, the trick is to take the analysis one small step at a time.

■ **Industry analysis is an ongoing process.** Preparing the industry and market analyses for the firm's business plan should only be the start of an information-gathering process that is never completed. The essence of operating and managing a business is planning and decision-making, and a necessary part of these critical management functions is gathering, analyzing, and evaluating timely information on the firm's industry and market(s). Unless this information is updated to reflect the changes that are continually taking place in the firm's rapidly changing environment, the business will quickly become passé.

SAMPLE INDUSTRY ANALYSIS

The following sample illustrates how the Standard Industrial Classification (SIC) System (see Chapter 4) can be used in conjunction with secondary information sources to gather industry and market information. To illustrate, assume a small software developer, the Creative Software Company (CSC), has written a new software program for computerized machine tool manufacturing. In order to develop the marketing strategy for the new software, management must make an estimate of its market potential as measured by the number of possible customers (machine tool manufacturers) and sales volume. To do so requires data and qualitative information on the machine tool industry.

The CSC researcher assigned the task of performing the analysis starts by identifying the SIC code number for the machine tool industry. The *SIC Manual* indicates that machine tool manufacturers are classified by code number 3541. Since the manual furnishes no additional industry or market information, the CSC researcher turns to other secondary sources. An abbreviated list of sources that catalogue industry and market information by SIC code are shown at Table 5-2.

The CSC researcher begins gathering data by first determining how many U.S. firms are included in the 3541 industry classification. By surveying the sources listed at Table 5-2, she discovers that this information is available in the *U.S. Census of Manufacturers*. This valuable reference identifies such pertinent industry information as:

■ The number of firms with this SIC code in each state.
■ The number of employees used by these firms.
■ The total manufacturing value added to finished machine tool products by these firms.
■ The total cost of materials purchased by these firms.
■ The total units shipped by these firms.
■ The value of the units shipped by these firms.
■ The total annual capital expenditures made by these firms.

TABLE 5-2
Leading SIC Coded Data Sources

SIC Source	Possible Applications
SIC Manual	Obtaining the SIC code number for industry classifications.
U.S. Census of Manufactures	Determining information useful for estimating market size, growth rates, areas of geographic concentration, and number of firms in an area.
U.S. Industrial Outlook	Determining number of firms in an industry, areas of geographic concentration, past industry trends, and projected industry forecasts.
Predicasts Forecasts	Obtaining information and data on a wide variety of industry and market topics including size, growth rates, performance indicators, and forecasts through the index of publications.
Sales & Marketing Management's "Survey of Industrial & Commercial Buying Power"	Obtaining market analysis data by SIC code and county such as age distribution, income distribution, and number of firms.
Dun's Census of American Business	Obtaining descriptive business firm data such as state and county location, number of firms, sales volume, and number of employees.

The next task for the CSC researcher is to determine whether the machine tool industry has been growing over the past five years and how this growth rate compares to the growth rates of the economy, total manufacturing, or other cyclical industries. She begins by examining the historical performance data for the machine tool industry shown in the *U.S. Census of Manufacturers*. To support the evidence of historical industry growth, the CSC researcher adds explanations of why these trends have developed. She gathers this qualitative information from sources such as Standard & Poor's *Industry Surveys*, from periodicals published by the machine tool industry trade associations, and from a variety of articles on the machine tool industry indexed by *Predicasts* (see Tables 5-1 and 5-2).

In order to enhance the historical growth perspective she has developed, the CSC researcher compares the trends of key performance indicators for the machine tool industry with those for total manufacturing in the United States, for broad-based economic indicators such as GDP, and for an industry with economic, operating, and financial characteristics similar to those of the machine tool industry. To make the broad-based comparisons with the machine tool data, the CSC researcher obtains total manufacturing and aggregate economic data from the *Federal Reserve Bulletin* (see Table 5-1). Her selection of a suitable comparison industry is made after reviewing various industry analyses in Standard & Poor's *Industry Surveys*. To gather data for her choice, the heavy equipment manufacturing industry, she repeats the steps used in the machine tool industry analysis.

When the historical analysis is complete, the CSC researcher directs her attention to the outlook for growth in the machine tool industry as indicated by industry sales and the number of new firms entering the industry. Information for this purpose can be obtained from a number of excellent sources. Prominent among these are the *U.S. Industrial Outlook* (see Tables 5-1 and 5-2), Standard & Poor's *Industry Surveys,* machine tool industry trade association publications, research department releases of large stock brokerage firms, and the many articles on the machine tool industry indexed in *Predicasts*.

The next step in the analysis is to make a realistic sales forecast for the new software. The CSC researcher chooses to approach this task by identifying all U.S. machine tool firms by name and location and then using a combination of mail, telephone, and personal contact to determine the extent of their interest in the new software. To obtain the necessary data, the CSC researcher consults Dun & Bradstreet's *Census of American Business* or *Million Dollar Directory*, and state industrial directories such as the *Georgia Manufacturing Directory* or the *Directory of Florida Industries* (see Tables 5-1 and 5-2). She could, if she so desired, purchase this information in computer-readable form from companies such as Dun & Bradstreet or one of the many marketing research firms that compile and sell mailing lists.

While the CSC researcher used only a few of the many SIC-coded industry and market information sources available, the effort provided a detailed picture of the machine tool industry. The data and qualitative information she compiled allows management to make a realistic projection of the market potential for the software and to establish sales goals, sales quotas, and contacts for sales personnel. Equally important, the research provides verifiable supporting documentation for these projections.

CHAPTER PERSPECTIVE

Because industry performance is one of the more important determinants of the firm's commercial success, an industry analyis is an essential component of the business plan. An industry analysis is a study of the factors that define and influence the group of primary and secondary businesses that make up the firm's industry. It usually consists of a description of the economic sector and classification to which the industry belongs; the product or service it provides; geographical boundaries of its markets; its major suppliers, customers, and distributors; the major firms in the industry; the product or service that directly or indirectly competes with the industry's product or service; the historical performance of sales and profits; the future outlook for industry performance; and the strategic opportunity the industry offers for the firm.

The Market Analysis and Sales Forecast

WHAT IS A MARKET ANALYSIS AND A SALES FORECAST?

The market analysis and sales forecast are the necessary companions to the industry analysis and are related steps in the process of validating commercial feasibility or success. If the firm is to attain commercial success, its industry must provide a strategic opportunity and its market must provide a profitable niche. The sales forecast, which is the ultimate measure of commercial feasibility, converts market potential into the numerical targets that are the driving force for all planned activity in the firm.

As commonly used in business, the term *market* refers to the geographical boundaries encompassing the firm's target market and the competition it faces. Its geographical boundaries may be as limited as a specific district within a metropolitan area or as large as a domestic or international market. The firm's *target market* is the group of potential customers with characteristics, needs, and expectations to which the firm's product or service should appeal.

Market competition refers to the direct and indirect competitive threats faced by the firm. As discussed in Chapter 5, *direct competition* refers to substitute products or services, such as accommodations offered by major motel chains. *Indirect competition* refers to the alternative choices available to consumers, such as eating chicken instead of beef.

A *market analysis*, then, is a study of the basic factors that define the market for the firm's product or service and how the firm must position itself to take advantage of the opportunity that is available. These factors include:

- The geographic boundaries of the market.
- The economic, competitive, and social factors that influence activity in this market.
- The specific market niche in which the firm does business.
- The specific characteristics that define the target market for the firm's product or service.

■ The sales potential for the identified target market.

■ The businesses and products or services that directly and indirectly compete with that of the firm.

The sales forecast is an estimate, based on a given set of assumptions about the firm's environment and market, of expected sales volume for specific future time periods. This estimate is an important indication of a new firm's potential for commercial success and, as such, is the criterion by which the venture's feasibility is assessed. Also, since all activity in a business is ultimately predicated on sales volume, the sales forecast is also critical data for other components of the business plan.

After studying the material in this chapter, you will:

■ Understand the role of the market analysis and sales forecast.

■ Know the information needed to do a market analysis and a sales forecast and the major sources of this information.

■ Know the steps to preparing a market analysis.

■ Understand the basics of the Metropolitan Category System, which is used by the Census Bureau to classify market segments by population density.

■ Know the major sales forecasting techniques.

WHEN TO INCLUDE THESE COMPONENTS IN THE BUSINESS PLAN

As is true of the industry analysis, the information provided by the market analysis and sales forecast is required in any well-prepared business plan. This is the case whether the business plan is used internally, whether the presentation package is limited to a loan proposal and summary updates from selected business plan components, or whether a complete business plan is presented to the intended reader. Market information, when combined with information on the firm's industry, is critical to both an assessment of commercial feasibility and to the internal management process.

Without comprehensive information on the forces that drive its market and a realistic estimate of the sales potential this market offers, neither the entrepreneur nor the intended reader of the business plan can effectively evaluate the firm's potential for commercial success. Equally important, the entrepreneur needs a continuous supply of market information to develop the firm's marketing strategy and to make the many day-to-day marketing decisions that are an essential part of planning and operating the business.

INFORMATION NEEDED TO PREPARE THESE COMPONENTS

In order to prepare a convincing marketing analysis, a variety of information on the firm's external environment, its industry, its target market, and its competition are needed. The questions listed below provide guidelines for identifying what information is required.

■ Where is the market for the product or service located, and how large is this market in terms of potential sales?

■ What demographic factors characterize this market?

■ What are the key economic, social, and legal factors that influence business activity in this market, and what are the historical and future trends of these factors?

■ What is the outlook for this market in terms of sales, profits, and growth potential?

■ What market niche does the firm seek to fill or exploit?

■ What marketing strategy will be used to exploit the intended market niche?

■ What demographic, psychographic, and behavioral characteristics describe the firm's target customer group?

■ How will the firm reach its target market, and what message will be used to do so?

■ Why will the target customer group buy from the firm rather than from its competitors?

■ What sales volume should this market niche and target customer group generate for the firm?

■ Which products or services and which businesses represent the strongest competitive threat to the firm?

■ On what basis (price, quality, service, etc.) does the firm's product or service compete?

■ What competitive advantage does the firm hold over its competition?

STEPS TO PREPARING THE MARKET ANALYSIS

Chapter 5 indicated that a complex process is simplified when viewed and treated as a series of small tasks performed in logical sequence. This approach is also recommended for preparing the market analysis. The ordering of the seven steps discussed below offers a logical approach for doing so.

1. **Market analysis and sales forecast summary.** This optional section *may* be used when the analysis and forecast are prepared for outside presentation. The summary is a convenience for the reader and should be no longer than what is needed for him or her to gain a basic understanding of the firm's market, the factors that affect it, and the sales outlook. This can usually be accomplished in one paragraph.

2. **Define the firm's market location.** *Market location* refers to the geographic boundaries within which the firm does business.

While the ultimate focus of the market analysis is the firm's target market, a clear understanding of the geographical limits of the market in which the firm operates is important for the following reasons.

- The aggregate forces that influence the broad market area will, to varying degrees, affect the firm's target customer group as well. For example, the large reduction in U.S. government defense spending adversely affected the concentration of defense contractors and military installations in southern California. Because of the widespread ripple effect from military base closings, lost contract revenues, and massive employee layoffs, the entire southern California market area suffered a prolonged business slump.
- The physical size of a given market area sets the upper limit for the potential number of customers the firm may attract.
- Geographic boundaries are often an important basis for market segmentation. *Market segmentation* refers to subdividing a larger market into smaller segments according to shared consumer attributes or characteristics. When markets are divided by geographical boundaries, the process is referred to as *geographic market segmentation.*

Geographic market segmentation is most often done on the basis of population concentrations. For example, the greater Atlanta metropolitan area, the Pacific Northwest region, or the sunbelt states are typical examples of markets defined by population concentrations. The most widely used method of classifying market segments by population density is the *Metropolitan Category System* devised by the U.S. Bureau of the Census. A metropolitan category is an area that surrounds and is economically and socially tied to what the Bureau refers to as a center city. The Bureau of the Census identifies three basic metropolitan categories:

- **Standard Metropolitan Statistical Areas (SMSAs):** These are free-standing areas that are not closely associated with other SMSAs. Most often, SMSAs are surrounded by nonmetropolitan counties. For an area to qualify for recognition as an SMSA it must be either (a) a city or urbanized area with a population of at least 50,000 or (b) a total metropolitan area with a population of at least 100,000. For example, Albany, Georgia, and Tallahassee, Florida, are SMSAs.
- **Primary Metropolitan Statistical Areas (PMSAs):** A PMSA is a population area of more than 1,000,000 that consists of either (a) a large urbanized county or (b) a cluster of counties with strong economic and social links. PMSAs often have close ties to neighboring CMSAs or PMSAs. For example, the cities

of Gary/Hammond, Indiana, constitute a PSMA with close ties to the Chicago, Illinois, CMSA.

- **Consolidated Metropolitan Statistical Areas (CMSAs):** These are large areas that include several PMSAs as components. For example, under the SMSA classification scheme, Anaheim/Santa Ana, Los Angeles/Long Beach, Oxnard/Ventura, and Riverside/San Bernardino are the PMSAs that make up the Los Angeles CMSA.

The Metropolitan Category System designations are used in many secondary information sources to identify specific geographic areas. For example, the wide array of consumer and business statistics published in the "Survey of Industrial & Commercial Buying Power" are organized using the Metropolitan Category System classification system.

Other commonly used bases for geographical segmentation are political boundaries, such as countries, states, or cities; regions, such as the Pacific Northwest; and climate differences, such as cold or hot climate zones.

3. **Understand market forces.** One major goal of market analysis is to identify the forces that influence the firm's market and understand how these forces do so. To gain this insight, the entrepreneur must gather the information necessary to answer questions such as the following:

- What is the primary source of business activity in the market area? For example, is the main driving force agriculture, commercial and financial, manufacturing, tourism?
- What is the total volume of business activity in the market area as measured by such indicators as retail sales, sales tax revenue, total payroll, or number of people employed? What is the outlook for these indicators?
- What are the major business firms, governmental agencies, or organizations that account for the largest percentages of business activity in the market area? What are the sales and/or employment projections for these entities?
- What is the average unemployment rate in the market area, and how does this rate compare to the national average? What is the current outlook for this indicator?
- How does the average price level and living standard for this market area compare to the national average for these statistics?
- How sensitive is business activity in the market area to changes in overall economic activity? Which major economic indicators have the largest impact on business activity in the market area?
- Is the tax and regulatory environment in the market area favorable to business?

- What are the key demographic factors that characterize the market? For example, answers to questions such as the following will provide the entrepreneur with a demographic profile. What is the current population of the market area? Is the population trend growing or declining? What is per capita income, and how does it compare with the national average or the averages of other market areas? What are consumer expenditures by retail category in this market area? What is the gender, age, and ethnic makeup of the population in the market area?

- What are the major social or cultural factors that shape or influence buying habits in the market? Is there evidence that these trends are changing? For example, answers to questions such as the following will provide a social/cultural profile of the market. What are the most dominant social goals in the market area? What are the prominent attitudes on religion, family, and education in the market area? What social value system is most dominant in the market area? What is the breakdown of major social classes (e.g., upper class, middle class, or working class) in the market area?

4. **Identify the firm's market niche.** A *market niche* is a specific segment of a larger consumer or business market that the firm can profitably exploit. It is identified by a target customer group (target market) having needs and expectations to which the firm can appeal. If the niche is to be commercially successful, the firm must establish a competitive position through careful matching of its strengths and capabilities with the needs and wants of its identified target market. Examples of successful market-niche positioning abound. For instance, sales of Rolls Royce automobiles have been successfully directed toward the elite segments of the retail automobile market; Pepsi-Cola has been successful in targeting its marketing effort at the youth segment of the soft drink market; and Porsche obtains a premium price for its cars by appealing to a loyal group of aficionados who feel no other automobile offers the desired bundle of product/service/membership benefits.

A market niche can be segmented in terms of various combinations of possible attributes or characteristics. The major categories of segmenting variables used to partition consumer markets are shown on Table 6-1; those used for business markets are shown on Table 6-2.

Fortunately, there is no one best strategy or approach to successful market-niche segmentation. A commercially successful market niche can be established with such diverse strategies as offering a new or technologically more efficient product or service, having a convenient

TABLE 6-1
Major Categories of Segmenting Variables for Consumer Markets

Geographic	Demographic	Socioeconomic	Psychographic
• Political boundaries • Climatic regions • Population boundaries	• Age • Gender • Race • Ethnicity • Marital status • Family size • Family life cycle	• Occupation • Education • Income • Social class	• Lifestyle • Activities • Interests • Hobbies • Opinions • Values • Religion

Behavior Patterns	Consumption Patterns	Consumer Predispositions	
• Type of store • Shopping location • Shopping frequency • Time of purchase • Size of purchase • Media habits	• Occasion for use (birthday, anniversary, etc.) • Frequency of use (heavy vs. light) • Types of products owned or services used • Product or service price level • Brand loyalty	• Product knowledge • Benefits sought • Reasons for purchase • Beliefs about products and brands	

location, selling at lower prices or providing better service than competitors, maintaining a superior product image, or tapping a market segment that has been ignored by other businesses.

While the vast array of domestic and international markets offers countless opportunities for developing a market niche, not all are realistic for a given firm. Identifying a potential market opportunity is only one-half the equation for commercial success. The other is the firm's capacity for capitalizing on the opportunity. Before attempting to enter and develop a market niche, the entrepreneur should have satisfactory answers to questions such as the following:

- Is the market opportunity consistent with the firm's basic strategy?
- Are the sales and profit potential of this opportunity sufficient to provide a compensatory rate of return?

TABLE 6-2
Major Categories of Segmenting Variables for Business Markets

Purchasing Characteristics	Financial Characteristics	Operating Characteristics
• Order frequency • Order size • Centralized or decentralized purchasing • Purchasing criteria—cost, quality, reliability, service • Purchasing attitude—see product as routine purchase, moderately important, critical	• Account size • Credit rating • Payment practices • Likelihood of default • Profitability of account	• Type of technology employed (labor-intensive or captial-intensive) • Frequency of use • Operating capacity • Continuous or seasonal operations • Delivery lead time required

Geographic Characteristics	Demographic Characteristics
• Geographic regions • Political boundaries • National boundaries • Climatic regions	• Industry classification • Type of business • Company size • Location

- What clearly defined competitive advantage does the firm have to justify entry into this market?
- Does the firm have the ability to make the opportunity successful? Does it have the necessary technical know-how, production capacity, management and staff expertise, employee skills, and financial resources?
- Does the firm have any weaknesses that affect its chance for commercial success? If so, how can the weaknesses be overcome?
- What pitfalls or risks are associated with this market opportunity, and can precautions be taken to minimize their impact?

5. **Define the firm's target market.** A target market or target customer group is that segment of the market having defined characteristics, needs, and expectations to which the firm's product or service is expected to appeal and toward which its marketing effort is aimed. The reasons for identifying the characteristics that distinguish the firm's target market from other consumers are:

- **To capitalize on these differences.** Consumers buy a specific product or brand name or use a particular service because it satisfies some perceived want, need, or expectation. The key to identifying a potentially successful market niche is, therefore, understanding these motives and how the firm can take advantage of them.
- **To provide justification for commercial success.** By demonstrating an understanding of the factors influencing purchases of the target customer group and how the firm's product or service can meet their needs, the entrepreneur provides the type of supporting evidence that is needed to make the business plan convincing.
- **To provide evidence of managerial ability.** By demonstrating marketing knowledge, the entrepreneur provides evidence of managerial ability. Again, this is evidence the intended reader expects to find.
- **To develop the marketing plan.** As discussed in Chapter 7, one important purpose of the firm's marketing plan is to decide how the firm will reach and motivate its target customer group. Unless the wants, needs, and expectations of the target market are clearly understood, it is impossible to create an effective plan for reaching them.

The most effective method for presenting the entrepreneur's characterization of the firm's target market is the *customer profile*. A customer profile identifies the geographic, demographic, psychographic, and behavioral characteristics that distinguish the target market from other consumers. These characteristics are explained below, and two examples of customer profiles are shown on Tables 6-3 and 6-4. The first profile, shown on Table 6-3, reflects the findings from a segmentation study of coffee drinkers. The data reveal three distinct segments in this category of consumer: those drinking decaffeinated, caffeinated, and ground coffee. The customer profile shown on Table 6-4 identifies the breakdown of the two primary demographic variables, age and income level, used by a bank to segment its retail customers.

As previously discussed, *geographic segmentation* involves the subdivision of a market into distinct geographical units such as national, state, regional, county, city, or neighborhood boundaries.

Demographic Characteristics are the general-population characteristics that distinguish the target market from other consumers. Included here are commonly used segmenting variables such as age, gender, race, ethnic background, income level, occupation, education level, and religious preference. Marketing experts suggest that demographics characteristics are the primary set of influences driving the

TABLE 6-3
Coffee Market Segment Profiles

Attribute	Decaffeinated	Caffeinated	Ground
Percentage of Total Users	35%	33%	32%
Frequency of Use	Light user	Medium user	Heavy user
Distinguishing Benefits Desired	Does not cause nervousness or lost sleep, concentrated form, prepared quickly	Helps people to wake up, provides lift, easy to prepare, convenient packaging, brand name	Non-concentrated form, taste, aroma indifferent on preparation requirements, indifferent on equipment require-ments, indifferent on packaging
Form Desired	Instant	Both instant and ground	Ground
Demographics	Older, widowed, low income, more minorities	Average age, divorced, average income, more minorities	Younger, married, higher income, fewer minorities

TABLE 6-4
Bank Customers Segmented by Age and Income Level

		AGE	
	Under 39	40–65	Over 65
Below $16,000	Young, Low Income	Middle-Aged, Low Income	Retired, Low Income
$16,000–44,000	Young, Middle Income	Middle-Aged, Middle Income	Retired, Middle Income
Above $44,000	Young, High Income	Middle-Aged, High Income	Retired, High Income

INCOME

purchase of consumer goods and services and the easiest of the segmenting variables to measure. There are numerous examples of how demographic variables are used by marketers to reach specific market segments. For instance, much of the marketing efforts of major breweries are aimed at the blue-collar worker because this group accounts for the largest percentage of total beer sales. General Foods has effectively used a segmentation strategy based on the age and life-cycle stage of a typical dog to market its Cycle 1 through Cycle 4 dog foods to concerned pet owners. Segmentation based on gender has long been applied to the marketing of such products and services as clothing, hairdressing, cosmetics, and magazines.

Psychographic characteristics are the segmenting variables that identify the consumer's social class, lifestyle, or personality makeup. Experienced marketers agree that what consumers buy and the reasons for their purchases are strongly effected by their psychological makeup. For example, marketers have discovered that social class has a strong influence on consumer preferences in cars, clothing, home furnishing, leisure activities, and reading activities. Publishers and marketers of magazines rely heavily on lifestyle segmentation to reach an identified target market. Likewise, marketers rely heavily on identifying the values, attitudes, and beliefs that identify consumer personality. This knowledge allows them to endow their products or services with brand personalities that correspond to the personalities of their target markets.

Behavioral variables refer to consumers' attitudes, habits, or responses to a product or service. For example, automobile buyers can be segmented by the perceived benefits provided by ownership, such as the degree of functional utility received, how well the vehicle fits the buyer's lifestyle or self-image, or the degree of brand loyalty demonstrated by consumers. Consumers can also be categorized by the occasions that prompt a purchase, such as Christmas presents or wedding gifts; by user status, such as first-time user, regular user, or potential user; or by usage rate, such as light, medium, or heavy. Many marketing experts believe that behavioral characteristics are the most logical starting point for identifying a market segment or niche.

As this overview of segmentation suggests, there are numerous ways to segment a market. Not all, however, are practical. For example, the customers of a commercial print shop could be segmented by hair color, race, or age. Yet none of these characteristics are useful for identifying who uses the service and why or how often it is used. To be effective, a market segment or niche should exhibit the three characteristics identified below. Equally important, the justification for commercial success presented in the business plan should explicitly or implicitly include these characteristics. To be effective, a market niche or segment should be:

- **Measurable.** It must be possible to identify and measure the characteristics, size, and purchasing power of the target market if this customer group is to be distinguished from others.
- **Significant.** The segment or niche must be sufficiently large and profitable to warrant the marketing effort.
- **Accessible.** It must be possible to effectively reach and serve the segment or niche.

For the typical entrepreneur, the information needed to define a target market may come from secondary information sources, personal observation, personally or professionally conducted market research, or some combination of these. Market segmentation, target market analysis, and consumer behavior are widely discussed marketing topics, and there are numerous sources of secondary information available on these subjects. The places to start researching these topics are industry or trade journals and other sources of topic-specific articles.

Entrepreneurs from smaller firms can often conduct their own marketing research to segment a market by target customer group. This effort can take a variety of forms ranging from something as simple as observing traffic patterns at various city intersections to conducting face-to-face or mail-out customer-opinion surveys.

Target market information can also be obtained through the services of a professional market research firm. If the venture for which the business plan is prepared has sufficient potential, hiring a market research specialist to gather information on market feasibility may be cost-effective.

6. **Identify the competition.** One of the few business certainties on which the entrepreneur can depend is the existence of competition. The degree of competition faced by the firm and the extent to which the entrepreneur can effectively combat competitive forces are important determinants of commercial success. Since the intended reader of the business plan will carefully evaluate the section describing the firm's competition, it should detail:

- The substitute products or services that pose competitive threats to the firm's sales and how the entrepreneur will counter these threats.
- The major businesses that compete directly with the firm and their relative strengths and weaknesses.
- The competitive advantage the firm holds over its rivals.

Some information on the firm's competition may be obtained from published sources such as trade journals. For many businesses, however, the most effective method of assessing competition is by direct observation. In these cases, the entrepreneur can assess a competitor's strengths and weaknesses by visiting that business; observing its method of operation; and speaking with customers, suppliers, and others that deal with it. The competitor assessment should focus on characteristics such as the following:

- Product or service differentiation.
- Product or service quality.
- Selling price.
- The type and quality of customer service.
- Customer relations.
- Credit policy.
- Reputation and image.
- Location and appearance.
- Advertising effectiveness.
- Quality of employees.
- Financial strength.

A simple yet effective tool for organizing competitor information is a column-and-row worksheet. This simple device is illustrated in the sample market analysis at the end of this chapter.

7. **Forecast sales and prepare the marketing plan.** Sales forecasting is discussed in the next section of this chapter. Preparation of the marketing plan is the subject of Chapter 7.

PREPARING THE SALES FORECAST

The ultimate aim of researching the firm's industry and its market is to gather the information necessary to make a realistic sales forecast. This forecast is the single most critical piece of information contained in the business plan. It is important to both the intended reader of the plan and to the entrepreneur for the following reasons:

■ Since sales volume is the most obvious indicator of commercial success, the sales forecast and its underlying assumptions will be carefully evaluated by the reader of the plan. A questionable sales forecast creates suspicion about the entrepreneur's claim of commercial success.

■ For the new business, sales potential is the ultimate criterion for judging the feasibility of the venture. If the target market cannot be expected to produce a profitable sales volume, then the venture is doomed from the outset.

■ The sales forecast is essential information for other components of the business plan. For example, expected sales volume is the starting point in the financial plan for estimating asset needs and period-by-period cash flow. Likewise, the planned level of operations as developed in the operating plan, the planned level of promotion and advertising as indicated in the marketing plan, and the estimated number of employees needed to produce and sell planned output as shown in the organization plan, are all dependent on the sales estimate.

■ Since virtually all business planning and operating activity in the firm are predicated on sales or the expectation of sales, the sales forecast is essential information for the internal planning and decision-making required to operate the business.

Forecasting is the art of estimating what is likely to happen given some assumed set of conditions. A sales forecast, then, is an informed estimate, based on a given set of assumptions about the future, of sales volume for a specific market, a target market, a firm, a group of firms, or an entire industry. The forecast may be stated in terms of either sales revenue or units, and the time period covered by the forecast may be short, such as the monthly or weekly forecasts used in preparing a cash budget, or the planning horizon may extend to as much as five years.

Both the term "art" and the phrase "assumed set of conditions" are critical to the sales forecasting process. Forecasting, unfortunately, is not a precise science. Rather, good forecasting is a blend of relevant information about the past and future, sound forecasting tools, the judgment of an experienced entrepreneur, and the learning and expertise that comes from preparing forecasts.

The entrepreneur should understand from the outset that sales of very few products or services lend themselves to easy forecasting. Only those having a stable sales trend, such as the demand for electricity experienced by the typical public utility, are relatively easy to predict. What's more, since a forecast deals with an unknown future, any forecast is subject to varying degrees of uncertainty or forecasting error. The extent of the error inherent in a sales forecast depends on the type of business for which the forecast is prepared, its age, and the circumstances under which it operates. In general, the degree of accuracy in a sales forecast increases, or forecasting error declines, if the firm is established, operates in a relatively stable market, has experienced management, and has an experienced and informed person making the forecast. Conversely, if the firm is new, if the entrepreneur or the forecaster has limited experience, or if the product is unique or the market volatile, forecasts are subject to much greater uncertainty.

In order for the sales forecast to be viewed as credible by the reader of the business plan, the assumptions on which the forecast is built must be sound and carefully detailed. As discussed in the previous sections, the firm's sales are affected by a variety of external and internal influences. Unless specific assumptions about the impact and future status of these influences are clearly spelled out, the sales forecast as well as other components of the business plan using this number will be labeled meaningless exaggeration.

THE SALES FORECASTING PROCESS

Preparing the firm's sales forecast is typically a four-stage process. A forecast is prepared for the following:

- The national economy.
- The firm's industry.
- The firm's market or target customer group.
- The firm and its individual products.

Since general economic conditions and industry sales affect the firm and its market, the sales forecasting process should begin with the entrepreneur's assumptions about these two important external variables. The forecast for the economy, the firm's industry, and possibly its market will usually not have to be made personally. Acceptable projections are readily available in numerous business, trade, and government publications. The information gleaned from these sources can be used to make the assumptions that serve as the backdrop for the entrepreneur's sales forecast.

SALES FORECASTING TECHNIQUES

A sales forecast for the firm is made using information from one or both of two possible sources: what buyers have done in the past and what potential buyers are likely to do in the future. The data and other information gleaned from these sources can be used with virtually any forecasting technique.

Forecasting methods can be grouped into two basic categories: (a) the quantitative tools used to extend past behavior and (b) the qualitative or quantitative tools used to predict future behavior. In the case of an existing business, either or both types of forecasting methods can be used. Forecasting sales for the new venture is, by necessity, limited to techniques from the latter category.

Forecasts themselves fall into three general categories: qualitative or judgmental forecasts, which depend heavily on the informed judgment and intuition of the forecaster; quantitative forecasts, which apply mathematics to historical or estimated data; or some combination of the two. *A qualitative sales forecast* is an estimate based on the expertise and experience of an informed forecaster. Where possible, qualitative forecasts should be enhanced by the quantitative analysis of historical or projected sales data.

There are essentially two types of *quantitative forecasts*: (a) projections produced by extending or projecting trends and patterns found in historical sales data and (b) projections produced by predicting future sales using the relationship between sales and an influencing variable or group of variables. The more commonly used methods in each category are described below.

Extrapolating Past Sales

The sales forecasting process for an existing business typically starts with a detailed analysis of past sales. This review provides management with background information needed to understand why sales behaved as they did and the forecaster with the basis for extrapolating the past.

The various quantitative forecasting methods used with historical data are generally referred to as *time-series methods*. A time series is simply a collection of data that occurred or was measured in regular time intervals such as months, quarters, or years. In general, the mathematical tools used in time-series analysis identify recurring patterns and random or nonrecurring movements in the data; smooth the random influences around the identified patterns; and project the smoothed patterns into the future. Time-series patterns can be separated into the following components:

▬ **Basic trend:** A trend represents the long-term movement of sales through time. It is represented as a smooth, mathematically or graphically fitted line of historical or projected sales. Since the trend-smoothing process strips all cyclical, seasonal, and random movements from the trendline, this line is often referred to as the line of average relationships. That is, it reflects the impact of an average of all the factors affecting sales through time. For example, if sales have grown at the long-term trend rate of 10% per year, sales for each of the forecast years are assumed to grow at this same 10% rate.

▬ **Cyclical movements:** Cyclical patterns are the intermediate-term, periodic, wave-like movements of sales. These waves have clearly defined peaks and troughs and usually reflect the strong influence of general swings in overall economic activity (business cycles). Since the typical business cycle lasts from one to three years, identifying cyclical patterns in sales is important for intermediate-range forecasting.

▬ **Seasonal patterns:** Seasonal patterns refer to the consistent, periodic movement of sales within the year. The term *seasonal* describes any recurring hourly, daily, weekly, monthly, or quarterly sales pattern. Seasonal patterns are usually related to holidays, trade practices, weather, or the influence of predominant social customs.

The recognition of seasonal patterns in sales data is essential to the accuracy of short-term sales forecasts.

Extrapolating historical data by relating sales to time periods is a common method of sales forecasting. It can work well for mature firms selling products or services in markets that are relatively free from dynamic change. In these cases, the method is especially effective when used to make the monthly sales estimates needed for cash budgeting and for projecting the firm's long-term sales trend.

Before leaving this section, two important points should be noted. First, it is clear that any time-series forecast, regardless of the level of technical sophistication employed, implicitly assumes that the conditions causing historical sales patterns will continue into the future. Since any forecast is only as good as its underlying assumptions, a sales projection based on time-series analysis can be realistic only if the past is a good indicator of the future. Where circumstances are changing, any mechanical projection of sales should be considered no more than a starting point for the sales forecast. Projected sales values should be adjusted for the impact of what management expects to occur.

Second, while a detailed discussion of time-series techniques is beyond the scope of this book, the topic is covered in books on forecasting or statistics. Also, and of more importance to the entrepreneur preparing a business plan, there are numerous user-friendly, software packages available that feature forecasting techniques. Many of these packages require neither prior knowledge of forecasting techniques nor computer sophistication.

Estimating Market Potential and Market Share

Obtaining a sales projection from historical data is not the end of the forecasting process. Rather, it is usually the starting point. As indicated above, even when historical data are available, it is desirable to tie the sales forecast to a variable or variables other than time. A common method for doing so involves estimating the sales potential of a market segment, a geographic target area, or a target customer group, and then estimating the share of that total to be captured by the firm. The forecast values produced by this approach can stand alone or they can be used as checks on, or refinements of, the results produced by other forecasting techniques.

The most common approaches to estimating market potential and market share are the *market build-up method* and the *market factor method.* The former approach is most often used to estimate sales of business-related products or services, and the latter is most often used to estimate sales of consumer-related goods and services.

Market Build-up Method: Forecasting sales using the market build-up method involves identifying the potential business buyers of the firm's product/service in each market and then estimating the purchase potential of each. The estimates for individual markets are totaled to arrive at the sales forecast for the firm.

One variation of this approach is explained in the following example. It uses Standard Industrial Classification (SIC) codes to identify potential purchasers and Standard Metropolitan Statistical Area (SMSA) to identify market areas.

To illustrate, assume the management of XYZ Company, a hypothetical manufacturer of packaging material, is considering expanding into the southeast market. Their first goal is to estimate sales potential for this regional market. They begin by dividing the southeast region into sub-markets according to SMSA designations. The contrived sales and employment data for product-user-groups (SIC codes) in one hypothetical SMSA are shown in the first three columns of Table 6-5.

The first calculation is average packaging sales per worker in each user group. These values are shown in Column 4 and are calculated by dividing the Column 2 value by that of Column 3. For example, the Food group purchased $586,164,000 of packing material and employs 1,587,305 workers nationwide. Average sales per employee in the Food group is, therefore, $371.

Estimated packaging material sales are obtained by multiplying Sales Per Worker by the number of workers employed in that industry group. For example, the $1,845,000 sales estimate for the Food group, Column 6, is calculated as the Sales Per Worker of $371 times the 4,973 Food group workers employed in the SMSA (Column 5). Total estimated sales for the SMSA, $2,387,000, is obtained by summing the estimated sales for each industry group. This process would be repeated for each SMSA in the southeast region. The sales of individual SMSAs are then totaled to obtain the sales estimate for the southeast market. Given this estimate, management's next task would be to estimate the share of this market they believe the firm could capture.

Alternative Methods: One alternative method of forecasting business sales involves calculating the historical percentage relationship between the firm's sales and total industry sales (firm sales/industry sales). This percentage, which represents the firm's share of the industry, is then applied to an industry sales forecast to obtain estimated sales for the firm. Industry sales forecasts are available from a number of secondary sources of published information, such as those identified in Chapter 5.

TABLE 6-5

Estimated Sales of Packaging Materials in a Hypothetical Market

(1) Product Users By SIC Group Code	(2) Value Of Product Used ($000)	(3) Number Of Workers By User Group	(4) Sales Per Worker By User Group	(5) Workers By User Group In SMSA	(6) Est. SMSA Sales By User ($000)
20 Food	$586,164	1,587,305	371	4,973	$1,845
21 Tobacco	17,432	74,557	233	None	None
22 Textile	91,520	874,677	104	250	26
23 Apparel	34,865	1,252,443	27	1,974	53
24 Lumber	19,611	526,622	37	690	26
25 Furniture	89,341	364,166	245	616	151
26 Paper	211,368	587,882	359	190	68
27 Printing & Publishing	32,686	904,208	36	2,876	104
28 Chemicals	128,564	772,169	166	488	81
29 Petroleum	28,328	161,367	175	None	None
30 Rubber & Plastics	67,551	387,997	174	190	33
Total					$2,387

Another alternative for estimating business sales would be to purchase total sales and brand sales reports from marketing research firms such as the A. C. Nielsen Company. These data can be used to calculate the firm's historical share of the market. For example, Nielsen audits retail sales in supermarkets and drug stores for various product categories. The percentage of this total captured by the firm can be applied to published estimates of industry sales to obtain forecast sales for the firm.

Market Factor Method: When the factor method is used to estimate sales of consumer goods, the forecast is made by relating sales behavior to the behavior of a factor or a set of factors that is highly correlated with sales. A factor is simply a variable that relates the behavior of one item to that of the item being forecast.

Assume, for example, that the management of a wholesale bakery company in Jacksonville, Florida, has determined from historical records that the firm's sales average one-half of one percent (.005) of the total retail sales in the Jacksonville SMSA. Management can forecast sales for the firm by multiplying .005 by an estimate of retail sales for the Jacksonville SMSA. For instance, if total retail sales for Jacksonville are estimated to be $120,000,000 next year, the sales forecast for the bakery is $600,000 (.005 × $120,000,000). Retail sales estimates for SMSAs are published by *Sales & Marketing Management* in its "Survey of Buying Power" issue.

The single-factor approach illustrated above is often expanded to include a logically related set of factors that are combined into an index. The advantage of using multiple factors stems from using more information to describe sales behavior. One widely used multiple factor index is the "Buying Power Index" published in the *Survey of Buying Power*. This index reflects the relative consumer buying power in different regions, states, and SMSAs. It is a weighted index of the three most important factors determining consumer buying power: income, retail sales, and population. A similar index for industrial purchasing power is also published by *Sales & Marketing Management*.

The Survey of Buying Power Index is readily available and easy to use. Suppose, for example, that the Buying Power Index for the Jacksonville SMSA were published as .95% (a hypothetical figure). This index value means that .95% of the retail sales in the United States are made in the Jacksonville SMSA. Thus, if a cosmetics manufacturer were estimating the market potential for the Jacksonville SMSA, it could be expected that approximately .95% of the cosmetics sales in the United States would take place in that SMSA.

Other Forecasting Methods

Other forecasting methods fall into either of two broad categories: (a) forecasts designed to measure consumer response to a product or service and (b) expert or judgmental forecasts. Response measurements include various forms of consumer surveys and test marketing. These techniques are used to gather information on what consumers are likely to do. They are based on the assumption that a reliable indicator of potential sales to a given target customer group can be obtained by garnering the opinions and reactions of a representative sample of target market consumers.

Consumer surveys can be used to gather sales information for existing businesses or new ventures and for either business or consumer products or services. The techniques employed vary in sophistication from simple direct questioning to intricately designed consumer interviews, panels, or questionnaires. The more sophisticated approaches are usually conducted by marketing research firms or other marketing experts. Surveys are especially valuable if consumers have clearly formulated intentions and are able to describe them. For example, a former client of the authors was interested in opening a neighborhood fresh-seafood market. To determine the number of potential customers in the area and their purchasing habits, he conducted personal-contact interviews with residents in an eight-block radius of the intended site. The data gathered provided a clear indication of potential target market sales and an estimate of the likelihood for the success of his proposed venture.

Test marketing is often used to measure potential sales when the product is new or expert or judgmental forecasts are not reliable. The technique involves selling the product or service in a representative market area or to a sample of targeted customers using the same marketing program that is intended for the broad-scale campaign. Test marketing is useful for measuring consumer reaction to the product, the extent to which the product is repurchased after the initial trial, and the effectiveness of various advertising and promotion techniques.

While test marketing is effective for estimating market potential, it requires expertise to administer and, therefore, may be cost-prohibitive for many firms. In the correct situation, however, the expense incurred may be worth the sacrifice. The hard sales data produced by test marketing is the most convincing evidence of sales potential for a new product or service that can be used in a business plan.

Forecasting the level of sales required to ensure commercial success for a new business venture or a new product or service is often done using the judgmental estimate of a marketing expert or an informed entrepreneur. Experts include such diverse groups as sales personnel, distributors, suppliers, retailers, wholesalers, marketing consultants, marketing research firms, trade associations, and firms that specialize in making industry and market forecasts, such as Data Resources, Chase Econometric, and Wharton Econometric. The estimates can be obtained using various information-gathering techniques such as interviews, questionnaires, or panel discussions. Again, expert opinion is an effective form of documenting the entrepreneur's claim of commercial success.

TIPS FOR PREPARING THE MARKET ANALYSIS AND SALES FORECAST

■■ **Don't assume a market exists.** There is a natural tendency for an entrepreneur excited about the firm's product or service to assume consumers will be equally enthusiastic. While the entrepreneur's excitement is important to success, emotions are not a substitute for evidence that willing customers exist. The reader of the business plan will expect to see solid supporting documentation and not unsupported claims.

■■ **Don't slight this component.** Along with the industry analysis, the market analysis and sales forecast are critical to the question of commercial success. The intended reader will carefully evaluate the quantity and quality of information presented in this section, and it is important that the entrepreneur do his or her homework before it is prepared.

■■ **Do this analysis second for new ventures.** Before committing time and energy to preparing a complete business plan for a new venture, do a quick market feasibility study after completing the preliminary industry analysis. By making this effort early, the entrepreneur gets a clear indication of whether the venture has sufficient merit to justify preparing a complete business plan.

■■ **Make multiple sales forecasts.** Since a forecast is only as accurate as the assumptions upon which it is built, it is wise to create three variations of the sales forecast. One forecast should be based on pessimistic assumptions, the worst-case scenario; one based on optimistic assumptions, the best-case scenario; and one based on the most likely set of conditions. There are two basic advantages to this "what if" approach to forecasting and planning. First, multiple sales forecasts clarify the distinction between what is deemed most likely to occur and what is possible. Second, the entrepreneur sends another strong message about management ability. Using the "what if" forecasting and planning indicates that he or she understands and prepares for the uncertainty associated with projecting the future.

■■ **Contact suppliers for information.** The potential suppliers of a new business have a vested interest in its success. In many cases, they have information that will help the entrepreneur estimate sales volume. Some suppliers also have sophisticated models for estimating sales for a given type of business. This is true, for example, with suppliers of restaurants, feed stores, department stores, automobile dealerships, and many fast-food franchise operations.

━━ **Contact industry trade associations for information.** Most industry trade associations have a wealth of data that are useful for developing a sales forecast. Some trade associations also have sophisticated sales forecasting models that can assist the entrepreneur.

━━ **Study similar sales experiences.** It is often possible to estimate sales potential by evaluating the sales experiences of others, including competitors, other new firms in the industry, or similar products or services. For example, assume XYZ Software Company develops a totally new and revolutionary computer program. Since the program is unique, there are no direct sales comparisons available. Yet, valuable insights for estimating sales of the new program can be gained by examining the sales history of other successful software.

━━ **Use graphics.** Some portions of the market analysis and sales forecast will necessarily deal with quantitative data. The message in these data is delivered more effectively when verbal explanations are supplemented with tables, graphs, and charts.

SAMPLE MARKET ANALYSIS AND SALES FORECAST

Assume Ms. Karen Martin intends to open a new retail furniture store in a major southeast Standard Metropolitan Statistical Area (her target SMSA). She expects the medium-priced to high-priced bold furniture and bedding lines the store will carry to appeal to the upper-income consumer. The store will offer delivery and home decorating services and will extend installment credit to qualified buyers.

Since this is a new business, she wishes to (a) determine whether sufficient market potential exists to support the business and (b) make a realistic sales estimate that can be used in her business plan. To do so, Ms. Martin first conducts an industry and market analysis. The key points from these studies are summarized as part of the following six-step process.

1. **Identify the firm's industry.** Realizing that the retail furniture industry includes a number of different SIC codes, Ms. Martin begins the analysis by reviewing the description of the business and its intended operations as explained in the business summary component of her business plan. She then examines the various descriptions of the retail furniture group in the *SIC Manual* and identifies 5712 as the proper SIC code for her business.

Using this SIC code, Ms. Martin begins her investigation of the retail furniture industry by researching secondary information sources selected from those listed in Chapter 5. Primary among these are industry trade association publications, published articles on the retail furniture industry, Standard and Poor's *Industry Surveys*, the *Census of Retail Trade*, and *A Guide to Consumer Markets*. In order to identify relevant published articles on the furniture industry, Ms. Martin consults *Predicasts Forecasts*. She uses *Gale's Encyclopedia of Associations* and the *Small Business Sourcebook* to identify appropriate trade association publications.

This research provides a wealth of information about her industry. For example, Ms. Martin discovers the following key facts about retail furniture sales.

- The consumer demand for furniture is closely linked to new housing construction and the level of disposable personal income (DPI). DPI, which is a measure of the consumer's ability and willingness to spend, is a widely published economic statistic. It is reported quarterly along with gross domestic product (GDP) and other aggregate economic data.
- The surge in demand for home furnishings lags increases in new housing construction by about one year.
- The demand for home furnishings is closely linked to general economic conditions. This demand rises during economic upswings as DPI and GDP increase, and declines during downswings.
- The key factors that influence consumer spending for furniture are: the population growth rate, the level and distribution of personal income, age distribution of the population, the number of households, the rate of new household formations, and overall consumer retail spending.

Information such as this has given Ms. Martin a working knowledge of the industry. She now understands the industry's cyclical nature, its sensitivity to changes in economic activity, the primary factors influencing industry performance, and the major indicators of industry success. Her research also producesa realistic forecast of the industry's long-term growth rate and industry sales and profits for each of the next three years. Of greatest importance, Ms. Martin has identified which secondary information sources should be monitored in the future to keep abreast of industry developments.

2. **Identify the firm's market area.** Ms. Martin's next task is to define the specific geographic area the furniture store will serve. Based on personal observation, market demographics, the expected rates of economic and demographic growth, the recommendations

from published market research, and readings from other selected secondary information sources on various market areas in the southeast, she has decided on the target SMSA as the best choice. Ms. Martin further reasons that because home furnishings are considered shopping goods, the store has the potential to attract customers from a relatively large geographic area. On the basis of this information, she defines her market as the entire target SMSA. This geographic area consists of five counties with a combined population of approximately 2,000,000 residents.

3. **Define the firm's target market.** To begin her analysis of an appropriate target market, Ms. Martin consults the publication entitled *A Guide to Consumer Markets*. This publication provides invaluable information on consumer spending habits. From this source she learns that heads of households in the 25-year to 44-year age group spend more for furniture and home furnishings than any other age group. To determine the age distribution and purchasing habits of furniture and home furnishing consumers in the target SMSA, she uses census data obtained from the *Census of Population: General Population Characteristics* published by the Bureau of the Census, "The Survey of Buying Power" published by *Sales and Marketing Management Magazine*, various state and municipal publications, and selected articles on the geographic area in which her target SMSA is located. From these publications she learns these important facts:

- Households in the 25–44 age group make up about 20% of the population in the target SMSA.
- Approximately 22% of the households in the 25–44 age group in the target SMSA earn at least $40,000 annually.
- Households in the 25–44 age group in the target SMSA earning $40,000 or more spend an average of $350 annually on furniture and home furnishings.
- The total population, number of new households, and total retail sales in the target SMSA are increasing at an 8% annual growth rate. This growth pattern is expected to continue for at least the next ten years.
- The trend of new-home construction in the target SMSA is increasing at the long-term average growth rate of 10%. This growth pattern is also expected to continue for at least the next ten years.

Given her intention to focus on the upper-income buyer, Ms. Martin concludes that her primary target market should consist of those households in the 25–44 age group having an annual income of $40,000 or more.

4. **Identify and evaluate the firm's competition.** Some useful information on competition may be found in secondary sources such as industry and trade association publications or those of appropriate state and municipal agencies. Also, data sources such as the *Census of Retail Trade* provide useful quantitative information on competition in a specific SMSA. In the case of a retailer of consumer items, however, the most reliable source of information on competition is personal contact. Using this approach, Ms. Martin conducts informal interviews with furniture customers in the target SMSA and visits those stores she identifies as direct competition. From her visits, she gathers information on competitor product lines, services, pricing policy, number of employees, store size, customer philosophy, and location.

In order to better organize and evaluate this information, Ms. Martin compiles her data using the simple competitive-information form shown on Table 6-6. This table simplifies the evaluation process and is an invaluable aid to decision-making.

5. **Estimate market sales potential.** Ms. Martin realizes that before the annual sales estimates for her store can be made, she must make an estimate of the sales potential for the target SMSA and/or for her target customer group. There are several sources that provide useful information for estimating current sales by product line in a given market area. The two most noted are the "Survey of Buying Power" and the *Census of Retail Trade*. From the "Survey of Buying Power," she is able to determine that the retail category "Furniture and Sleep Equipment" generated $40,000,000 of sales in the target SMSA last year. Assuming sales in this category will grow at the same rate as that projected for new household formations, 10%, Ms. Martin estimates total furniture and sleep equipment sales in the target SMSA next year to be $44,000,000 ($40,000,000 × 1.10).

As an alternative, Ms. Martin could have made the estimate of potential market sales by multiplying the "Average Dollars Spent Per Household on Furniture Products" by the number of households in the target SMSA. The former figure can be obtained from *A Guide to Consumer Markets* and the latter from the *Census of Retail Trade*.

To develop an estimate of the sales potential for the target market group, Ms. Martin uses two approaches. The first involves multiplying the $44,000,000 estimate of total furniture and sleep equipment sales for the target SMSA by the percentage of that total represented by sales of medium-priced to high-priced items. From her research, Ms. Martin estimates that approximately 60% of total sales of home furnishings fall in the upper one-half of the price range. Using these numbers, she arrives at a target market sales estimate of $26,400,000 ($44,000,000 × .60).

TABLE 6-6
Summary Competitive Information

Characteristic	A	B	C	D	E	F	G	H	I
Products Offered									
Bedding	X		X	X		X	X		
Furniture		X						X	X
Appliances		X						X	X
Carpeting		X							
Product Quality									
Low	X								
Medium		X		X		X	X		X
High			X		X			X	
Pricing Policy									
Low	X								
Medium		X		X		X	X		X
High			X		X			X	
Services Offered									
Delivery	X								
Credit		X		X		X	X		X
Decorating			X		X			X	
Store Size									
Under 5000 sq. ft.	X								
5000 to 9999 sq. ft.		X		X		X	X		X
10000 to 14999 sq. ft.					X				
15000 to 20000 sq. ft.			X					X	
Number of Employees									
5 or less	X								
6 to 10		X		X		X	X		X
11 to 15					X				
More than 15			X					X	
Location									
Mall		X				X	X		X
Shopping strip	X			X	X				
Other			X					X	

For her second approach to estimating target market sales, Ms. Martin uses the demographic data obtained from her research on target market characteristics. The target SMSA currently has a total population of 2,000,000 and this number is expected to increase by 8% next year. This growth rate would result in a total population of 2,160,000. She also discovers that households in the 25–44 age group make up about 20% of the population in the target SMSA. Applying this percentage to the total population estimate results in an estimated 432,000 households in the 25–44 age group. Since she has targeted households in this age group with incomes of $40,000 or more and approximately 22% of the households in the 25–44 age group in the target SMSA fall into this category, the target market group has an estimated size of 95,040 households (432,000 × .22). Given an average annual expenditure on home furnishings by this group of $350, the alternative estimate for target market sales is $33,264,000 ($350 × 95,040).

Since the estimates from the two approaches are reasonably close, Ms. Martin decides to use the average of the two for any subsequent calculations. This figure is $29,832,000 [($26,400,000 + $33,264,000)/2].

6. **Forecasting sales for the business.** In order to compete effectively and capture a profitable share of estimated sales volume for a target market, the entrepreneur must be able to distinguish his or her business from the competition. This differentiation can take many forms, including lower prices, better service, better location, or a unique product line. Ms. Martin is confident that the exclusive distributor rights to a new and bold product line will provide the product differentiation her store needs to compete successfully. Her task, then, is to make an estimate of the share of total target market sales the store can capture. To do so, she combines the results of several different methods of estimating initial sales for the business.

One approach is to calculate the average sales figure per competitor in the market area. She begins by consulting the *Census of Retail Trade*. From this source she learns that there are 76 retail furniture stores in the target SMSA. Based on her reading and from her experience evaluating the competition, Ms. Martin estimates that 21 of the 76 stores now compete for the same target customer group. Adding one to this figure for the addition of her store, she divides this total into the $29,832,000 average of the two target market sales estimates. The result is an average sales figure per store of $1,356,000 ($29,832,000/22).

Ms. Martin then uses two alternative methods of estimating sales to check the validity of the previous result. The first involves using average sales per square foot, and the second average inventory turnover. From trade journals, Ms. Martin identifies the average sales per square foot of floor space for a typical retail furniture store. She multiplies this number by the number of planned square feet in her store to obtain an additional sales estimate. Ms. Martin also consults *Robert Morris Associates Annual Statement Studies* to obtain the average inventory turnover (sales/inventory) figure for retail furniture stores in her size category. She multiplies this number by the planned level of inventory for her store to obtain the third sales estimate. Since the sales figures produced by the three alternative methods are reasonably close, Ms. Martin uses the average of the three as an estimate of the most likely sales volume for her store.

CHAPTER PERSPECTIVE

The market analysis and sales forecast are an extension of the industry analysis. A market analysis provides the information needed to convert an assessment of market potential into a realistic sales forecast. It is a study of the basic factors that define and affect the market for the firm's product or service and what the firm must do to effectively position itself to take advantage of the opportunity that is available. A market analysis usually consists of a description of its geographic location, the firm's market niche, the target market the firm expects to reach, the firm's competition, and an estimate of the sales potential the market should provide. The sales forecast is a guage of the firm's ability to achieve commercial success and, because all activity in the firm is ultimately related to sales, it is the basis for all other plans and projections.

The Marketing Plan

MARKETING AND PLANNING

This chapter is the first in the series that applies planning to one of the basic functions of a business firm. In this case, that function is marketing. Planning involves deciding what must be done, how it will be done, when it needs to be done, and by whom it will be done. The marketing function in a business firm is responsible for establishing the plans, policies, and procedures that will get the right goods or services to the right people, at the right place, time, and price, using the right promotion techniques. The marketing plan, which combines these functions, is the basic strategy for satisfying the needs and wants of the firm's target customer group.

After studying the material in this chapter you will:

■ Understand what planning is and the basic steps in the planning process.

■ Understand the role of the marketing plan.

■ Know the information needed to prepare the marketing plan.

■ Understand the steps to preparing the marketing plan.

■ Understand what a marketing-mix strategy is and the role it plays in the marketing plan.

WHAT IS PLANNING?

The cornerstone of the management process and the most important function any manager performs is planning. Planning is the art and science of deciding what course of action the firm will take to meet established objectives. Through planning, a manager:

■ Gathers the information needed to evaluate the firm's strengths, weaknesses, and opportunities.

■ Sets realistic long-term objectives and short-term operating goals.

■ Develops long-term strategies that capitalize on the firm's strengths and minimize its threats and weaknesses.

■ Develops the short-term operating plans that identify the resources and activities that will be employed to meet strategic aims.

The necessary corollary to planning is the management function of control. It involves monitoring activity to ensure that actual results are consistent with planned expectations and, when necessary, that corrective action is taken.

A MODEL OF THE PLANNING PROCESS

Planning, as true of any complex activity, is not a single act but rather a process consisting of interrelated steps. These steps and their interrelationships are depicted in Figure 7-1. The process starts with the entrepreneur's statement of the firm's business philosophy and its intended mission. These basics form the personality and character of the firm, identify the image to be projected, determine the general direction the business will take, and establish the foundation from which the firm's strategic and operating plans are determined.

FIGURE 7-1 *The flow of activities in the planning process*

In order to develop operating plans that effectively carry out adopted strategies, the entrepreneur must have reliable information on the firm and its environment. This information is used to prepare the forecast on which detailed operating plans and budgets are developed.

Figure 7-1 also indicates the importance of the control function. Plans are developed using assumptions and forecasts about the future. Since the future is uncertain, it is necessary to monitor actual results and these outcomes to what has been anticipated. Doing so puts the entrepreneur in position to take corrective action before problems become crises. Corrective actions can range from a simple fine-tuning of operations to a complete remake of assumptions, forecasts, and plans.

WHAT IS A MARKETING PLAN?

A marketing plan is a coordinated action program that describes how the firm's target customer group will be motivated to purchase its product/service. This document details the marketing goals to be achieved, the marketing-mix strategy that will position the firm's product/service in its market, and the marketing and selling programs required to achieve marketing goals. A well-prepared marketing plan serves two important purposes:

■ It is critical to validating commercial success and to convincing the intended reader of the merits of the business plan.

■ It is an integral part of the firm's internal planning and decision-making process.

INFORMATION NEEDED TO PREPARE THE MARKETING PLAN

In order to develop a convincing marketing plan, a variety of information on the firm's external environment, its industry, markets, competition, and target market are needed. The questions listed below provide guidelines for identifying what information is required.

■ What is the firm's basic business philosophy and what is its basic mission statement?

■ What market opportunity exists for the firm's product or service?

■ What key factors influence sales in this market?

■ What opportunity exists to establish a niche in this market?

■ Who are the consumers of the type of product or service the firm sells, how much do they buy, and why do they buy this product or service?

■ How do consumers perceive the product or service in terms of value, quality, benefits, and price?

■ From whom does the target market now buy the product or service, and why do they buy from these firms?

■■ What are customers' attitudes toward the firm's competitors?

■■ What advertising and promotion techniques are used by competitors, which have been most effective, and which have been least effective?

■■ At what price does the competition sell its product or service?

■■ What advantages or disadvantages do the firm's competitors have?

■■ What competitive advantage does the firm have?

■■ What current channels of distribution are used by competitors to supply customers, and how effectively do these channels function?

■■ What channels of distribution does the firm use, and what advantages, if any, do they offer over competition?

■■ How will the target market be made aware of the firm and the product or service it offers.

■■ What marketing-mix strategy can be employed to reach the target market and to motivate them to buy the firm's product or service?

■■ What marketing program will be employed to carry out the adopted marketing-mix strategy?

■■ What are historical sales for the firm (if it is an existing business) and what factors have influenced these sales?

■■ What are the firm's sales and profit goals?

■■ What are forecast sales for the firm for each of the next twelve months and for each of the next three years?

As suggested by these questions, the information needed to prepare the marketing plan should come from the market analysis and sales component of the business plan.

WHEN TO INCLUDE A MARKETING PLAN WITH THE BUSINESS PLAN

Since the marketing plan is an essential component of a convincing business plan, the information it provides is a required part of the document. This is true whether a complete business plan is prepared for outside presentation, whether the presentation package is limited to select business plan information, or whether the marketing plan is used internally. The intended use of the marketing plan does, however, determine the amount and detail of its content. If the marketing plan is used as part of an outside financing request, only the information needed to explain the adopted marketing strategy should be included. On the other hand, a highly detailed marketing plan is needed for internal planning and decision-making.

STEPS TO PREPARING A MARKETING PLAN

Marketing planning is predicated on the firm's market and target customer group. Unless the entrepreneur understands what constitutes the market for the firm's product or service and the characteristics, perceptions, and motivations of the target customer group, it is impossible to devise an effective plan for satisfying customer needs and expectations. The six steps to preparing a marketing plan outlined below reflect this basic fact.

1. **Consider a marketing plan summary.** This optional section of the marketing plan *may* be used when the plan is prepared for outside presentation. It serves as a convenience for the reader and, if included, should be no longer than what is needed by the reader to gain a quick grasp of the plan's major thrust. Normally, this can be accomplished in one paragraph.

2. **Prepare a situational review.** The purpose of the situational review is to establish the groundwork for the key components of the marketing plan. As such, this section should summarize the important findings and conclusions from the industry analysis and market analysis and sales forecast components of the business plan. Included are a synopsis of the the firm's market, the market niche that is available, the competitive advantage held by the firm, the target market, the competition, and the outlook for sales. Also, if the firm has major competitive weaknesses these should be identified along with an explanation of how the entrepreneur plans to combat them. If the business plan is prepared for an existing business, this section should also include historical sales data for the past three to five years and a brief summary of the key factors that influenced this sales performance.

3. **Identify marketing goals.** A marketing plan, as is true of all business plans, cannot be effective unless planned activity is geared to clearly defined, realistic, measurable goals. Goals serve several important purposes.

- They define objectives toward which all activity is coordinated and directed.
- They provide incentives for motivating management and employee efforts.
- They serve as standards or targets for measuring progress toward planned outcomes.
- They are the criteria used to identify deviations from the plan that require remedial action.

In order to ensure that marketing efforts are tied to the firm's overall objectives, marketing goals should be established with careful consideration given to the firm's business philosophy and mission statement, the needs and expectations of its target market, the firm and product images management wishes to project, and the sales and financial goals to which marketing activity will contribute. Marketing goal statements can be expressed in the form of quantitative targets, such as expected sales volume or percentage share of the market, or as qualitative objectives, such as increasing the consumer product-awareness level or establishing an ongoing sales training program.

Regardless of the form in which marketing goals are expressed, goal statements should be sufficiently specific and detailed to allow progress to be measured. For example, note the difference between the following poorly expressed and effectively stated goals:

- **Poor goal statement:** We expect to increase sales for our product by lowering price.
- **Effective goal statement:** We expect sales to increase at a compound growth rate of 10% per year over the next five years. This target growth rate will be accomplished by (a) opening a branch location in the rapidly growing northeast section of the county; (b) doubling the size of our mailout promotion list; (c) increasing mailout promotions to four per year; and (d) increasing attendance and displays at industry trade shows to three per year.

It is also important that marketing plans be coordinated with and contribute to the firm's overall financial goals. Financial goals set the ultimate performance standards the entrepreneur wishes the firm to achieve. Marketing goals, in turn, should convert financial goals into specific marketing accomplishments. For example, assume the XYZ Company has established a net profit goal of $1,000,000 and a minimum net profit margin goal of 10% of sales as two of its overall financial goals. In order to meet the profit goal and maintain a 10% net profit margin, sales revenue of $10,000,000 would have to be generated ($1,000,000/10%) and, if the intended selling price for their product is $369, then 27,100 units must be sold ($10,000,000/$369).

4. **Explain the intended marketing strategy.** *Marketing strategy* is the firm's broad-scaled plan for reaching and motivating targeted consumers and for positioning the firm's product/service relative to the firm's identified competition. The focal point of marketing strategy should be the firm's marketing mix. *Marketing mix* is the combination of controllable marketing variables identified by the entrepreneur as best able to meet the needs and expectations of the target market. These marketing variables, or decision areas, include what is traditionally referred to in marketing as the "Four P's": *product/service, price, place,* and *promotion.*

The *product/service decision* involves identifying the product/service or product/service mix that meets the defined needs and expectations of the target market and, at the same time, is consistent with the firm's adopted philosophy, its mission, and strategic objectives. For example, if the entrepreneur has decided the firm will be a high-quality, high-price operation and this combination meets the expectations of the target market, the product/service offered must be consistent with this image.

As shown on Tables 7-1 and 7-2, there are various product classes within the basic consumer goods and industrial (business) goods categories that are an important part of this decision. The consumer goods product classes identified on Table 7-1 are defined as follows:

- **Convenience products** are goods the consumer needs but is unwilling to spend much time, effort, or planning to shop for or purchase. These products are purchased frequently, require little or no selling effort, are often inexpensive, and are often purchased out of habit. Included in this category are such commonplace items as table salt, soft drinks, and magazines.
- **Shopping products** are goods the consumer feels are worth spending the time and effort needed for careful planning and comparison shopping. These include products such as furniture, stereo equipment, and appliances.
- **Specialty products** are goods the consumer wants and for which he or she is willing to make a special effort to find. While specialty products are not necessarily expensive products, they are often brand name items that serve as status symbols or fit the consumer's self-image. Specialty products include recognizable items such as Calvin Klein jeans, ethnic foods, or automobiles.
- **Unsought products** are goods unknown to the consumer.
- **Services** are specialized assistance provided for a fee.

The industrial goods product classes identified on Table 7-2 are defined as follows:

- **Installations** are major capital expenditures that have a long economic life, such as land or standard or custom-made heavy equipment, machinery, buildings.
- **Accessory equipment** includes short-lived capital expenditure items such as tools, equipment, computers, and vehicles.
- **Raw materials** are unprocessed expense items such as iron ore, crude oil, and cotton that are used in the firm's finished product.
- **Components** are preprocessed, custom-made, or standardized items that are used in and become part of the finished product such as disk drives for a computer or motors for appliances.
- **Supplies** are routine maintenance and repair items such as paint or lubricating oil.
- **Professional services** are specialized skills that support the operations of a business, such as accounting, legal, or engineering services.

TABLE 7-1

Consumer Product Classification and Marketing-Mix Decisions

Product Class	Product Type Included	Marketing Considerations
Convenience Goods	Staples Impulse products Emergency products	In general, these goods require widespread distribution and maximum exposure. Staples require low selling price and impulse and emergency goods need preferred display and counter positions.
Shopping Goods	Homogeneous Heterogeneous	Both product types need enough exposure to facilitate price comparison and should have adequate representation in major shopping districts or large shopping centers near other, similar shopping products.
Specialty Goods	N/A	This product may have limited exposure, but in general should be treated as a convenience or shopping good in order to reach persons not yet sold on its specialty status.
Unsought Goods	N/A	These products need attention directed to their existence and aggressive promotion in outlets, or in places where similar products are sought.
Services	Personal Professional	Effective selling requires widespread availability and aggressive and widespread promotion through technically competent contact personnel.

TABLE 7-2
Industrial Product Classification and Marketing-Mix Decisions

Product Class	Product Type Included	Marketing Considerations
Installations	Long-lived capital expenditures	Effective selling requires widespread, knowledgeable, technically competent contact and selling effort by well-trained personnel.
Accessories	Short-lived capital expenditures	Effective selling requires fairly widespread and numerous contacts and selling effort by knowledgeable, well-trained, and sometimes technically competent personnel.
Raw Materials	Unprocessed items used in product production or service rendering	Effective selling requires widespread contacts, reliable distribution channels, uniform quality and grading, and competitive pricing.
Components	Preprocessed, custom-made, or standardized items used in product production or service rendering	Effective selling requires widespread contacts by knowledgeable, well-trained, technically competent personnel, reliable distribution channels, uniform quality, and competitive pricing.
Supplies	Low cost, routine maintenance and repair items	Effective selling requires widespread contacts and distribution and prompt, reliable delivery, at competitive prices.
Services	Out-of-house specialized skills	Effective selling requires widespread availability, sales and contact efforts conducted by well-trained, technically competent personnel, and reputation for expertise and reliability.

Attention to differences between product classes is important because consumers and industrial users view, shop for, and buy products/services differently, and these differences affect how a product/service should be marketed. Examples of the considerations associated with the various product classes and types are shown in the last columns of Tables 7-1 and 7-2.

Note also from the last column that the considerations for offering a service to targeted customers differs from those for a product. Services are, by their nature, intangible, inseparable, and perishable. Since a service is not tangible and must be performed anew on each occasion, it is virtually impossible to separate the quality of the service from the supplier. Since service firms live or die by their reputations, the marketing of a service must focus on the firm's good name, expertise, and quality of work provided. It is up to the entrepreneur to create and maintain this image.

It is critical to both the preparation of a convincing business plan and to the success and viability of the firm that the decision on an appropriate marketing mix reflect the entrepreneur's understanding of the target market. Without this knowledge it is impossible to develop a realistic, consumer-oriented marketing strategy that is tied directly to the needs, expectations, and perceptions of targeted customers. For example, where the firm's selling efforts are concentrated, how a product/service is positioned, and where and to whom it is promoted and advertised depends, to a large extent, on demographic characteristics. Or, the type of product/service offered by the firm, its value, the customer's preference for personal contact during the selling process, and the frequency and regularity of purchase affect the decision on selling price, the advertising and promotion message, and the number and type of middlemen used in the distribution process. Table 7-3 lists examples of some of the many possible marketing-mix decisions that are related to and affected by target market characteristics.

The *pricing decision* is important to the marketing-mix strategy for two reasons. First is the issue of product/service image and how the established price is perceived by the target market. As true of the product/service itself, selling price should be consistent with the consumer perceptions the entrepreneur is attempting to influence. If, for example, the goal is to have consumers associate the firm with the concept of a low-cost, high-volume seller, the selling price of the product/service must be lower than that of competitive products/services. If the product is aimed at the upscale, image-conscious consumer, the product would not be priced low and marketed through discount stores.

TABLE 7-3
*Relationship Between Target Market Characteristics
and Marketing-Mix Decisions*

Target Market Characteristics	Decision Variables Affected
1. Geographic location and other demographic characteristics.	Affects *size* and economic potential of target market; the *place* where products should be made available; and where and to whom the product is *promoted*.
2. Behavioral needs and attitudes, and how present and potential products/services fit into customers' consumption patterns.	Affects *product* image, design, packaging, and depth of product line; and the information conveyed and appeals used in *promoting* the product/service.
3. Product expectations and perceived value and benefits.	Affects *product* image, design, packaging, and depth of product/service line; the product/service selling *price*; and the information conveyed and appeals used in *promotion*.
4. Consumers' urgency to get need satisfied and their desire to compare and shop.	Affects *place*—how directly products are distributed from producer to consumer, how extensively they are made available, and the level of service needed— and *price,* or how much potential customers are willing to pay for product or service.

The second major consideration surrounding pricing strategy is profit margin. The established selling price must be sufficient to provide the firm a compensatory profit margin at the expected sales volume. That is, the selling price must be sufficient to cover the cost of both producing/rendering the product/service and other directly related cost elements. For example, cost considerations such as discounts offered, credit extended, and the degree of service provided after the sale must be factored into the pricing decision.

While there are no mechanical formulas for making pricing decisions, the following basic guidelines will help the entrepreneur establish a rational pricing strategy.

- **Know your full costs.** While this advice may appear obvious, research indicates that new entrepreneurs rarely understand the full cost of operating their businesses. The most effective method for understanding cost is to perform a breakeven analysis (see Chapter 10) for the business as a whole and for individual products/services or product lines.
- **Price, image, and goals are interrelated.** Pricing policy cannot be established in a vacuum. The selling price of the product/service should be consistent with the entrepreneur's marketing goals, the image he or she is attempting to project, and the perceptions and expectations of the target market.
- **Price, product differentiation, and market power.** The ability to set price independent of competition depends on the degree of differentiation the product/service commands and the market power of the firm. The more difficult it is to differentiate the product/service from that of the competition, the more likely it is the firm will have to accept the going market price as a given. The same is true of market power. Larger firms and industry leaders have more flexibility in setting selling price than smaller firms and industry followers.
- **Price and non-price perceptions.** While selling price is an important influence on consumer purchases, it is not the main reason consumers buy. More important is how price and non-price considerations are perceived by consumers. In general, price, quality, value, and service are closely interrelated in the mind of consumers.

The *place* component of the firm's marketing-mix strategy involves deciding which channels of distribution will be used to get the product in the right place at the right time. *Distribution channels* are the interconnecting steps used to move the product from producer to the ultimate user. A channel may consist of one or more marketing middlemen, such as selling representatives, brokers, wholesalers, and retailers, or the product may move directly from producer to consumer.

Distribution channels play an important role in the marketing process. As shown on Table 7-4, they perform three basic functions that benefit manufacturers, suppliers, and consumers: physical distribution, communication, and facilitation.

The following factors should be considered by the entrepreneur when selecting a distribution channel.

- **Cost.** The marketing intermediaries through which goods are moved are specialists that perform functions essential to the marketing process. While it is possible to eliminate the middleman by performing the functions in-house, it may not be cost-effective. Specialists are usually able to perform a unique function at a lower cost. This benefit must be weighed against the loss of control that occurs when the function is handed over to an outsider. For example, it may be cost-effective to use sales representatives to sell the product or service. The trade-off is the risk of having less selling interest and motivation than that of the firm's sales force.

- **Product class.** As discussed above and shown in Tables 7-1 and 7-2, the type of product or service offered the buyer or consumer often dictates the channel of distribution. For example, effective selling of consumer convenience goods or industrial supplies dictates widespread distribution. Therefore, these products are usually marketed through a large number of wholesalers and retailers.

- **Degree of exposure required.** Ideally, the appropriate goal for deciding the number of intermediaries used in the distribution channel and/or the number of outlets for a given intermediary is just enough product availability to satisfy the target market. Too much exposure needlessly increases marketing costs and too little results in lost sales.

TABLE 7-4

Services Performed by Intermediaries for Suppliers and Customers

Marketing Function	Performed for Suppliers	Performed for Buyers
Physical Distribution	Breaking bulk Accumulating bulk Creating assortments Transportation Storage	Sorting by quantity Assorting by type Storage Delivery
Communication	Impart product information Gather market information Gather consumer information	Identify needs Buy based on needs Advise Impart information
Facilitation	Take product risk through ownership Provide personalized services Finance customer purchases	Business management assistance Extend credit Provide repair services

- **Other marketing-mix considerations.** As true with other components of the marketing-mix strategy, a decision on the appropriate distribution channel cannot be made in a vacuum. The choice of a distribution channel is interrelated with product image, selling price, and promotion and advertising strategy. For example, a high-quality, high-priced status product would not be distributed through discount retailers.
- **Market characteristics.** The nature and characteristics of the firm's market and targeted customer group often influence the distribution channel. For example, the number of customers in a given market and the size of the average purchase influence the number of intermediaries in the distribution channel (i.e., the length of the channel). In general, the fewer the number of large-scale purchasers, the shorter and more direct the channel. Conversely, if there are a large number of small purchasers, distribution channels tend to be long.
- **Service marketing.** A service is defined as a bundle of benefits provided the user. In this sense a service is essentially a product. Because it is intangible and usually rendered directly to the end user by the supplier, it often appears that no distribution channel exists. While there is normally no intermediary involved in the delivery of a service, the marketing-mix functions necessary to render a service for the end user are still required. As is true of tangible goods, the type of service provided must be consistent with the image and business philosophy of the firm; a price consistent with market forces and firm image must be established; information regarding the existence and nature of the service must be communicated; and the service must be promoted and advertised.

Promotion involves a decision on the strategy and techniques that are used to communicate product/service information between seller and prospective buyer. The ultimate goal for transmitting this information is influencing consumer attitudes and behavior. Promotion is, in short, communication with a purpose: telling and selling the customer. It includes the mix of activities surrounding sales promotion, sales strategy, and advertising.

- **Sales promotion** involves the methods used to communicate information about the firm and its product/service and to provide out-of-the-ordinary incentives to purchase. Non-routine purchase incentives are inducements such as coupon deals, offers for free goods, point-of-purchase displays, or free in-house or video tape demonstrations.
- **Sales strategy** involves the procedures used to make sales. The

appropriate goal for this strategy is to use cost-effective selling methods that make it easy for the customer to buy from the firm. These methods can range from highly personal selling using trained, knowledgeable personnel to contact the customer either in-house or on-site to mass selling through the use of telemarketing.

- **Advertising** is any paid form of nonpersonal, persuasive message delivered through mass media. The primary purpose of advertising is to influence purchaser behavior.

Promotion should detail how, given the image and message to be projected, the entrepreneur will zero in on targeted customers. The strategy should focus on how targeted customers will be influenced to think of the firm when they want to buy the type of product/service it sells; how they are motivated to buy from the firm; and what selling approach will be used to close the sale. As is true of the other components of the firm's marketing mix, developing the appropriate promotion strategy begins with a clear understanding of the target market. It is the defined characteristics of this customer group that should determine the specific methods used to accomplish promotional goals.

Common examples of promotion activities often used for each of the four basic target market groups are shown on Table 7-5. The important point made by these examples is that different blends of promotion mix are needed for different target markets. By identifying its target market, the entrepreneur not only establishes the primary area of marketing emphasis but is able to concentrate scarce marketing dollars into a mix of promotion methods, time, and media combinations that most directly hit the target audience.

The following questions can be used as a guide to developing and presenting promotion strategy.

- What are the perceived needs, wants, and expectations of the target customer group?
- Does the target market know the firm is in business, and what evidence is there to this effect? If not, how will they be informed?
- Is the target market aware of what the firm sells, and what evidence is there to this effect?
- If the target group must be educated as to what the firm sells, how will this be done?
- What promotional methods will be used to reach the target market?
- What message will be used to persuade the target customer group that the firm can meet their needs?
- What selling strategy and techniques will be used to achieve sales?

TABLE 7-5
Promotion Activities by Target Market Group

Group	Objective	Strategy	Methods
Final consumer	Reach, inform, persuade, and motivate numerous customers	Mass promotion and selling	Area media advertising Mailouts 800 number Catalogues Free merchandise Samples & coupons Contests Aisle displays Point-of-purchase displays Sponsor special events
Industrial user	Reach and inform limited number of customers	Personalized promotion and selling	Trained contact & sales personnel Trade publication ads Trade shows National media advertising Product information mailouts
Middlemen	Reach, inform, and persuade limited number of intermediaries	Personalized promotion and selling	Trained contact & sales personnel Trade shows Trade publication ads Promotion deals Price deals Gifts Sales contests Provide sales training Provide technical liaison personnel
Retailer	Reach numerous outlets Transmit product information, persuade and motivate	Personalized promotion and selling	Trained contact & sales personnel Trade shows Trade publication ads Price deals Promotion deals Sales contests Financing or credit extension Provide market & customer advice Sponsor special events

5. **Preparing the marketing budget.** Effective planning must also consider the cost of implementing what is to be done. The process for determining the financial feasibility of the firm's strategic and operating plans is known as budgeting. A *budget* is simply a plan expressed in quantitative terms such as estimated dollars of expense, expected sales revenue, sales in units, the number of services performed, or dollars of expected profit. These budgeted figures are the results of decisions on how scarce dollars will be allocated and, as such, serve as standards against which the efficiency and effectiveness of actual operations is measured.

The marketing budget should detail both estimated revenues and expenditures. The revenue estimates consist of forecast sales in units (or number of service units performed) and the selling price per unit. On the expense side, the budget should detail the dollar amount and timing of all marketing-related expenditures. The difference between forecast revenue and expenses is the projected marketing profit goal.

The commonly used approaches to budgeting marketing programs are the *percent-of-sales*, *matching*, *default or affordable*, and *objective and task* methods. The first three budgeting methods, while offering the advantage of simplicity, suffer from flawed logic. Each contradicts the rationale behind business planning. The percent-of-sales method establishes the amount to be spent on marketing by assigning an arbitrarily established percentage-of-sales value to the forecast sales figure for the period. For example, if 5% of sales is judged a reasonable amount to spend on marketing activities and forecast sales total $100,000, the budget allocation for marketing would be $5,000. The matching method uses the same procedure but bases the percent-of-sales figure on what competitors or other firms in the industry are using.

Both the percent-of-sales and matching methods imply that marketing activities are the consequence of sales. That is, sales occur without any marketing effort. The reality is, however, that sales are the result of effective marketing. What's more, either method produces marketing expenditures in amounts that often run counter to what is needed. When sales decline, marketing expenditures decline as well. Yet, this may be the time when increased marketing activity is needed to boost lagging sales.

With the default or affordable approach, the amount spent on marketing activities is determined by the cash flow remaining after the firm's mandatory obligations and management priorities are met. This approach also defies sound business logic. The funds spent on marketing activities are an investment. As is true of the investment in any business asset, planned marketing expenditures should generate a return on investment (ROI) that justifies the funds used.

It is the expected rate of return on the dollars that could be invested in the marketing program that should determine the amount actually spent and not how much money remains after spending priorities have been satisfied. In theory, dollars should be committed to an investment as long as the expected return is greater than the cost of the funds invested.

The objective and task method involves the application of planning principles to the budgeting process. With this method, the dollars to be allocated are determined by the task(s) that must be completed to achieve an established marketing objective. Application of this method involves (a) setting marketing goals according to what can realistically be accomplished, (b) identifying the marketing activities that must be performed to achieve the objectives, and (c) estimating the cost of performing each task. The estimated costs of each task are totaled to arrive at the total marketing budget.

6. **Establish marketing controls.** Any experienced entrepreneur, manager, or reader of a business plan knows that the planning process does not end with the finished document. Planning is not complete, nor can it be effective, until the control procedures are put in place and used on a regular basis. Control is as essential to successful marketing planning as the plan itself, and the control procedures that will be used should be clearly spelled out in the last section of the marketing plan.

Control involves the monitoring and evaluation of actual and planned results in order to keep operations on course. The performance standards used in the control process are budgeted goals and activities. Through the periodic comparison of actual and planned results, the entrepreneur ensures that plans are executed, that changing conditions have not invalidated planning assumptions, that the firm is on course to meet planned objectives or, if these are not the case, that remedial actions are taken.

Marketing controls take three basic forms: sales standards, cost standards, and profit standards. The tools used to compare actual performance against these standards are sales analysis, cost analysis, and profit analysis. Sales analysis is the breakdown and evaluation of sales data in order to determine the effectiveness of the marketing effort. The manner in which sales data are disaggregated for analysis depends on the nature of the business, the product/service, the market(s), the customer, and the information needed to accurately assess performance. The four most common methods of disaggregating sales data are shown on Table 7-6, along with examples of control variables used in the monitoring and control process.

TABLE 7-6

Types of Sales Breakdowns and Control Variables

General Sales Analysis	Analysis By Customer	Geographic Sales Analysis	Analysis By Product
Annual sales dollars	Customer classes	By state, city, county	Product class
Annual unit sales	Customer SIC code	By zip code or area code	Product line
Monthly sales dollars	Percentage cash versus credit purchase	By sales territory	Product
Monthly unit sales	Percentage old versus new customer	By salesperson	Product defect
Seasonal sales	Average purchase size	By product type	Product return
Sales by product life cycle	Frequency of purchase	Sales per call	Price
Comparative sales by year, month, or season		Percent of quota	Packaging
Average sale size		Promotion dollars	Promotion dollars
Average order size		Advertising dollars	Advertising dollars
Average sales per sales call			

Cost analysis is similar to sales analysis. It involves the breakdown and restructuring of marketing costs in order to evaluate the efficiency of the marketing effort. The process of restructuring costs begins with the breakdown of the marketing costs shown on the traditional accounting income statement into two cost categories: direct costs and indirect or common costs. The restructured direct costs are then assigned to the activity being analyzed. This activity may be a specific sales category, a particular marketing activity, or a given marketing segment of the business. Indirect costs are allocated to a common overhead category.

Direct costs are those that can be directly traced to or associated with a given activity. They are easily identified by answering the following question: Would this cost be incurred if the activity under analysis were no longer performed? If the answer to the question is no, that is, the cost would disappear if the activity were discontinued, then the cost item is directly related to that activity and would be assigned as such. If the answer is that the cost would not disappear if the activity were discontinued, it is an indirect cost and would be assigned to a common pool of marketing overhead costs.

For example, assume XYZ Company has a multi-product product line and the sales force is paid a monthly base salary plus a bonus in the form of sales commissions. Sales commissions are structured by individual product. If management were considering dropping a poorly performing product from the product line, the sales commissions on that product would no longer be paid (they would disappear), but the base salary expense would still be incurred unless the sales position were also dropped. For this particular analysis, sales commissions are a direct cost item and sales salaries are an indirect cost. The first column of Table 7-7 contains examples of commonly incurred direct and indirect marketing costs.

TABLE 7-7
Examples of Direct and Indirect Marketing Costs

Direct Cost Items	Indirect Cost Items
Sales commissions	Marketing manager's salary
Shipping costs	Marketing clerical salaries
Packaging costs	Sales salaries
Purchase discounts	Travel allowance expense
Product promotion	Vehicle expense
Product advertising	Company-wide promotion
Product liability	Company-wide advertising
	Depreciation expense on selling equipment

Profit analysis is the breakdown and evaluation of sales revenue and cost charges by activity. The focus of the analysis may be the profitability of a product or geographical territory, a particular marketing activity such as advertising, or the marketing department itself. The most effective tool for this purpose is a *contribution format income statement*. An example of a contribution format statement prepared for each of the products in the XYZ Company's product line is shown in Table 7-8. As indicated there, when the contribution format is used for marketing analysis and control, direct costs are assigned to the sales revenue items to which they are related. Indirect costs are assigned to the common marketing-overhead-cost pool. Profitability is measured at two levels: the contribution margin of individual products and the contribution of the total marketing effort to overall company profits. The former item measures the direct or incremental profit produced by each product. It is the additional dollars of profit that remain after the direct cost associated with the sale of a given product are deducted. The total product contribution ($9,330) is the sum of the individual product contributions ($4,510 + $2,620 + $2,200). The total marketing contribution indicates the contribution to overall company profits that remains after the deduction of both direct and indirect marketing costs.

TABLE 7-8
The XYZ Company
By-Product Sales Breakdown and Marketing Cost Analysis
(000 omitted)

Item	Product A	Product B	Product C
Sales Revenue	$ 6,000	$ 3,500	$ 4,000
Direct Costs:			
Product promotion	100	-0-	300
Product advertising	450	500	760
Sales commissions	600	200	440
Packaging costs	65	55	100
Shipping costs	155	75	120
Purchase discounts	120	50	80
Total Direct Cost	$ 1,490	$ 880	$ 1,800
Product Contribution	$ 4,510	$ 2,620	$ 2,200

Indirect Marketing Costs

Total Product Contribution	$ 9,330
Indirect Marketing Costs:	
Marketing management salaries	400
Marketing clerical salaries	70
Sales salaries	525
Travel allowance	65
Vehicle expense	130
Company-wide promotion	235
Company-wide advertising	1,000
Selling equipment depreciation	75
Total Indirect Marketing Costs	$ 2,500
Total Marketing Profit Contribution	$ 6,830

TIPS FOR PREPARING THE MARKETING PLAN
■■ **Use help in developing the marketing plan.** In addition to using primary and secondary sources of information to prepare the marketing plan, the entrepreneur should take advantage of available assistance. Agencies such as chambers of commerce, area planning and

development commissions, small business developments centers, the U.S. Small Business Administration, and college and university schools of business administration often provide planning information and/or assistance at little or no cost. Also, if the cost can be justified, the entrepreneur may consider using a professional marketing consultant to assist with the marketing plan. While this alternative may be costly, the cost may be justified, if for example, the plan is to be presented outside the firm as part of a critical financing proposal.

■ **Planning is not a one-time job.** Planning is a basic function of management, and the entrepreneur's planning effort should not end when the business plan is completed. Rather, planning should be a continuous process that includes monitoring the firm's internal and external environment, gathering information, preparing strategic and operating plans, and comparing the results of actual operations against planned expectations. Since an outside reader will expect to find evidence of the entrepreneur's understanding of the importance of sound planning, the business plan should indicate how planning will become an integral part of the entrepreneur's management process.

■ **Good plans are based on good information.** As is true of forecasting, plans are only as good as the underlying assumptions. While the entrepreneur's creativity, insight, experience, and intuition play an important part in the planning process, sound plans cannot be developed without sound information. The business plan should make clear the entrepreneur's intention to monitor key sources of planning information on a continuous basis.

■ **Documentation is critical.** Plans are, by necessity, built on assumptions about the future environment in which they will be implemented and conducted. In order for plans to be accepted as realistic and to serve as effective guides for operating the business, these assumptions must be clearly stated and periodically reviewed. If underlying assumptions are not made clear or they are unrealistic, plans will be considered nothing more than pipe dreams.

■ **Why marketing plans fail.** Marketing plans can fail for a variety of reasons. Some of the more common causes that can be avoided or controlled are identified below.

- **The plan is prepared for the wrong purpose.** When the entrepreneur is not convinced of the value of sound planning, preparation of the marketing plan will be viewed as a one-time, necessary evil. This attitude virtually ensures that marketing planning and control will not become a routine part of the management process. The result is a business whose success is dependent on good luck rather than good management.

- **The plan is poorly prepared.** When the effort put into planning is inadequate, the plan will be shallow and lack the substance and detail necessary to make it an effective guide for decision-making.
- **The environmental analysis is deficient.** When the firm's external and internal environment are not sufficiently analyzed or understood, the entrepreneur lacks the background necessary to prepare a marketing plan that will be viewed as realistic.
- **Goals and objectives are unrealistic.** When the entrepreneur does not have a clear understanding of the realities of the firm's market, target market, or competitive environment, established marketing goals will be seen as impractical or unattainable.
- **There is a failure to understand the limitations of planning.** Inexperienced entrepreneurs often fail to appreciate the realities of planning. While planning is a powerful tool capable of providing positive results for the firm, it is not a panacea. Planning is not a substitute for sound judgment developed from experience; it will not endow management with the ability to predict the future with certainty; it will not prevent mistakes from being made in the future; and plans, once developed, are not permanently and immutably fixed. Planning does, however, force the entrepreneur to understand the environment in which the firm operates and to identify the factors that lead to success or failure.
- **There is a failure to monitor results.** Diligent monitoring of actual results and periodic comparison of these results to planned expectations is critical to effective planning. The firm's environment is constantly changing and monitoring allows the entrepreneur to identify and prepare for change.

■ **Reach the target market one step at a time.** Marketing experts suggest that promotion and advertising should be designed to move customers toward the purchase in a series of steps. This means the entrepreneur should make certain the marketing plan clearly indicates the steps to be followed in the adopted promoting and advertising scheme. For example, first identify what image will be projected. Next indicate how targeted customers will be made aware of the firm and its product or service. Third, discuss how the firm will attempt to convince targeted customers that the firm's product or service can meet their needs. Last, make clear how targeted customers will be motivated to buy the firm's product or service.

■ **Avoid advertising myths.** There are three popular advertising misconceptions to which new entrepreneurs often fall prey. The first suggests that only creative, clever advertising can be effective. In reality, advertising is most effective when it sends the appropriate message, when the message is properly directed, and when it is done consistently rather than haphazardly. The second myth suggests that the firm can rely on word of mouth rather than media advertising to send the message. While the praises sung by satisfied customers are important, this vehicle is not a substitute for effective advertising. Available research indicates that ten satisfied customers tell an average of only about eight other people about the positive experience. Third, it is often suggested that the entrepreneur can save money by doing his or her own advertising. Again, research indicates that unless the entrepreneur is an experienced marketer, do-it-yourself advertising is usually ineffective and proves to be a costly mistake.

■■■ **Focus on the customer.** There is a natural tendency for new entrepreneurs to feel that the business and its product or service are the most important elements in the profit equation. In reality, there is nothing more important to the success of the business than its customers. Without customers there is no business. The entrepreneur's understanding of this basic fact should be clearly conveyed in the marketing plan and, even more important, should be the foundation of the entrepreneur's business philosophy.

■■■ **Be cautious about extending credit.** While extending credit may enhance sales, its effects can be bittersweet. Extending credit is equivalent to making a loan to the customer. The immediate effect is a cash drain and an added cost of doing business. What's more, the long-term effects can be disastrous if the customer base contains an inordinate number of slow- and non-pays. Before establishing a credit policy for the firm, the entrepreneur should be certain that financial resources are adequate; that profit margins are sufficient to cover the cost of extending credit; that someone in the firm is capable of evaluating a customer's credit risk; and that someone in the firm can collect on slow-paying accounts. Since the reader of the business plan will have reservations about the extension of credit, justification for its intended use should be clear and forceful.

SAMPLE MARKETING PLAN

The Pegasus Electronics Company is a hypothetical medium-sized manufacturer of sophisticated electronic components. Until recently, approximately 80% of total company sales were to defense industry firms and only 20% were made to the private sector. Given the government's recent large cutbacks in defense spending, Pegasus's management has changed the firm's basic strategy. Its goal is to reverse the proportions of defense and private sector sales over the next three years.

Pegasus engineers have recently made a major research breakthrough in the manufacture of audio system componentry. They have developed a highly sophisticated audio component that outperforms the popular Dolby surround-sound feature used in large and expensive stereo systems. As opposed to the Dolby system, Pegasus's componentry is compatible with the popular compact or mini-system stereo. The company intends to capitalize on this breakthrough by marketing a high-quality, complete mini-system with the model name of Paragon. This system will offer greater sound output and superior sound quality than are possible in existing compact units. Pegasus's management feels that these features, coupled with a cost and selling price considerably lower than competitive high-quality mini-systems, will give Paragon a decided market advantage.

The Paragon prototype has been demonstrated at various dealer trade shows over the past year and the response has been excellent. Based on dealer reaction and other market research information, management has developed a complete marketing strategy for the Paragon model. The major features of this plan are highlighted below.

It should be noted that while only the key points of the Pegasus plan are presented here, the amount of detail that should be included in the marketing plan is dictated by the purpose that it is to serve. If the plan will be presented to an outside reader, the marketing plan needs only enough detail to adequately inform the reader about what is intended and how it will be done. Additional information, if needed, can be supplied at the reader's request. If, however, the plan is to be used internally as a guide to decision-making, it should be fully developed.

FIGURE 7-2 *Pegasus Electronics*
The Marketing Plan For The Paragon Stereo System

Marketing Plan Summary

The Paragon marketing plan outlines the strategy that will be used to market the product and control marketing activities over the next three years. Sales of this advanced, high-quality compact stereo system are targeted for the middle- and upper-income audiophile. It will be distributed through retailers specializing in high-quality product lines. Anticipated sales should produce contribution margin, net of direct and indirect marketing costs, that is sufficient to break even the first year, and in the amounts of $7,500,000 and $10,000,000 in the next two years. The

FIGURE 7-2 *continued*

expected three-year sales volume from Paragon will increase Pegasus's private sector business to at least 40% of total sales.

Situational Review

The Market. Approximately 50% of U.S. households currently own audio systems, and about 5% of this group replace or upgrade existing systems each year. In addition, nearly 30% of the new household formations each year become stereo system owners within three years to five years. Compact system sales currently account for approximately $80,000,000 of the $400,000,000 of total industry sales. Over the past three years, mini-system sales have grown by 15% per year, and industry experts expect at least this rate of growth over the next three years.

The major buyers of compact systems are low-, middle- and upper-income consumers in the 20-year to 50-year age range. Their primary motivations for purchase are:

1. The desire to avoid the higher cost of a larger stereo system.

2. The desire for high-quality sound without the expense of purchasing the more costly modular systems.

3. The desire for quality sound from a system that is suited to living space or design limitations.

4. The desire for a second stereo system.

Distribution. Mini-systems are commonly distributed through a variety of retail outlets including audio specialty stores, department stores, appliance stores, discount stores, furniture stores, radio/TV stores, music stores, and mail order businesses. High-quality mini-systems are retailed primarily through audio specialty stores, department stores, and high-quality mail order retailers. To avoid the common perception of lower price and lower quality, discount stores, radio/TV, and music stores are normally not used.

Competition. The intention to market Paragon in the high-quality niche will put the product in direct competition with the established brand names commonly associated with high quality and high price. Because of the value Paragon offers consumers, however, management conservatively estimates that the product will capture 10% of its target market the first year of the three-year planning horizon, and from 50% to 65% of this market by the end of the three-year period. Opinions of dealers surveyed at trade shows and the market research conducted for Pegasus by an outside consulting firm substantiate these estimates.

Strategic Opportunities and Threats.

The Paragon model offers the following strategic advantages and opportunities.

- Consumers have shown an increased interest in high-quality compact systems. Sales in this segment of the audio market have grown faster than all other segments combined over the past five years.
- Paragon has a significant advantage over its competition. The system offers superior features, better sound quality, and lower manufacturing costs. The cost advantage allows Paragon to be sold at a retail price that is dramatically lower than other high-quality mini-systems.
- Pegasus currently possesses the technical expertise and resources needed to provide the high-quality warranty and repair service expected by sophisticated, high-end audio consumers.
- Pegasus has signed exclusive-dealer agreements with two national department store chains and one national audio-store chains. These agreements alone are expected to produce over 50% of expected sales during the planning horizon.
- Pegasus currently has a staff of highly trained, experienced sales personnel. While this experience has been primarily in industrial sales, both management and the salespeople involved feel that the transition to consumer selling will not require extensive retraining time or cost.

The Company and the Paragon model face the following strategic threats.

- Pegasus and the Paragon model have no established image in the retail consumer market.
- The Paragon brand name is unknown to consumers.
- The Paragon system is not yet positioned relative to its direct competition.
- The research breakthrough made by Pegasus engineers is expected to be duplicated by competitors in three to five years.

FIGURE 7-2 *continued*

- There is some evidence of a growing trend toward modular purchases by upscale, sophisticated stereo consumers.

Marketing Goals

Pegasus requires that all marketing goals be expressed as a combination of financial and marketing objectives. For the Paragon system the following goals have been established:

Financial Goals

1. Earn an annual rate of return on invested dollars in the Paragon system of at least 20%.

2. Generate Gross Contribution Margin (Sales minus Production and Direct Marketing Costs) during each year of the planning horizon of at least 20% of sales.

3. Generate Net Contribution Margin (Gross Contribution Margin minus Indirect Marketing Costs) sufficient to break even in 19X1, and in the amounts of $7,500,000 in 19X2, and $10,000,000 in 19X3. These amounts should represent a Net Contribution Margin that is at least 10% of sales.

Marketing Goals

1. Given Paragon's intended retail selling price of $499 and the goal to provide dealers a gross profit margin of 35%, the selling price to the dealer will be $369. The 35% gross profit margin for dealers exceeds the 30% used throughout the industry and provides Pegasus with an added competitive advantage.

2. Capture 10% of target market sales in the first year of the planning horizon, and between 50% and 65% by the end of the third year.

3. Generate sales revenue on the Paragon model of $9,200,000 the first year of the planning horizon, $40,000,000 to $45,000,000 in the second year, and $55,000,000 to $65,000,000 in the third year.

4. Conduct a wide-scale, institutional (company) promotion and advertising campaign designed to create the image of Pegasus as a new leader in the high-quality consumer audio market. The goal for this campaign is to expand target market awareness of the Company name to 95% over the three-year planning period.

5. Expand the number of exclusive dealer agreements and distribution outlets by 20% each year over the three-year planning period.

Marketing Strategy

The important features of the marketing strategy developed for Paragon are listed below.

- **Target Market:** Upscale households with particular emphasis on young professionals in the 25-year to 40-year age range.
- **Positioning:** The Paragon mini-system has a strong competitive advantage over existing systems. It has features and sound quality that are superior to the leading high-quality systems and a retail price that is approximately $100 less than competition.
- **Product:** Initial entry into the consumer audio market will be made with the compact Paragon system. This system offers the highest sound quality currently available regardless of component size. The complete system consists of a 60-watt amplifier with the surround-sound feature, five speakers, a five-in-one CD player, and a dual cassette deck. The decision to enter two other segments of the audio market has also been made. Scheduled for production and market entry in October of 200X is a high-quality surround-sound system for automobiles, trucks, utility, and recreational vehicles. In 200X, the Company will enter the growing modular component market with a full line of high-quality tuners, amplifiers, speakers, and tape and CD players.
- **Service:** Pegasus will operate a quick-turnaround repair service for both warranty and non-warranty work. It is the intention of management to maintain a level of service that is consistent with the high-quality image of Paragon and other planned products.
- **Price:** The dealer price on the complete Paragon system will be $369. This price allows dealers a comfortable 35% markup above cost when the model is sold at the suggested retail price of $499. The 35% markup exceeds the industry norm of 30% and provides Pegasus with an added competitive advantage over existing high-quality systems.
- **Distribution:** Paragon will be distributed through audio specialty stores, department stores, and high-quality mail order retailers under exclusive-dealer arrangements. Lower-priced retailing outlets will not be used.
- **Salesforce:** Pegasus's existing sales force will be used. This staff is well-trained and experienced, and the

FIGURE 7-2 *continued*

transition to private-sector sales will require only minor, inexpensive, reorientation.

- **Promotion:** Paragon's entry into the market will be accompanied by an intense six-month promotion campaign consisting of increased presence at industry trade shows; a combination of dealer sign-on and sales contest incentives; and retail-customer sales contests promoted through dealer establishments. The total promotion budget for the first year of the planning horizon is $1,400,000. This amount will be reduced by 90% in the second and third years if market acceptance rates and sales targets are met.

- **Advertising:** An outside advertising agency has been employed to develop and implement an advertising campaign that supports the high quality, superior features, and attractive pricing strategy for Paragon. The total advertising budget for the first year of the planning horizon is $600,000. This amount should be increased by 20% in each of the remaining two years of the horizon.

Marketing Budget

The marketing budget consists of annual pro forma, contribution format income statements for each year of the planning horizon. The annual pro forma statement for the first year is partitioned into 12 monthly statements. This breakdown allows more frequent and detailed monitoring of key budgeted amounts.

To ensure that planning and budgeting at Pegasus is done on a continuous basis, a rolling-budget procedure is used. As each month or year of actual operations is completed, the statement for that period is dropped from the planning horizon and a new monthly or annual projection is added. By so doing, management always has current 12-month and 3-year annual budgets to guide and control operations.

The annual pro forma statement for the first year of the planning horizon is shown below on Table 7-9. Although the 12-month statement for the first year and the annual statements for the remaining two years of the planning horizon are not shown, they are prepared using the identical format.

TABLE 7-9
Pegasus Electronics
The Paragon System Annual Budget[1] for Pro Forma 19X1

	Budgeted	% Of Sales	Actual	Variance
Unit Sales[2]	24,932			
Price	$ 369			
Sales Revenue[3]	$9,200,000	100.0%		
Direct Costs:				
Production[4]	$5,360,610	58.3%		
Packaging Costs	99,729	1.1		
Shipping Costs	124,661	1.4		
Product Promotion	1,000,000	10.9		
Product Advertising	500,000	5.4		
Sales Commissions	230,000	2.5		
Total Direct Costs	$7,315,000	79.5%		
Gross Contribution Margin	$1,885,000	20.5%		
Indirect Marketing Costs:				
Marketing Mgmt Salaries	$ 400,000	4.3%		
Sales Salaries	800,000	8.7		
Clerical Salaries	35,000	0.4		
Travel Expense	150,000	1.6		
Company-wide Promotion	400,000	4.3		
Company-wide Advertising	100,000	1.1		
Total Indirect Costs	$1,885,000	20.5%		
Net Contribution Margin	$ -0-	0.0%		

Notes:
1. The Budget has been prepared under the primary assumptions that no major recession will occur over the three-year planning horizon and the economy's expansion phase of the current business cycle will continue over the planning horizon.
2. Unit sales forecasts are based on the assumption that the strong competitive advantages of the Paragon system will allow 10% of target market sales to be captured the first year and up to 65% over the next two years.
3. Since current sales by all manufacturers to the compact stereo market total about $80,000,000 and these sales are expected to grow at a rate of 15% per year, the estimate of a 10% market share generates first-year revenues of approximately $9,200,000 ($80,000,000 × 1.15 × 10%).
4. While total production costs of the Paragon system are not under the direct control of the marketing department and technically are not a marketing budget item, the figure has been included here in order to accurately portray contribution margin goals.

Marketing Controls

The sales and profit performance of Paragon will be monitored and evaluated on a monthly basis. The primary tool used for this purpose is the monthly budget. Projected monthly values serve as targets against which actual monthly data are compared and evaluated. The monthly comparisons are made by calculating a variance for each budget item. The variances for revenue or inflow items are calculated as the actual value minus the budgeted value. The variance calculations for expense or outflow items are reversed. Thus, a positive-valued variance indicates a favorable occurrence and a negative-valued variance an unfavorable outcome.

In addition to budget values, several additional performance indicators are monitored. These include the Booking to Billing Ratio (the orders taken relative to the sales that have been billed), Sales by Type of Distributor, Retail Sales by Type of Dealer, Dealer Inventory Level, Retail Sales by Customer Characteristic, and Market Acceptance Rate (the extent to which consumers are aware of, have tried, or have purchased the product).

CHAPTER PERSPECTIVE

Planning is as a process consisting of interrelated steps that begin with the firm's mission statement and a forecast of its external and internal environment and end with control and feedback. The marketing plan is an action program that describes how the firm's target customer group will be motivated to purchase its product/service. It details the marketing goals to be achieved, the marketing-mix strategy that will position the firm's product/service in its market, and the marketing and selling programs required to achieve established marketing goals. The heart of the firm's marketing strategy is its marketing mix. Marketing mix is the set of variables, or the Four P's of marketing, directly under management's control. They are product/service, price, place, and promotion.

The Operating Plan

CHAPTER

8

WHAT IS AN OPERATING PLAN?

The term *operations* is usually associated with a production process or a manufacturing firm. While production is one form of operations, it is not the only one. Operations is an essential function of every business, whether the firm produces a product, provides a service, or merchandises (retails or wholesales) consumer or industrial goods. As the noted management expert Peter Drucker has suggested, operations is simply the application of logic to work.

Operations can be defined as the process or system through which resource inputs such as raw materials, creative talent, labor, selling skills, or a convenient location are converted to useful outputs. Outputs may take the form of products, services, information, or the consumer satisfaction that results from effective merchandising. In short, the operating function determines how the firm creates value for its customers and the operating plan describes the planned procedures and flow of activities required to do so.

After studying the material in this chapter, you will:

- Understand the role of the operating plan.
- Know what information is needed to prepare the operating plan.
- Know the steps to preparing the operating plan.
- Understand the basic differences between operations for a manufacturing, service, and merchandising business.

INFORMATION NEEDED TO PREPARE AN OPERATING PLAN

As is true of each component of the business plan, the operating plan should be written as a miniature feasibility study. It is the vehicle that provides the intended reader with an understanding of the process that creates value and how this process contributes to the success of the firm. To accomplish these objectives, the operating plan should provide information for the following key questions:

- **What value does the firm create?** This means identifying the firm's primary output: the product that is produced, the service that is performed, or the goods that are merchandised.

━━ **How is value created?** This question is answered by determining the essential functions that make up the firm's normal operating activities.

━━ **What resources are used in creating value?** This means identifying the primary physical, human, informational, and financial assets that are required to conduct normal operations.

━━ **Where is value created?** This means identifying both the physical location of the business and the boundaries of its market(s).

━━ **How does operations contribute to the firm's success?** In other words, what unique advantage or benefit does the operating function provide? This contribution may take a variety of forms such as lower production cost, a good location, a new product or service, or more efficient distribution.

━━ **What factors influence operations?** This means identifying the variables that determine the success or failure of the firm's operations.

WHEN TO INCLUDE AN OPERATING PLAN WITH THE BUSINESS PLAN

In general, an operating plan is included as a separate component of a business plan when one or more of the following conditions exist.

━━ When operations, or an important part of operations, is unique, highly technical, or complicated.

━━ When operations is critical to the firm's success.

━━ When a major change in operations is intended.

If none of these conditions is present, the extent to which operating procedures are discussed is a matter of judgment. For example, if the firm's method of operations is uncomplicated or self-evident, reference to operations may be omitted entirely. Or, if some mention of operations is warranted, a summarization could be included in the business description section of the business plan.

STEPS TO PREPARING AN OPERATING PLAN

The eight steps identified and discussed below offer a logical sequence for gathering information and preparing an operating plan. However, since operations differ among different types of businesses, each step may not be included in every operating plan. Some steps may be omitted because they are inappropriate, some may be combined under one title for clarity or convenience, or some may be renamed to make them more descriptive of the situation. For example, if the operating plan is prepared for a traditional retailing business, it is unlikely that such topics as distribution and quality control will be discussed. On the other hand, these sections are usually critical to the description of operations in a manufacturing firm.

As an aid to gathering information and preparing the operating plan, guideline questions are included, where appropriate, with a given step. Also, an operating plan for a hypothetical business appears at the end of this chapter as Figure 8-1.

1. **Consider an operating plan summary.** This optional section *may* be used when the operating plan is prepared for outside presentation. The summary is a convenience for the reader and should be no longer than what is needed for him or her to gain an understanding of the plan's major thrust. This can usually be accomplished in a paragraph that summarizes the essential functions that make up the firm's operations.

2. **Prepare a situational review.** Normally, this section serves either of two purposes. It may be used to describe a major change that has occurred or is intended to occur in the operations of an existing firm; or, in the case of a new venture, the review may be used to describe how operating procedures were developed and the current stage of that development.

3. **Identify the firm's location.** Location is a factor that can mean the difference between success and failure of a business. This is especially true for the new venture and for firms that are highly dependent on proximity to either its resource needs or its customers.

The underlying theme for this section of the operating plan should be providing answers to the implicit questions of *where* and *why*. *Where* refers to the site of operations and *why* refers to the reason(s) this site was selected. As indicated in both the following discussion and the guideline questions for this section, these reasons may include such considerations as competitive advantage, favorable traffic patterns, accessibility to shipping and distribution facilities, or a plentiful labor supply.

The six location factors discussed below are, to varying degrees, a consideration for all businesses. Table 8-1 lists the major factors that should be considered in selecting a city, an area within a city, and a site within an area. Note that service businesses are combined with merchandising and production firms on Table 8-1 because the location needs of these businesses often overlap both categories.

- **Location of customers:** To virtually all merchandising firms and many consumer service firms, a location that is accessible to the target customer group is critical to success. Such firms depend heavily on customers who are drawn into the place of business, and their location is influenced by such considerations as population clusters, traffic or pedestrian movement patterns, and customer needs. Service firms that are able to take the service to customer locations have somewhat more flexibility than retailers, but even in these cases population clusters are important to having cost-effective operations.

TABLE 8-1
Major Location Factors

Factors Affecting The Selection Of:

A City	An Area In A City	A Specific Site
Retail & Service:		
Size of Trade Area	Area Potential	Cost of Site
Potential of Area	Access Routes	Auto Traffic Volume
Population Trends	Zoning Regulations	Pedestrian Volume
Purchasing Power	Appearance	Appearance
Competition	Competition	Related Shopping
Related Shopping	Amenities	Customer Convenience
	Related Shopping	Parking
Production & Service:		
Cost	Cost	Cost
Market Location	Zoning	Zoning
Vendor Location	Transportation	Utilities
Labor Supply	Compatible	Transportation
Transportation	Businesses	Employee Convenience
Utilities		Waste Disposal
Taxes		
Government Regulations		
Government Incentives		
Community Amenities		

Producers are typically more concerned with proximity or access to suppliers than customers. Yet, customer location is often critical to manufacturers that sell to firms using a just-in-time inventory system or whose products are perishable or expensive to ship. In these cases, a convenient location is an important consideration in measuring the cost of operations.

- **Location of suppliers:** For many businesses the cost, time, or certainty of supplying its inventory needs mandates a location close to its suppliers. For example, producers of foodstuffs, such as canneries, locate near the source of the perishables on which they rely. Likewise, manufacturers that use just-in-time production systems are concerned with proximity to major suppliers.
- **Location of labor supply:** The availability of human resources having appropriate, cost-effective skills is a consideration for most businesses. For example, producers of high-tech products that rely on a well-educated labor force tend to concentrate near major educational centers. On the other hand, firms that use

predominately unskilled labor often seek areas characterized by low standards of living and a minimum threat of unionization.

- **Access to transportation:** The cost and availability of different modes of transportation influence the location of many businesses. Manufacturing firms often rely heavily on controlling the cost and time involved in shipping the raw materials used. For example, manufacturers using low-unit-cost, bulky raw materials such as coal or basic steel locate near low-cost transportation. Or the producers of some perishable goods such as greenhouses typically locate near fast or specialized modes of transportation.

    The availability of appropriate transportation is also a location requirement for many merchandising and service firms. Retailers and service firms whose success depends on heavy automobile traffic such as manufacturers' outlet stores, restaurants, and motels, locate near major highway systems. Firms dependent on local, high-flow automobile or pedestrian traffic would choose locations having negotiable city streets and safe, pleasant access walks.

- **Services, taxes, and regulations:** A firm's location is often heavily influenced by governmental considerations such as the rates and types of taxes levied or the tax incentives granted. Other considerations such as zoning requirements; building codes; and restrictions on pollution, waste disposal, and industrial growth can make a location more or less desirable. In many cases, state or local governments, governmental agencies, or industrial authorities may provide a number of valuable services as an inducement to locating in a given area. For example, municipalities may raise the capital necessary for the construction of production facilities, assist firms in raising low-cost capital, or provide long term, rent-free leases on land.

- **Community features:** An important location requirement for many businesses is the quality of life the community can provide for the firm and its workers. Living conditions and community amenities such as educational facilities, cultural and recreational activities, and climate may make the difference when deciding between locations.

The following guideline questions should help the entrepreneur identify the type of information needed to develop an effective plan for locating the firm.

- Where is the business located?
- How and why does this site contribute to the success of the business?

- What competitive advantage(s) does this site offer?
- Are rental costs, lease costs, or purchase prices for land and buildings reasonable for this location?
- Do local authorities offer benefits such as tax breaks or financial assistance for locating businesses?
- Does this area provide an adequate supply of trained or trainable labor?
- Does this area have adequate educational facilities for the firm's labor force and their dependents?
- Is the location convenient to cost-effective transportation?
- Is there an adequate supply of cost-effective energy available to this location?
- Are city, county, and state taxes reasonable for this location?
- How much time and cost are involved in delivering to customers from this location?
- Does this location minimize the risk of product perishability?
- Is the location suitable to major customers using just-in-time inventory systems?
- Is the location conveniently accessible for the firm's suppliers?
- Is the location suitable given the firm's inventory needs?
- Is the location convenient to the firm's target customer group?
- Is there sufficient customer demand for the product or service in this area to support the business?
- Is there sufficient customer purchasing power in this area to support the business?
- Is the location suited to customer needs such as parking, transportation, and pleasant, safe surroundings?
- Is the volume of automobile and/or pedestrian traffic adequate at this location?
- Is the business clearly visible to automobile and pedestrian traffic at this location?
- Are adequate, cost-effective facilities available in the area of highest population cluster and people flow?

4. **Exploring operating procedures.** Once the issue of location has been decided, the policies and procedures that determine how value is created and how day-to-day operating procedures are conducted must be developed. If the operating plan is prepared for internal use, policies and procedures must be described in sufficient detail to guide employee and supervisory work efforts. If the plan is prepared for outside presentation, it is important that the operating process is made clear for the reader. In general, the more technical, the more complicated, or the more unique the firm's operations, the more descriptive this section of the plan must be. If a financier

cannot understand the firm's operations, financing will not be forth-coming.

It is also important that this section of the operating plan include a discussion of how the entrepreneur will balance the critical trade-off between creating value and the cost of doing so. The ability to effectively maximize difficult cost/benefit trade-offs such as those associated with operations is a management quality for which the intended reader will be searching.

The questions on the next few pages should serve as guidelines for identifying the type of information that is needed to prepare the operating plan. Since operations differ for different types of businesses, the guideline questions are divided into manufacturing, service, and merchandising (retail, wholesale, or distribution) categories.

The following guideline questions should help the entrepreneur identify the type of information needed to develop an operations plan for a manufacturing firm.

- What product(s) does the firm produce?
- What is the planned level of product output per unit of time (hour, day, week, etc.)?
- What major pieces of machinery and equipment are needed to produce the anticipated level of output?
- What is the maximum output per unit of time the facilities can accommodate?
- What are the major steps or stages in the firm's production process?
- How does work flow from the beginning to the end of the production process?
- Why is this work flow efficient and cost-effective?
- What transformations take place at each stage in the production process?
- Which raw materials are required to produce the product?
- What is the per-unit cost of raw materials?
- How stable are raw materials prices?
- Which labor skills are required to produce the product?
- What wage levels will these labor skills command?
- What is the materials and labor cost per unit of output?
- What is the expected level of productivity (output per man-hour) of the manufacturing process?
- What unique or competitive advantage (lower cost, better quality, etc.) does the firm's production process provide?
- What is the key to success for the production process?
- How does the production process contribute to the overall success of the business?

- What new technologies or unique production techniques are employed, and why do they provide an advantage for the firm?
- Are the subcomponents used in the firm's product manufactured in-house, or are they sourced outside the firm?
- How is production volume planned and scheduled?
- What cost savings or other production advantages does this scheduling procedure provide?
- Is the production process more dependent on labor (labor-intensive) or on machinery and equipment (capital-intensive)?
- What are the direct labor, direct materials, and overhead costs of producing the firm's product(s)?
- What percentage of the firm's total production cost does variable cost (those costs that change as production and sales levels change) represent, and what percentage does fixed cost (those costs that remain unchanged over longer time periods or over a reasonable range of production volume) represent?
- What is the contribution margin (selling price minus variable production cost) of the firm's product(s) or product lines?
- What is the firm's breakeven volume of production or sales?
- What is the gross profit margin (selling price minus cost of goods sold) of the firm's product(s) or product lines?
- What measures are used to monitor and control production costs?

The following guideline questions should help the entrepreneur identify the type of information needed to develop an operations plan for a service firm.

- What service does the firm provide?
- How is the service performed?
- What steps are involved at each stage of providing the service?
- What unique or competitive advantage does the service provide?
- What is the key to success for the service process?
- What in-house manufacturing is associated with rendering the service?
- Which components used in providing the service are subcontracted?
- What portion of the total cost of providing the service does in-house manufacturing or subcontracting represent?
- How many service representatives are required to provide the service?
- What guarantees, warranties, or maintenance agreements if any, accompany the service provided?
- What is the cost per man-hour or per employee to provide the service?

- What percentages of the total cost of providing the service do variable and fixed costs represent?
- What is the contribution margin of the service provided?
- What is the breakeven level of service revenue for the firm?
- What measures are used to monitor and control the cost of performing the service?

The following guideline questions should help the entrepreneur identify the type of information needed to develop an operations plan for a merchandising firm.

- To what merchandising category (specialty store, department store, off-price retailer, discount store, direct seller, wholesaler, etc.) does the business belong?
- What product or product line is sold?
- How does this product or product line provide a unique or competitive advantage?
- What are the major activities and procedures that make up the firm's merchandising process?
- What aspect, if any, of the merchandising process is unique?
- What is the key to success for the merchandising operation?
- How is product selection and purchasing conducted?
- What is the firm's sales and pricing strategy (low profit margin/high volume, quality, service, etc.), and why is it successful?
- What are the firm's sales figures per square foot of selling area, per labor dollar, and per sales employee?
- What percentages of the firm's total cost do variable and fixed costs represent?
- What is the contribution margin of major products or product lines?
- What is the firm's breakeven sales volume?
- What is the gross profit margin for the firm?
- What measures are used to monitor and control operating costs?

5. **Describing operating facilities and layout.** A successful operation requires sufficient space and an efficient combination and deployment of physical and human resources. Physical resources include such assets as buildings, machinery, equipment, fixtures, and vehicles. Human resources are the labor and administrative skills needed to create value and manage the business. Whether operating activities take place in a store, office, or plant, there must be sufficient, correctly designed space to accommodate the flow of work and the movement of workers, materials, or customers. The primary objective in deciding the size of the work area needed to accommodate operations is the planned volume of output, the efficient placement of physical assets, and movement of people.

There are a number of ways to plan the layout of operations. Most, however, use some form of scaled model. For example, a diagram of the floor and wall space can be prepared and then templates or scaled models are used to represent the amount of space that each requires. The templates or models are then correctly located to determine whether a smooth flow of activity results. Computerized versions of this approach are readily available in the form of computer assisted drawing or design (CAD) programs.

There are three basic types of operating layouts: product, process, and some combination of the two. With a *product layout,* the arrangement of physical and human resources follows the sequence of operations to be performed. Products, people or work-flow move forward from one stage of operations to the next with little or no backtracking. One well-known production process using the product layout is an automobile assembly line. The food line and customer flow in a typical cafeteria are arranged as a product layout. In general, the advantages of the product layout include faster movement, specialization of workers and machines, lower space requirements, and lower inventory requirements.

The *process layout* is based on the principle of grouping related functions. For instance, machines performing the same type of work, workers with similar skills or performing similar tasks, or merchandise serving the same function are grouped together. Common examples of process layouts include secretarial pools in offices, merchandise arrangements in department stores, or the grouping of special-purpose machinery and equipment in a machine shop. The primary advantages of the process layout relative to a product layout include more efficient use of machines, labor, and time; the flexibility to handle variety and change; and the potential for higher productivity or lower cost through grouping similar functions.

Few layouts are all product or all process. Rather, well-designed layouts attempt to capture the benefits of each. For example, the process layout typically reduces idle or down time compared to the product layout but often results in higher inventory cost. Combining the features of each may allow a balance that maximizes trade-offs such as this.

The following guideline questions should help the entrepreneur identify the type of information needed to develop a plan for a firm's operating facilities and layout.

- What type of facility is required to produce the planned volume of output or to maximize sales?
- Are the facilities leased or owned? If leased, identify the lessor and describe the significant terms of the lease. If owned,

identify outstanding liens against the asset, the lien holder, and the amount of the outstanding balance(s).

- How much space is required to effectively conduct operations?
- Has adequate space been allowed for people or product movement under normal and extreme conditions?
- What physical assets (building, machinery and equipment, vehicles, etc.) are required to conduct operations?
- How much space is required for the placement of physical assets?
- What is the most effective layout of physical assets, people, and work-flow?
- What aspects of the required facility or layout are unique or provide a competitive advantage?
- Why are facilities and layout cost-effective?
- How do facilities and layout contribute to the overall success of the business?
- What percentage of the firm's total assets do fixed (plant) assets represent?
- Are equipment, vehicles, and machinery leased or owned? If leased, identify the lessor and describe the significant terms of the lease. If owned, identify any outstanding liens against the assets, the lien holder, and the outstanding balance(s).
- What are the ages, expected useful lives, and operating condition of major fixed assets?
- Are the building and equipment adequately covered by insurance?
- Do the facilities, layout, and work-flow adequately meet safety and environmental standards and regulations?
- Do the facilities, layout, and work-flow meet reasonable standards for cleanliness and aesthetics?
- What procedures have been established to monitor and control efficiency of work-flow?

6. **Describe purchasing procedures.** In order to produce and/or sell a product or service, the typical business firm requires some form of incoming materials or finished goods. The process used to acquire these items is referred to as the *purchasing function*. In some businesses, purchasing may involve nothing more complicated than placing orders with sales representatives. In other firms, purchasing is complicated by the nature, assortment, volume, and price of the goods purchased. For example, some firms use basic raw materials and others use finished components; some use standardized products, while some use specially designed items; some materials must be stored, but others are not.

While such diversity rules out the possibility of one best purchasing system, there are two basic considerations that apply to any complicated purchasing function. First, the purchasing function should be a carefully designed process or system consisting of an established set of procedures. Second, the system should provide the desired quality of goods, in the correct amount, when they are needed, and at the least cost.

The following guideline questions should help the entrepreneur identify the type of information needed to develop a plan for a firm's purchasing procedures.

- Which purchases are critical to the firm's operation and why?
- What event indicates a purchase should be made, or which person makes this determination?
- How are purchase quantities determined?
- Are key items available from a limited number of suppliers or are they widely available?
- What vendors are used by the firm, and what criteria influence this choice?
- How reliable are these suppliers in terms of product availability, meeting lead times, service, and quality control?
- What alternative sources of supply are available?
- If only a limited number of suppliers exist, what contingency plans have been made to avoid a disruption of operations?
- What procedures are in place to check incoming shipments for accuracy, quality, etc.
- What percentage of the firm's total operating cost does the purchasing function represent?
- What measures are employed to monitor and control purchasing costs?
- What record-keeping system is used to track purchase orders from the time an order is placed to the time the goods are received and stocked?
- What aspect, if any, of the purchasing function is unique or provides a competitive advantage?
- Does the firm purchase through an outside buying group?
- What unique or competitive advantage does purchasing through the outside buying group provide?
- What methods are used to ensure that suppliers are paid promptly and cash discounts are taken when available?

7. **Explain inventory management procedures.** Inventory requirements vary by type of firm and how operations are conducted. The typical manufacturing firm has three levels of inventory: unprocessed raw materials inventory; partially processed work-in-

process inventory; and finished goods inventory. On the other hand, merchandising firms, such as retailers and wholesalers, carry only finished goods inventory. Service firms fall somewhere in between the two. Some service firms use raw materials or finished goods in rendering their service, while others have no inventory.

For those firms using inventory, purchases are typically made in advance of the time they are used in the operating process. This creates inventory levels which, for many firms, represent a sizable investment and a major cost item. For these reasons, it is important that inventory is carefully managed and controlled.

Sound inventory management is a prerequisite for maintaining satisfactory profit margins, minimizing invested dollars, minimizing operating costs, and avoiding cash-flow crises. Effective inventory management is also necessary to balance the important trade-off between the cost of carrying too much inventory and the cost of carrying too little. The former condition means cash, credit, or borrowed funds being needlessly tied up in excessive inventory, while the latter means stock-outs that result in lost sales or disruptions to production schedules.

The four major requirements for an effective inventory management are:

- Effective sales forecasting.
- Sound policies controlling which inventory items are carried, what inventory levels are maintained, the point at which inventory is ordered, the amount that is ordered, and the safety stock that is carried.
- An information system that provides reliable and timely inventory information from the point of purchase through the point of transformation and/or sale.
- Careful monitoring of the information produced by the inventory management system.

For those firms whose inventory represents a sizable investment of funds, it is essential that the operating plan clearly detail the procedures used to manage this valuable asset. The intended reader of the business plan will search for this information because it signals the entrepreneur's understanding of the importance of inventory control and makes a statement about his or her managerial ability.

The following guideline questions should help the entrepreneur identify the type of information needed to develop inventory management procedures.

- What techniques are used to forecast sales and project inventory needs?
- How are inventory projections related to the sales forecast?
- What inventory items are critical to the operation of the business?

- What is the average daily usage or sales rate of key inventory items?
- What is the minimum level of inventory needed to conduct operations efficiently and to avoid disrupting production or losing sales?
- What measures have been established to identify when the minimum level has been reached and when the necessary purchase order should be placed?
- What controls have been established to ensure that a purchase order is placed when the minimum stock level is reached?
- What techniques are used to control the costs of ordering and carrying inventory?
- How is information on inventory status (purchase dates, balances on hand, inventory age, usage or turnover rates, etc.) generated and used in the inventory control process?
- What automated techniques are used in inventory control? For example, is the process computerized, is a just-in-time inventory system used, is a point-of-sale device such as an optical scanner or an automated cash register used as part of the inventory control system?
- How are inventory costs monitored?
- How often is inventory control information reviewed by the person(s) responsible for inventory management?
- When and how often are gross profit margins (sales minus cost of sales) or contribution margins (sales minus variable cost) reviewed?
- What methods are used to prevent inventory theft by employees?
- Why is the firm's inventory management and control system effective?
- What unique or competitive advantage does this inventory management system provide?

8. **Establish quality control and customer service procedures.** By necessity, the first goal of operations is the effective and efficient creation of value. Planning an effective operating process does not, however, end here. An important part of operations is maintaining an acceptable level of product quality and customer service. These ingredients are often as important to the success of the business as having the product or service available. When consumers can choose from a large number of substitutes, or when the firm operates in highly competitive markets, meeting the quality and service expectations of customers may be the firm's only key to success.

As is true of operations, quality control is often thought of only in the context of manufacturing. Again, this perspective is too narrow.

In general, *quality* refers to conformity with perceived standards and *quality control* can be defined as the process of measuring and comparing the firm's product or service against standards set by management and the customer.

At one time, quality control was thought of as a means of correcting problems after they had been discovered. For example, goods were checked for defects only after production, or customer complaints were not investigated until a large number were received. Closely related to this thinking was the idea that productivity, quality control, and customer satisfaction were separate and mutually exclusive goals. Today, this thinking has changed and much of the credit for this change is attributed to Dr. W. Edwards Deming.

Dr. Deming pioneered the idea that quality, productivity, and customer satisfaction are closely linked. In his view, quality cannot be "inspected into" a product after the fact. To be effective, quality control must be considered a *preventive* process. For example, in a manufacturing firm, the quality of a product begins with the goals set by management, the product's design, the design of the operations that produce it, and the attitude about quality of the operating personnel involved. In a merchandising or service firm, the quality of output begins with an organizational commitment to customer satisfaction and the recognition that it is the customer that must ultimately set the standards that define quality. The entrepreneur must take the steps necessary to identify customer expectations and to select and train personnel to be concerned with meeting these expectations.

As is true of other facets of the firm's operations, maintaining quality and customer satisfaction involves a cost/benefit trade-off. The costs associated with controlling quality or achieving customer satisfaction must be weighed against the benefits derived from meeting customer expectations. Again, the intended reader will search for evidence of this understanding.

The following guideline questions should help the entrepreneur identify the type of information needed to develop the firm's quality control and customer service procedures.

- What policies have been established to ensure an acceptable level of quality and customer satisfaction?
- What methods are used to transmit the intent of these policies to managers and employees?
- How are customer attitudes about product quality and service determined?
- How are customer service needs determined?
- What quality standards have been established?
- How is output measured against these quality standards?

- At what point(s) in the operating process is output inspected and compared to quality standards?
- What methods are used to implement quality control and customer satisfaction standards?
- How is information on the effectiveness of quality control and customer satisfaction generated and used?
- What precautions have been taken to ensure that customer orders are handled properly from the point of sale to the point of delivery?
- What techniques or measures are taken to minimize the response time from order point to shipment date?
- What follow-up procedures are used to determine customer satisfaction subsequent to the sale?
- What percentage of orders are returned or require further attention because of customer dissatisfaction?
- How are quality control and customer service costs identified and measured?
- Why is the firm's quality control and customer service program effective?
- What unique or competitive advantage does the firm's quality control program provide?

TIPS FOR PREPARING THE OPERATING PLAN

▬ An effective operation means effective management. The operating plan not only provides the intended reader with an understanding of how the business operates, but also serves as an indicator of the entrepreneur's managerial ability. The most effective method for conveying this message is to identify the cost/benefit trade-offs that are associated with operations and how the entrepreneur intends to balance them.

▬ Explain how costs are controlled. The intended reader of the operating plan will also be keenly interested in how the cost of operations will be controlled. The method used may consist of nothing more complicated than a systematic review of operating-cost data, or it may consist of a sophisticated computerized cost control system. Of most concern is evidence that the entrepreneur understands the need for cost control and has established effective control procedures.

▬ Explain how inventory is controlled. For firms that carry inventory, control of this asset is as critical to successful operations as controlling costs. Excessive or obsolete inventory increases the cost of operations and is a major drain on cash flow and profits. Again, the particular inventory control method used is not as important as evidence that the entrepreneur understands the need for it and has established effective control procedures.

▬ **Use graphic aids.** If operating activities are highly technical, visual aids such as layout sketches, schematic drawings, or flow charts are valuable tools for enhancing verbal descriptions. Even when a manufacturing process is not unusually complicated, a simple flow chart depicting the steps in the value-creating process promotes understanding with a minimum of writing. Care must be taken, however, that graphics do not become an unintended substitute for substance.

SAMPLE OPERATING PLAN

The following operating plan is for a hypothetical food preparation and delivery firm, Masterful Meals (MM). The firm offers a unique combination of fresh, packaged meals and home delivery service. This business concept is the creation of the firm's founders, Chris and Lisa Shaw. Both entrepreneurs have strong backgrounds in the food industry and restaurant management fields.

MM's target market is the harried, two-income household. The majority of households in this target customer group consist of young and middle-aged urban professionals. The Shaws' market research revealed that while this target group is interested in appetizing, nutritious alternatives to fast foods or extensive dining out, they often lack the time, energy, or inclination to do grocery shopping and meal preparation for weeknight dinners. MM seized this opportunity by offering the combination of well-balanced, pre-prepared, single-dinner and five-dinner gourmet meal packages with home delivery. The customer is able to select from a menu containing a wide variety of traditional and gourmet meals. These meals can be heated and consumed immediately or frozen for later consumption.

MM has been in operation for two years and its success has exceeded the Shaws' expectations. This success prompted a large-scale expansion along with plans for franchising the business within three years. MM's operating plan is one component of a detailed business plan that will first be used to obtain bank financing for the anticipated growth over the next three years, and then for obtaining venture-capital financing to support the planned franchise operation.

FIGURE 8-1 *The Operating Plan Of Masterful Meals, Inc.*

Operating Plan Summary

This operating plan describes the business concept and operating strategy that have been the primary reasons for the success of Masterful Meals. The high level of productivity enjoyed at each stage of operations, the quality of the end product, and the

---

FIGURE 8-1 *(continued)*

high level of customer satisfaction have been achieved through rigid adherence to established standards and an ongoing process of evaluation and improvement. These operating procedures will be standardized as part of an operating policy manual, which will serve as the blueprint for franchised operations.

Situational Review

Masterful Meals, Inc., has operated in metro Atlanta, Georgia, since its inception. The rapid growth that MM has experienced, as well as its plans for future growth, have necessitated a recent move to a 5,000-square-foot building. This area will meet the firm's current need for space and will be required to accommodate the anticipated 220% increase in sales volume over the next three years. The new location is ideally situated midway between the northern and eastern sections of metro Atlanta. These two sections are the fastest-growing commercial and residential districts in this market area, and approximately 80% of MM's customers reside in these sections. This proximity reduces delivery cost and increases the speed with which customer orders can be filled.

Operations

MM's operations are divided into three basic steps: meal planning, meal preparation, and meal delivery. Menu choices for an entire month are planned and then converted into required food components. The food is prepared and the meals are assembled and packaged by three work teams of three persons each. The teams work under the control of one supervisor and the Shaws. These teams are capable of assembling and packaging over 500 weekly orders per day during the peak preparation period of Friday, Saturday, and Sunday. If the volume of orders necessitates additional help, MM's three delivery drivers, who are trained in meal assembly and packaging, provide that help.

Both the withdrawal of food inventory from storage areas and the meal assembly and packaging by the work teams are closely supervised. Close supervision and meticulous attention to detail increase productivity, minimize inventory loss, and ensure uniform meal quality.

Since taste is critical to the success of MM's product, approximately 70% of the food components in an average meal consist of fresh meats and produce. As a result, most food purchases and meal preparation take place on either the day of delivery or the day before delivery. To ensure that meals are fresh when received by the customer, MM uses insulated, temperature-controlled, containers to store meals during delivery. The delivery containers, vehicles, refrigerated storage equipment, ovens, and shrink-wrap machines make up about 90% of MM's fixed assets.

The number of meals to be assembled and packaged for delivery during a given week is determined by the number of customer telephone orders taken the previous week. To qualify for delivery by 5:00 P.M. on Sunday, orders for an upcoming week must be received by 12:00 P.M. on Saturday. Approximately 80% of MM's total sales revenue comes from weekly orders placed by the Saturday deadline. Daily (single-meal) orders must be placed by 12:00 P.M. on a given day to guarantee same-day delivery by 6:00 P.M.

Each of MM's menu choices are reviewed each month. In a typical month, several menu substitutions occur because of low demand or expressed customer interest in a particular meal, or to add greater variety. Menu selections are created by MM's in-house dietitian and the Shaws. The criteria used to create menu items are taste, gourmet flair, nutritional balance, customer acceptance, and cost. Through detailed planning, creative menu choices, and careful selection of fresh and processed food components, MM is able to maintain an average contribution margin on sales (sales minus variable cost) of 44%. Fixed cost makes up the remainder of the firm's total operating cost.

Facilities and Layout

Currently, about one-third of the available floor space is used for meal preparation and packaging and approximately one-fourth is used for inventory storage. Meal assembly and packaging take place on stainless-steel tables arranged in a "u" shape around refrigerated food lockers. This arrangement minimizes movement, simplifies food withdrawal, and provides for close supervision of work teams. Completed meals are packaged and placed in temperature controlled containers, which, when filled, are moved to delivery trucks.

Inventory Management

Since MM has the luxury of knowing the demand for weekly meals in advance and since the number of single-meal orders

FIGURE 8-1 *(continued)*

on a given day is highly predictable, the amount of inventory carried and inventory losses due to spoilage are minimal. In addition, management maintains close control over foodstuffs. Detailed records are kept of food deliveries and quantities used. These records are matched against weekly physical inventory counts to ensure that inventory usage is kept within intended limits, to track inventory costs, and to minimize the potential for theft. Using a personal computer and inventory management software, the Shaws and the dietitian are able to accurately calculate, monitor, and control the labor, food-component, and packaging costs of each meal.

Supply and Distribution

MM's raw materials consist of foodstuffs and, to a lesser extent, packaging materials. Fresh produce, meats, and bakery items make up approximately 90% of the typical prepared meal. The remainder consists of packaged foodstuffs. Since packaged items are nonperishable, MM is able to maintain a small, in-house inventory of frequently used items. On the other hand, only a minimal inventory of fresh foodstuffs is maintained. This inventory is necessary to meet the demand for nonscheduled, single-meal orders.

Produce, meats, and bakery items are purchased and delivered to MM's premises three times per week from local wholesalers. Because of MM's purchase volume and the competition that exists between the large number of wholesalers in metro Atlanta, MM is able to minimize raw materials cost without sacrificing quality.

Customers' weekly orders are delivered on Saturday and Sunday, and single-meal orders are delivered by 6:00 P.M. the day of the order. Deliveries are made by MM employees in three company-owned vehicles. Delivery routes and the delivery sequence are pre-scheduled by the Shaws and the delivery men. The careful scheduling of delivery routes minimizes the time and cost of delivery and ensures the critical qualities of meal taste and freshness.

Quality Control and Customer Service

Quality, service, and customer satisfaction are critical to MM's success. This philosophy is instilled in each employee when they are hired and trained. Food quality is controlled by using fresh foodstuffs where called for and by diligent inspection at the preparation and packaging steps. Customer satisfaction and quality service are achieved by offering a large variety of gourmet- and traditional-cuisine menu choices and by providing timely delivery service.

In order to stay apprised of customer expectations and the degree of customer satisfaction achieved, MM has established policies that include (a) conducting quarterly customer surveys using the pre-stamped questionnaires enclosed with meal orders, (b) adopting a "customer is always right" attitude in responding to complaints about meals or delivery, and (c) providing a free replacement meal or refund at the slightest hint of customer dissatisfaction or in the event of late delivery.

CHAPTER PERSPECTIVE

Operations can be defined as the system or set of processes and procedures used to convert resource inputs into a valuable product/service output. The operating plan details where the firm will locate, the procedures that will be used to conduct operations, the facilities and layout that will be required to conduct operations, how inventory will be purchased and managed, and how quality control and customer service will be conducted. The most effective method for addressing the issue of feasibility is to identify the cost/benefit trade-offs associated with operations and explain how they are balanced.

The Organization Plan

WHAT IS AN ORGANIZATION PLAN?

The management process concerned with the arrangement of human, physical, financial, and informational resources is referred to as *organizing*. The blueprint that results from this effort is the *organization plan*. An effective plan for organizing the various resources used by the firm is important to the success of every business. To the growing firm, however, it is crucial. Unless there are clearly defined links between authority, job responsibilities, and the flow of information and communication, it becomes virtually impossible to effectively coordinate efforts and to achieve organization goals as the firm increases in size.

The organization plan also serves as the vehicle through which the entrepreneur convinces the reader that his or her decisions on form of ownership, organization structure, and organization staffing will lead to the success of the business. A well-written organization plan is evidence that the entrepreneur understands the factors that affect organizational effectiveness and has carefully planned for the their design.

After studying the material in this chapter, you will:

▬ Understand the role of the organization plan.

▬ Know what information is needed to prepare the organization plan.

▬ Know the steps to preparing an organization plan.

▬ Understand the basic differences between the three major legal forms of business ownership.

▬ Understand the basic principles that guide the organizing function.

INFORMATION NEEDED TO PREPARE THE ORGANIZATION PLAN

The information needed to prepare an organization plan falls into three major categories: the firm's legal form of ownership; the design of the firm's internal organization structure; and the identification of the human skills needed to fill the positions within that structure. There are three basic legal forms of ownership: the sole proprietorship, the partnership, and the corporation. To make the proper choice, the entrepreneur must understand the legal, financial, and personal considerations surrounding each ownership form. Given the complexity of the decision, it is often advisable to use a qualified consultant to study the ramifications of each choice.

A fundamental task of business managers is to design an organization structure that provides the most efficient mechanism for meeting the firm's goals; an effective match between people, skills, job requirements, and authority/responsibility relationships; and the physical and informational resources job-holders need to meet assigned duties and responsibilities. Making sound decisions on organization structure requires information such as the following:

- The key jobs within the firm that must be filled.
- How the duties and responsibilities of each job are divided.
- How job authority and responsibilities are grouped.
- How formal authority flows through the organization.
- The most effective organizational design given the firm's *primary task*. The primary task is the activity or set of activities that form the firm's reason for existence.

In the view of most business experts, having productive employees is as important to the success of the firm as the product or service it provides. The reason is simple: An organization is only as effective as its people, and its people are only as effective as the managers that lead them. The management process that is concerned with personnel issues is referred to as *human resource management*. To perform this function effectively requires information such as the following:

- The requirements of each job in the organization.
- The qualifications needed to fill each job.
- The appropriate compensation for each job.
- The appropriate fringe benefits for each job.
- How capable employees will be recruited and trained.
- The standards by which job performance is measured and evaluated.

WHEN TO INCLUDE AN ORGANIZATION PLAN WITH THE BUSINESS PLAN

An organization plan will typically be included as a separate component of the business plan when one or more of the following conditions exist.

- The firm is large enough to require multiple management and staff positions.
- The firm's expected growth indicates that multiple management and staff positions will be needed.
- The firm's primary task is sufficiently technical or complex to require multiple staff and key operating positions.
- A major change in the organization structure is intended.

If these conditions are not present, the extent to which organizational considerations are discussed is a matter of judgment. Regardless of what is decided, resumes of the entrepreneur, the management team, and other key personnel in the firm should be included in the appendix to the business plan. The intended reader of the business plan will be concerned about the qualifications of key personnel. He or she knows that all businesses, whether new ventures or going concerns, will periodically encounter varying degrees of adversity. The difference between the firms that survive setbacks and those that do not is capable, productive, people.

STEPS TO PREPARING AN ORGANIZATIONAL PLAN

The eight steps identified and discussed below offer a logical approach to gathering information and preparing the organization plan. As an aid to this end, guideline questions are included where appropriate with a given step. Also, an organization plan for the hypothetical firm, Masterful Meals, appears at the end of this chapter as Figure 9-1.

1. **Consider an organization plan summary.** This optional section *may* be used when the organization plan is prepared for outside presentation. The summary is a convenience for the reader and should be no longer than what is needed to gain an understanding of the plan's major thrust. This can usually be accomplished in one paragraph.

2. **Prepare a situational review.** Normally, this section serves either of two purposes. It may be used to describe a major change that has occurred, or is intended to occur, in the organization of an existing firm; or, in the case of a new venture, the review may be used to describe the various stages of organization development that have been completed to date.

3. **Identify the legal form of ownership.** An important part of the organizing function is a decision on the appropriate legal form of business ownership. Since a number of legal, financial, and tax issues grow from this decision, it is important that the choice be carefully planned. The legal form of ownership should be matched to the basic mission of the firm, the firm's overall goals, and the entrepreneur's personal needs.

Various legal forms of ownership are available to the firm. Because some are appropriate only to specialized applications, only the characteristics, advantages, and disadvantages of three basic forms are discussed here. When considering these points, it is important to keep in mind that most of the features identified are *not* absolute. What is an advantage or disadvantage of an organization form is relative to the current and expected circumstances for that firm and that entrepreneur.

For example, while the federal corporate income tax rate is higher than the rate for an individual taxpayer, absolute size of the tax rate is not the only tax issue that must be considered when choosing between the sole proprietorship and corporation. The total tax bill under the various forms of organization will differ depending on such factors as expected profits and losses over the planning horizon; expected growth of the firm and the need for future financing; wage, salary, and Federal Insurance Contributions Act (FICA) tax considerations (i.e., for Social Security and Medicare) for the entrepreneur or his or her family members; and the entrepreneur's estate plan.

A *sole proprietorship* is a business firm established and owned by one person. Legally, and in the eyes of taxing authorities, a business organized as a sole proprietorship is indistinct from its owner. The firm's assets, liabilities, profits and losses, tax obligations, and legal responsibilities are also those of the owner. What's more, the life of the business is tied directly to the life of the owner. Technically, if the owner dies, the business dies as well.

The advantages generally associated with the sole proprietorship are:

- It is the easiest and least costly ownership form to organize and to dissolve.
- It is often the most appropriate form of ownership for a new business.
- The proprietor has total control and can make and implement decisions without interference from others.
- All profits belong to the proprietor.
- Relative to the regular corporate form, there may be a potential tax advantage when losses occur, because the losses flow through to the owner's personal tax return.
- Relative to the regular corporate form, owner's withdrawals of funds from the business are taxed only once, at the proprietor's individual tax rate.
- Unlike the regular corporate form, which, by law, is required to disclose financial information, a sole proprietor can maintain complete confidentiality.

The disadvantages generally associated with the sole proprietorship are:

- The assets of the business and the personal assets of its owner are subject to the claims of the firm's creditors. This characteristic is known as *unlimited liability*.
- Without prior provision for the allocation of business assets, the life of the business is limited to that of the owner.

- The financing available to the business is limited to what the proprietor can personally invest or borrow.
- Because of the firm's limited growth potential and the limited opportunity for employees to gain a share of the firm's ownership, it is often difficult for sole proprietors to attract and keep good employees and management talent.
- Since profits from the business flow through to the owner, there is no opportunity to protect cash flow retained in the business from income tax.
- Relative to the regular corporate form, there may be income tax disadvantages associated with income tax on the owner's or his or her family members' salary and FICA and medicare tax payments.

The *general partnership form of ownership* shares many of the characteristics of the sole proprietorship. A general partnership is an association of two or more persons conducting business as co-owners. As is true of the proprietorship, the general partnership is legally and for tax purposes inseparable from the owners (partners) themselves. Each general partner shares in the firm's profits and losses, has management equality, is liable for the business-related actions and decisions of other partners, and has unlimited liability for the debts of the business. Also, the life of the partnership is, technically, tied to that of each partner.

There are variations of the general partnership status. The most common are the limited partner, the silent partner, and the secret partner. The liability of a *limited partner* is limited to the investment in the business, and he or she typically has no voice in managing the business. A *silent partner*, like a general partner, has unlimited liability but does not have an active voice in managing the business. A *secret partner* is active in the firm's management and has unlimited liability, but is unknown to the public as a partner.

The advantages generally associated with the general partnership are:

- Partnerships, like sole proprietorships but to a somewhat lesser degree, have the advantage of ease and low cost of both organization and dissolution of the business.
- Because partners pool financial resources, partnerships often have access to greater amounts of capital than do sole proprietorships. For the same reason, partnerships often have better credit standing than sole proprietorships have.
- The partnership has greater potential than the sole proprietorship for attracting and keeping management talent and good employees.

- In comparison to the regular corporate form, there may be a tax advantage, because losses from the business flow through to the personal tax returns of the partners.
- Relative to the regular corporate form, a partner's withdrawals are taxed only once, at the partner's personal tax rate.
- Unlike the regular corporate form, which, by law is required to disclose financial information, the partnership can maintain complete confidentiality.

The disadvantages generally associated with the general partnership are:

- Each partner has unlimited liability for the obligations of the business.
- Each partner is responsible for the business actions of other partners.
- The potential for partnership disagreement and internal strife is great.
- Without prior provision for the disposition of the business in the event of a partner's death, the life of the business is limited to that of any partner.
- The financing available to the business is limited to what the partners can personally raise.
- Since profits from the business flow through to the partners, there is no opportunity to retain, free from income taxes, the cash flow from operations generated by the business.
- Relative to the regular corporate form, there may be income tax disadvantages associated with a partner's or his or her family members' salary, FICA, and medicare tax payments.

Several words of warning about forming a partnership are necessary. First, the potential for partnership conflicts is great. Business experts agree that long-term partnerships are the rare exception rather than the rule. Consequently, it will take much stronger justification to convince the intended reader that a partnership can be more successful than other ownership forms. Second, a partnership is essentially a legal relationship between the partners. It is crucial, therefore, that the partners enter into an *articles of partnership* agreement. As indicated below, this agreement should define in detail the role, involvement, duties, and responsibilities of each partner. The most common provisions contained in the articles of partnership are:

- Date and duration of the agreement.
- Name and location of the firm and the nature of its business.
- Names of partners, their respective investments, and the agreed-upon distribution of profits and losses.

- Duties of each partner and the expected hours of personal service that are to be devoted to the business.
- Salary of each partner.
- Each partner's percentage distribution of profits and responsibility for losses.
- Limitations on withdrawals of funds from the business.
- Procedures to be followed in the event of a partner's withdrawal from the firm.
- Procedures to be followed in the event of a partner's death or incapacity.

The next form of ownership to be discussed is the *corporation*. A corporation is chartered by the laws of the state in which it is incorporated. As such, a corporation is a legal and taxable entity that has a life, existence, and duties and responsibilities separate and distinct from its owners. Technically, a corporation is governed by its board of directors. This group makes major policy decisions and appoints the firm's officers and top-level management. The owners of the corporation are its common stockholders. Stockholders elect the board of directors and are entitled to all profits remaining after other claims on income (such as wages, payments to vendors, interest payments, and taxes) have been satisfied.

The advantages associated with the corporate form of ownership are:

- The corporation is a legal entity that can sue and be sued, enter into contract, own assets, and borrow in its own name.
- The corporation has an unlimited legal life that is separate from that of its owners (stockholders).
- A stockholder's liability is limited to the amount of his or her investment.
- Professional managers with no share of ownership can be hired and fired by the board of directors.
- Relative to the sole proprietorship and partnership, earnings can be retained in the business without being taxed as income to stockholders.
- Shares of ownership (common stock) can be sold, making it easier to raise capital and expand the business.
- Shares of ownership can be sold or transferred, making it easier to extend ownership interest to valuable employees, and easier for the entrepreneur to do estate planning.

The disadvantages generally associated with the corporate form, as compared to the sole proprietorship or partnership, are:

- It is more difficult and costly to organize a corporation.
- Unless the corporation is small and has elected the S corporation

taxing option, it is subject to multiple taxation. Federal and state income taxes are levied on the corporation itself and on the dividends and salaries paid its stockholders. In addition to this *double taxation* of income, corporations may also pay franchise taxes as well as taxes or fees to other states in which it does business.

- Corporations must keep records and prepare reports for state and federal agencies. Also, if the corporation's stock is publicly traded, it must keep audited accounting records and prepare reports for the Securities and Exchange Commission (SEC) and the exchange, if any, on which its stock is listed.

The final form of ownership to be discussed is the Chapter S corporation. The Internal Revenue Service (IRS) allows a small, closely held corporation (35 or less stockholders) to be taxed as a sole proprietorship or partnership while, at the same time, keeping its legal status as a corporation. Known as S corporation status, this tax status eliminates the double taxation of income associated with the regular corporate form. The S corporation does not pay income tax. Instead, corporate profits (and losses) flow directly to the personal tax returns of shareholders and are taxed at the stockholder's personal tax rate. To obtain S corporation status, the board of directors must elect this option by making a specific request to the IRS.

With the above discussion in mind, the entrepreneur should consider the following *guideline questions regarding legal form of ownership*:

- What is the total cost of organizing the firm as a corporation as compared to organizing as a sole proprietorship or partnership?
- How will the entrepreneur's personal assets be protected from the firm's creditors if the corporate form is *not* used?
- Given the firm's growth prospects over the next one to five years, what is the estimated amount of income tax that would be paid under the various forms of ownership?
- Given the expectations for business profits, dividends (owner's withdrawals), salaries and wages, and FICA withholdings for the entrepreneur and working family members, what amount of tax would be paid under the various forms of ownership?
- In the event of the entrepreneur's death, how will ownership interests in the business be taxed and transferred to heirs under the various forms of ownership?
- If the corporate form of ownership is chosen, what relative tax advantages and disadvantages are associated with the S corporation election?
- If the sole proprietorship form of ownership is chosen, can management talent and other key personnel be hired and retained?

- If the corporate form is selected, who will serve on the board of directors, and what can each director contribute to the success of the firm?

4. **Management philosophy.** An important consideration in structuring the organization is the culture that will evolve to determine the values, beliefs, and patterns of behavior that are accepted and practiced by the organization's members. The culture that eventually evolves is, either consciously or unconsciously, the result of the entrepreneur's management philosophy: how the role of manager is perceived by the entrepreneur and the pattern of behavior exhibited when he or she makes decisions and exercises authority. While management philosophy is possibly more subtle than other determinants of the firm's success, it is no less important. How well the entrepreneur and other managers relate to those inside and outside of the business determines how well they can motivate and lead employees, win the loyalty of customers, creditors, and the surrounding community, and create a positive image of the firm.

Management experts suggest that the most important factor influencing the culture and management style that evolves in the firm is the entrepreneur's actions. What the entrepreneur says or writes is not as convincing as what he or she does. The following actions have been identified as having the most important influence.

- What the leader pays attention to, measures, and controls. For example, if the entrepreneur's actions enforce a customer-comes-first policy, employees will do so as well. By contrast, those things the entrepreneur ignores are perceived as unimportant by employees.
- How the leader reacts to critical situations. For example, assume that because of declining profits pay cuts are necessary for survival. If everyone from the CEO down takes pay cuts, the action emphasizes the belief that management and employees are, for better and for worse, on the same team. On the other hand, if only operating employees are made to sacrifice, the opposite message is sent.
- The leader serves as teacher and coach. By directly relating to and becoming involved with members of the organization, the leader establishes himself or herself as a role model.
- How the leader recognizes and rewards achievement. Leaders can quickly communicate their priorities by consistently linking pay increases and promotions, or the absence of pay increases and promotions, to particular behaviors.

Consider the following guideline questions regarding management philosophy:

- How would the entrepreneur like employees to feel about the firm, himself or herself, and other managers or supervisors in the firm?
- What steps will be taken to ensure that the employees will have positive feelings about the firm, the entrepreneur, and other managers?
- How will employees be motivated?
- How will employee achievements be recognized and rewarded?
- How will employees be disciplined?
- How will employee morale be gauged?
- To what extent should decision-making be centralized in one or a few top managers?
- To what extent should employees have a voice in planning, problem-solving, and decision-making?
- What philosophy should govern the firm's relationship with customers, suppliers, creditors, and the community?

5. **Organization structure.** An organization is a structured group of human, physical, informational, and financial resources combined to accomplish specific goals. The organizational design that results from this effort defines the relationships and formal lines of authority and communication that exist between people and positions.

The primary purpose of designing a formal organization structure is to effectively coordinate the efforts of each part of the firm. There are five basic principles or building blocks through which this is accomplished: division and specialization of labor, departmentalization, line and staff status, the hierarchy of authority, and span of control.

Division of labor refers to the process of partitioning jobs into smaller, manageable tasks and assigning these responsibilities to specific workers. *Specialization of labor* refers to dividing jobs into a set of tasks that can be repeated easily and efficiently.

Departmentalization is the process of grouping jobs into major work units and placing them under the authority and control of an identified manager. Decisions about how to departmentalize affect such important organizational considerations as the ways in which authority is delegated, responsibilities are assigned, resources are distributed, performance is evaluated, and information and communication flow.

One of the most basic principles of organization involves the distinction between line and staff authority. *Line authority* is the formal right to make decisions and issue orders. This authority flows from the top of the organization down. For example, the firm's CEO delegates defined limits of authority to the vice president of production who, in turn, redefines and delegates areas of authority to production supervisors. Conversely, the term *staff* refers to the right to advise and assist line managers or other staff personnel in the staff member's area of expertise. The degree to which the assistance or advice must be followed by line personnel depends on the amount of authority that has been delegated to the staff position.

Closely related to the concepts of line and staff authority are the principles of managerial hierarchy, chain of command, and unity of command. *Managerial hierarchy* refers to the levels of management within the organization, and the organization's *chain of command* defines the authority relationships between these levels. Typically, the chain of command flows from the top of the organization down. The principle of *unity of command* establishes that each worker reports to and gets instructions from only one boss.

The organizational concept referred to as *span of control* deals with the number of employees reporting to one manager. Once the work to be done has been divided into major work units, the number of managers needed to supervise the work and the people who perform it must be decided. While a good rule of thumb for determining a manageable span of control is five to nine employees, the number should be determined by the capabilities of the manager and the nature of the work involved. This number is affected by factors such as:

- **Nature of the task:** The more complex the task, the narrower the span of control should be.
- **Level of employee skill and motivation:** The higher the skill level and motivation of employees, the wider the span of control can be.
- **Location of employees:** The more work locations at which workers are stationed, the narrower the span of control should be.
- **The degree to which authority is delegated:** The greater the ability and willingness of management to delegate authority, the wider the span of control can be.
- **The degree of interaction required:** The more interaction and feedback needed between manager and employees, the narrower the span of control should be.

The ultimate design of the firm's organization structure should depend on its primary task. In general, there are five basic ways a business can be organized or structured around its primary task.

- **By product:** For example, a chemical manufacturer may organize activities into industrial and agricultural chemical product divisions.

- **By function:** For example, many firms are organized around their production, marketing, information, and finance functions.
- **By process:** For example, a hospital may be organized into process units based on the type of medical service provided (emergency care, cardiology, surgery, etc.).
- **By customer:** For example, an electronics firm may set up divisions to serve its military, industrial, and consumer target markets.
- **By territory:** For example, an international firm may establish strategic business units to serve the U.S., South American, and European markets.

If the firm's size necessitates multiple management and staff positions, the authority/responsibility relationships between them should be depicted in an organization chart. A partial chart for a firm organized by function is shown on Table 9-1.

TABLE 9-1
Baker Enterprises
Sample Organization Chart

The boxes shown on the organization chart represent positions in the organization as well as the functional areas of responsibility (Production, Finance, etc.) associated with each. The vertical lines depict the flow of authority through various levels of the organization.

The entrepreneur should consider the following guideline questions when making decisions regarding organization structure:

- What is the firm's primary task?
- Are the activities surrounding the primary task most logically related to function (production, marketing, etc.), product, process, type of customer, or geography?
- What are the top-level management positions in the firm?

- What are the staff and middle-level management positions in the firm?
- What are the specific duties and responsibilities associated with each management and staff position?
- What decisions must be made to fulfill the duties and responsibilities associated with each management position?
- What number of immediate, lower-level subordinates can effectively be supervised by each management and staff position?
- What level of authority is assigned to each management staff position?
- What are the authority relationships between each management position?
- Who holds each management position?
- How effectively does each management and staff position-holder delegate authority to immediate, lower-level subordinates?
- What are the major work units or departments into which the firm's primary task can be best divided and re-grouped?
- How many supervisors are required for each major work unit or department?
- What duties, responsibilities, and level of authority are associated with each supervisory position?

6. **Key-personnel assessment.** This section of the organization plan should contain a brief summary of the job-related attributes of each key position-holder in the organization. The summaries should be prepared from complete resumes for each person. The resumes should be included in an appendix to the business plan and their location appropriately referenced in this section.

As used here, the term *job-related attributes* refers to the background, skills, and accomplishments that enable the individual to effectively perform his or her assigned job. In order to correctly identify these attributes, the entrepreneur must first understand which skills and knowledge level are required for that position. This information is gathered through the process of *job analysis,* and the results are written into a formal document known as a *job description.* A sample job description for a hypothetical assistant store manager position is illustrated in Table 9-2.

In general, the job-related attributes summarized for each key position should include the following points:

- **Education:** As used here, *education* means training that is directly related to the job or duties performed. This may include such training as job-related military training, formal education, or the successful completion of executive development programs.

TABLE 9-2
Sample Job Description

Job Title: Assistant Store Manager

Reports To: Store Manager

General Description of the Job:
Manages the daily functions of a specialty department in the retail operations. The assistant store manager has responsibility for customer service, supervision of sales clerks, new employee training, merchandising, advising and coordinating purchases with purchasing manager, and inventory maintenance.

Principal Duties and Responsibilities:
1. Assists customers in merchandise selections, sales returns, and lay-aways as needed.
2. Clarifies any questions or problems that a sales clerk encounters.
3. Trains, coordinates, directs, and supervises department sales clerks daily.
4. Maintains inventory records.
5. Prepares the department for opening at the beginning of each day.
6. Ensures that the department remains professionally organized and orderly.

General Qualification Requirements:
1. Education:
   Minimum four-year college degree in marketing or related discipline from an accredited university.
2. Experience:
   Minimum of six months to one year in a retail environment.
   Preferred one to three years as sales clerk at [*Name of firm*].
3. Knowledge, Skills, Abilities:
   Basic math competency
   Effective interpersonal skills
   Good judgment and independent thought
   Highly motivated self-starter
   High integrity
4. Physical Requirements:
   Standing and walking for more than 90% of the work time.
   Ability to lift and carry boxes weighing about 15 pounds or less.

- **Qualifications:** These are the tangible job skills and intangible attributes needed to effectively perform a particular job. For example, a sales manager should have marketing skills, leadership ability, and managerial talent commensurate with the requirements of that position in a given organization. On the other hand, training and job experience as an electrical engineer, while admirable attributes, do not qualify one for a sales management position.

- **Experience:** This term refers to the individual's exposure to the duties and responsibilities that are directly or indirectly related to a particular job. The key to what is appropriate experience is job-related exposure. For example, experience as an aircraft mechanic's apprentice would qualify one for a mechanic's position. It does not, however, qualify one to fly a plane.

- **Successes:** This term refers to career or job-related accomplishments that indicate an individual's ability to succeed. Included are such considerations as superior work performance that has been recognized, promotions and awards received, and pay increases.

- **Strengths and weaknesses:** Strengths refer to the personal qualities an individual has that make him or her well-suited to a particular job. For example, if a particular management position were being filled, the candidate's ability to plan, motivate employees, and set and reach goals would be important strengths. Weaknesses refer to personal deficiencies that must be corrected to effectively perform the job. If individual weaknesses are identified, then a plan for correcting them should be included in this section as well.

Because the key-personnel assessment step and the next two steps are closely related, the guideline questions for all three are combined and appear at the end of Step 8.

7. **Planning human resource needs.** This section should describe the key positions that must be filled in the future and the reasons these positions will contribute to the success of the organization. The description should identify:

- Each position by job title.
- The duties, responsibilities, and degree of authority of each position.
- How the authority and responsibilities of each position fit into the organization structure.
- The job-related attributes needed to successfully carry out the duties and responsibilities of the position.
- How qualified people will be recruited to fill each position.

The discussion of why a particular position must be created and filled should focus on how and why it will add to the organization's existing strengths or correct its weaknesses. For example, the reason for creating a top-level marketing position may be stated as follows: "By hiring an experienced marketer, the firm would gain the expertise needed to establish realistic marketing goals and strategies, and to control its overall marketing activities."

For the guideline questions on human resources needs, see the end of Step 8.

8. **Compensation and incentives.** The intended reader of the business plan will be interested in the financial stake that management and other key personnel have or will have in the business. Consequently, information such as the following should be included for each key individual in the firm:

- The amount of personal financial investment in the business.
- The percentage of the total ownership interest in the firm that the individual's investment represents. If the firm is incorporated, this information should include the number of shares of stock held, the price at which they were acquired, the percentage of the total shares outstanding that the shares represent, and a description of the terms of stock options held.
- The base salary received.
- A description of any bonus or commission opportunities afforded the individual.
- A description of any profit-sharing opportunities afforded the individual.

If the firm has employment agreements or management contracts that legally bind the individual to the job, these should be identified, explained, and justified. Such agreements are often viewed suspiciously by financiers, especially venture capitalists, because they may be used as instruments for perpetuating managerial incompetence. If the firm has existing or planned management contracts or employment agreements, the justification should focus on how they contribute to the success of the firm. For example, a management contract may be the only way a highly qualified individual can be lured to the firm.

Also, if the firm is incorporated and has outside directors on the board, it is advisable to prepare a separate section that describes the qualifications of these individuals and the contribution that each makes to the success of the firm. Again, the intended reader will become suspicious if it appears that director positions (especially paid positions) are being used as havens for relatives and friends.

The description of each director should include information such as the following.

- The director's identity.
- The background and experience the director brings to the firm.
- The position-related qualifications the director brings to the firm.
- The policy-setting role the director plays.
- Any gap in management skills the director fills.

In preparing the sections for Steps 6, 7, and 8, key-personnel assessment, human resources needs, and compensation and incentives, the entrepreneur should consider the following guideline questions:

- What job title will be assigned each key position?
- What is the purpose of each position and what outputs should it produce?
- What duties and specific tasks must be performed by each position-holder?
- What responsibilities are associated with each key position?
- What authority is associated with each position?
- What level of education, knowledge, skill, and experience is needed to perform the duties and responsibilities of each key position effectively?
- What personality or behavioral characteristics are required to perform the duties and responsibilities of each position effectively?
- How much job education or training will be required in order for the duties and responsibilities of the position to be performed effectively after the person is hired?
- How will any additional education or training be provided?
- What materials and equipment must nonmanagement job-holders use?
- How much time is required to complete the important tasks associated with nonmanagement jobs?
- In what environment and under what working conditions will nonmanagement jobs be performed?
- What environmental hazards are associated with these jobs?
- How are workers protected against environmental hazards?
- Will these protections satisfy federal and state safety requirements?
- What salary or wage compensation, including fringe benefits, is assigned to the management and nonmanagement jobs?
- How is the compensation level for management and nonmanagement jobs established, and is this amount sufficiently competitive to attract qualified individuals?
- What monetary and other incentives will be used to motivate job-holders?
- How will qualified personnel be recruited?
- How will job recruits be evaluated and screened?
- How will job performance be evaluated?
- What promotion opportunities exist for each job-holder?

TIPS FOR PREPARING THE ORGANIZATION PLAN

■ **Stress feasibility.** The entrepreneur should not underestimate either the contribution a strong organization makes to the success of the firm or the significance the intended reader will attach to this factor. In all likelihood, the reader will understand the importance of capable people to the success of the firm. For this reason, he or she will pay particular attention to the qualifications of key personnel and to organizational needs that must be filled in the future. If the organization plan does not contain this information, it is impossible to make a convincing case for *why* the organization structure is feasible and *why* the business will succeed.

■ **Evidence a strong commitment.** The intended reader of the business plan will also know that the entrepreneur must make a strong personal commitment to the business if it is to be successful. An entrepreneur who is in a position to suffer a large personal loss if the firm fails will work hard to achieve success and is less likely to walk away from the business when adversity strikes. The entrepreneur's commitment to the business can be indicated in a number of ways, including the size of his or her personal financial investment, the personal assets the entrepreneur has or is willing to pledge as collateral for financing, the time devoted to the business, and how the entrepreneur deals with work and personal priorities, or balances business commitments with family responsibilities.

■ **Management experience is expected.** Usually, it is not enough that an entrepreneur has specific technical skills in his or her business area. The intended reader will also expect the entrepreneur to have management experience. He or she will carefully search the business plan and question the entrepreneur to verify that this experience exists or, if it does not, that the entrepreneur recognizes the deficiency and has a plan for correcting it.

■ **Do not exaggerate strengths.** The qualifications of the key position-holders in the firm are an important ingredient of a convincing organization plan. These qualifications should be presented as favorably as possible. In doing so, however, it is important to resist the temptation to exaggerate or misrepresent the facts. Anyone seriously considering a professional or financial interest in the business will verify what is written. Exaggerations or misrepresentations will be discovered and the discovery will destroy the entrepreneur's credibility.

■ **Do not whitewash weaknesses.** It is as self-defeating to hide or omit organizational weaknesses as it is to exaggerate strengths. If the entrepreneur or other key personnel have job-related deficiencies, they should be identified *along with* plans for correcting the problem. For example, an entrepreneur lacking certain managerial qualifications may compensate by using an outside consultant for major decisions, or by hiring an experienced person to fill the position. Hiding or failing to recognize weaknesses indicates a person who either cannot be trusted or, equally disastrous, one who does not recognize problems.

■■■ **Be prudent about employing friends and relatives.** Placing unqualified friends or relatives in key positions or creating unnecessary positions for them has been the death knell for all too many firms. A business represents a large investment of the entrepreneur's time and money. There is too much at stake not to select people who have the background and skills needed to contribute to the firm's success. The intended reader of the business plan will immediately be suspicious if there is a hint that the firm is being used as an employment sanctuary for unqualified people.

SAMPLE ORGANIZATION PLAN

The following organization plan is for the hypothetical firm, Masterful Meals (MM). As indicated in the background information for MM in Chapter 8, the level of success enjoyed by the firm over the past two years has prompted Chris and Lisa Shaw to make plans for expansion. The expansion will take two forms: start-up of company-owned operations in other cities and franchises awarded to qualified entrepreneurs. If the franchising operation is successful after five years, the Shaws intend to take the company public (to plan a public offering of the firm's common stock).

FIGURE 9-1 *The Organization Plan Of Masterful Meals, Inc.*

Organization Plan Summary

This plan describes the organization structure and key personnel that will be required to support MM's anticipated expansion and growth over the next three to five years. The expansion will take the form of additional company-owned locations in select cities and the franchising of the Masterful Meals (MM) name and operations to qualified franchisees. MM is incorporated in the state of Georgia.

Situational Review

MM's current organization structure reflects the limited needs of its one-location operation. The firm is currently organized by function and employs 13 people. An organization chart depict-

FIGURE 9-1 *(continued)*

ing its basic functional structure is shown as Table 9A-1 in the Appendix to this plan. Chris and Lisa Shaw share administrative and record-keeping duties, and the dietitian and the Shaws share meal planning and delivery scheduling responsibilities. The supervisor of operations oversees food preparation and delivery. (See TableA-1) A secretary/receptionist takes telephone orders and does general secretarial work.

Management Philosophy

Chris Shaw and Lisa Shaw, MM's CEO and Executive Vice President respectively, adhere to the philosophy that three groups are responsible for the firm's success: its customers, the people in the organization, and the management team that leads organizational personnel. The Shaws believe that it is top-level management's responsibility to create the atmosphere and establish the relationships that emphasize the importance of each member the firm, and their appreciation of the contribution made by each to the firm's success. The Shaws further believe that:

1. MM's customers are its lifeblood. Every customer must be treated by any MM representative as if he or she were the firm's best customer. At MM, the adage that the customer is always right means: The customer has the right to both a quality product and quality service. MM has the responsibility to see that these customer rights are fulfilled.

2. MM's employees are the firm's most important assets. Employees are vital members of the organizational team, and what the firm accomplishes is accomplished through them. It is the responsibility of all managers in the organization to treat subordinates with the same degree of dignity and respect that would be afforded the Shaws or any high-level professional hired by the firm. Each MM manager has the responsibility to create an atmosphere and work environment that allows subordinates the opportunity to be contributing, respected members of the team, and to perform to the best of his or her ability. This requires a manager, through word and deed, to be a leader. As a leader, a manager must positively influence the behavior of others. While a manager is ultimately responsible for the successful execution of his or her duties, that manager must act on the belief that these responsibilities cannot be met without the cooperative effort of motivated, productive subordinates.

3. Employee performance must be fairly evaluated. Employees have the right to expect that job performance is measured and evaluated by standards that are free from personal bias and reflect effort, results, attitude toward customers, and the degree to which the employee is a cooperative team player.

Key-Personnel Assessments

As indicated on the Current Organization Structure chart (Table A-1 in the Appendix to this plan), MM's key personnel consist of the CEO, the executive vice president, the supervisor of food planning, and the supervisor of operations. A summary of the background and qualifications of each position-holder is given below, and a complete resume for each appears in the Appendix to this plan. [*Note:* The resumes referred to here are not shown in the Appendix, which has been abbreviated to fit the focus of this chapter.]

Chief Operating Officer

Chris Shaw holds a B.A. in Management from the University of Georgia, an M.B.A. from the University of Virginia, and has completed training programs in food and restaurant management for two prominent restaurant chains. His 16 years of experience in the food and restaurant management field include positions as a location manager for a fast food chain; a regional manager for the same fast food chain; a regional manager for a full-service restaurant chain; and, for the three years prior to starting MM, the director of operations for the same restaurant chain. This last position is equivalent in authority and responsibility to what is typically a vice president position in many organizations. In that position, Mr. Shaw was responsible for the strategic planning, administration, and control of the 27 restaurant locations in the firm's chain.

Executive Vice President

Lisa Shaw holds a B.S. in Biology from the University of Georgia and a masters degree in Hotel & Restaurant Management from Florida State University. Her 13 years of experience in the hotel and food management field include positions as a management trainee with a large hotel chain; a hotel manager with the same chain; and, for the five years prior to starting MM, the director of food management with the same chain. In that position, Mrs. Shaw was responsible for the planning, administration, and control of restaurant operations for the entire chain.

FIGURE 9-1 *(continued)*

Supervisor of Food Planning

Megin Bradley, who was involved with the development and start-up of MM, holds a B.S. in Chemistry from Indiana University, a masters degree in Food Chemistry and Nutrition from Florida State University, and is a certified registered dietitian. She has 15 years of experience in the meal planning and food nutrition field, including positions as head dietitian in two hospitals and two nursing homes and director of food services at a large resort and health ranch. Ms. Bradley has particular expertise in the areas of meal planning and food acquisition, management, and control. Her meals feature the unique combination of nutrition, quality, taste, and flair.

Supervisor of Operations

Wade Nelson, who was involved with the development and start-up of MM, has eight years of experience in the food preparation field. During the last four years of this time span, he held the position of operating foreman for a large food packaging firm for two years and has been in his present position with MM for the other two years. Mr. Nelson was instrumental in designing and perfecting the operating methods now used by MM for preparing, packaging, and delivering meals.

Planned Organization Structure and Key-Personnel Needs

The key positions needed to support MM's planned expansion include vice presidents of food planning, accounting and finance, operations, and marketing and franchising. These positions are depicted on the planned organization chart shown as Table A-2 in the Appendix to this plan. Each planned position is described below.

Vice President of Food Planning

This position-holder will be heavily involved with the firm's strategic and operational planning and will have specific responsibility for, and authority over, menu planning, food acquisition and control, and the training of company and franchisee personnel in these areas. The individual who fills this position must have a bachelor's degree, be a certified dietitian, have experience in menu planning and food management, and have three to five years of experience in an administrative position. While in an administrative position, this person must have demonstrated an ability for planning, control, and personnel management. Ms. Bradley is the logical candidate for this position.

Vice President of Accounting and Finance

This position-holder will be heavily involved with the firm's strategic and operational planning and will have specific responsibility for, and authority over, the firm's financial management, planning, and control; its internal accounting system; internal auditing; the production of records and reports; and providing the financial expertise necessary for the firm's franchising activities and to take it public. The individual who fills this position must have at least a bachelor's degree in accounting/finance and, preferably, a master's degree in these areas or CPA certification. Three to five years of successful experience as a chief financial officer or controller, as well as experience with franchising and/or a public stock offering, is a mandatory requirement for the position. This individual will have to be recruited from outside the firm's current personnel.

Vice President of Operations

This position-holder will be heavily involved with the firm's strategic and operational planning (see Table A-2) and will have specific responsibility for, and authority over, the planning, organizing, and control of operations for company-owned and franchisee-owned locations. This person will also be responsible for standardizing MM's operating procedures, developing operating procedure manuals for use in all firm and franchisee locations, and training operating personnel for both. It is preferred, but not mandatory, that the individual who fills this position have a bachelor's degree in business administration. The individual must have three to five years of experience in food processing operations or a related area as well as experience in a supervisory or an administrative position. It is hoped that with satisfactory completion of selected executive development programs, Mr. Nelson can fill this position. If not, a qualified individual will be recruited from outside the firm.

Vice President of Marketing and Franchising

This position-holder will be heavily involved with the firm's strategic and operational planning and will have specific respon-

FIGURE 9-1 *(continued)*

sibility for, and authority over, developing marketing strategy, programs, and promotions for all company-operated and franchisee locations. In addition, the individual will have responsibility for, and authority over, the acquisition of franchisees and the planning, development, marketing, and promotion of MM's franchising operation. The individual who holds this position must have a bachelor's degree in business and, preferably, an M.B.A. Three to five years of successful administrative experience in marketing management and experience with the acquisition and marketing of franchising operations are required.

Compensation and Incentives

MM's corporate charter authorizes 500,000 shares of common stock. These shares have an assigned par value of $1.00. Only 280,000 shares, however, are outstanding. The distribution of these shares is as follows:

Chris and Lisa Shaw have a combined ownership of 250,000 shares, or 50% of the total shares outstanding. The total value of these shares represents compensation for the Shaws' time, effort, and expertise provided to the business and for the ownership risks assumed.

Megin Bradley, in return for her efforts with the development and start-up of the business, was compensated with 20,000 founder's shares.

Wade Nelson, in return for his efforts with the development and start-up of the business, was compensated with 10,000 founder's shares.

At the date of this writing, MM has no management contracts or employment agreements outstanding, nor do any employees hold stock options or profit-sharing or bonus incentive agreements. The Shaws fully realize, however, that in order to attract qualified people for the planned vice president positions, such considerations may be necessary.

At the date of this writing, MM has no outside members of the Board of Directors. The Shaws have, however, discussed seats on the Board with a local venture capitalist and a local financial consultant. Both individuals would bring much of the expertise, and possibly opportunities for financing, needed for the expansion into franchising and to take the company public. An annual stipend of $2,500 per individual has been discussed as possible compensation for their services.

Organization Plan Appendix

TABLE A-1
Master Meals, Inc.
Current Organization Structure

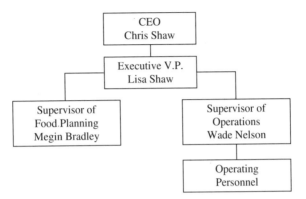

TABLE A-2
Master Meals, Inc.
Planned Organization Structure

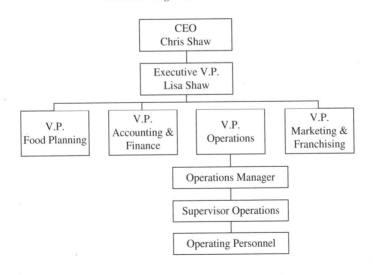

CHAPTER PERSPECTIVE

An organization plan details how the firm's resources will be organized and structured to coordinate activities and meet established goals. The organization structure that is chosen should give consideration to the most effective method for carrying out the firm's primary task, the duties and responsibilities of each key position in the firm, how authority should flow through the firm, and the most effective matching of job requirements and job qualifications. The typical organization plan contains a summary, a situational review, a statement of management philosophy, a description of the chosen legal form of ownership and organization structure, an assessment of key personnel and planned human resource needs, and a description of the compensation and incentives received by key personnel.

The Financial Plan

CHAPTER 10

WHAT IS A FINANCIAL PLAN?

The various operating plans prepared by the entrepreneur indicate where the firm is expected to go and how it is expected to get there. The mechanism used to estimate and plan for the financing needed to implement these intentions is the financial plan. It, along with the market analysis and marketing plan, is the most critical component of the business plan. A convincing financial plan answers the following key questions:

■■■ What amount of financing is needed to make plans feasible?
■■■ When and in what amounts will the financing be needed?
■■■ In what form will the financing be needed?
■■■ Who will provide this financing?

Generating convincing responses to these questions requires knowledge of how the business operates, the factors that determine the success or failure of its operation, a basic understanding of the financial side of the business, and the ability to translate this information into a sound financial game plan.

After studying the material in this chapter, you will:

■■■ Understand the role of the financial plan.
■■■ Know what information is required to prepare the financial plan.
■■■ Know the steps to preparing the financial plan.
■■■ Know how to prepare a cash budget and use this tool to estimate the firm's short-term financing needs.
■■■ Know how to prepare pro forma financial statements and use them to estimate the firm's long-term financing needs.
■■■ Understand the basic features of the major forms of financing.
■■■ Understand the basics of financial ratio analysis.

INFORMATION NEEDED TO PREPARE A FINANCIAL PLAN

Information for the financial plan comes from other sections of the business plan and, possibly, from published secondary sources. Included among these are:

▬ The firm's operating plans and budgets and the sales forecast that drives them. For example, the sales forecast is the starting point for the cash budget and pro forma (projected) financial statements; the marketing budget provides estimates of product revenues and marketing expenditures; and the operating budget provides data on asset requirements and production schedules.

▬ Historical financial statements and the cash budgets and pro forma financial statements prepared for previous planning periods. For the existing firm, these sources provide many of the key financial relationships needed to prepare planning documents.

▬ Published financial data such as *Annual Statement Studies*, published by Robert Morris and Associates, and *The Almanac of Business and Industrial Financial Ratios*, published by Prentice Hall. These references provide key financial statement data for large samples of firms in different size categories from a wide variety of industries.

▬ The firm's operating policies. For example, personnel policies determine the cost of fringe benefits such as holiday and vacation pay; inventory policy establishes appropriate inventory order quantities and purchasing procedures; and credit policy determines the average length of time accounts receivable (credit sales) are outstanding.

FORMS OF FINANCING

Before beginning the financial planning effort, the entrepreneur should be familiar with the major forms of financing used by businesses. In general, there are two major categories of financing: debt and equity; two basic sources of financing: internal and external; and four primary types of financing: seed money, start-up capital, working capital, and long-term financing.

Debt and Equity Capital

Debt financing represents funds borrowed from a creditor under a legally binding, contractual agreement. The contract obligates the borrower (debtor) to repay the obligation plus stipulated interest at some designated future date(s) and to honor all other specified provisions of the contract. While the debt agreement gives the creditor a legally enforceable claim on the firm's cash flow and assets, it also limits the creditor's relationship with the firm. Normally, a creditor has no voice in management; does not share in the firm's earnings beyond contractual payments; and has no ties to the firm beyond the duration of the debt agreement.

Debt financing used by business firms is generally thought of as having either a short-term or long-term maturity. *Short-term debt financing* usually takes the form of trade credit, which is credit extended by suppliers for purchased goods, and short-term loans from financial institutions. Obligations such as these appear on the firm's balance sheet in the current liabilities section.

Long-term debt financing may have maturities as long as 30 or more years and consists of such obligations as a term (installment) loan, mortgage loans for the purchase of real property, and bonds. These obligations appear on the firm's balance sheet in the long-term liability section.

Equity capital represents the ownership interest(s) in the business. It consists of funds invested by or stock purchases of the owner(s) and, if the firm is a going concern, the cash flow that has been retained in the business rather than paid out as dividends to the owner(s). In contrast to creditor's claims, the owner's claim is residual and, unless otherwise specifically agreed, is assumed to continue for the life of the firm. As residual claimant, the owner is entitled to all cash flows and asset values remaining after other claims on the firm have been satisfied.

Internal and External Financing

Internal financing refers to the funds generated by normal operations which remain after creditors and taxes are paid, or to the additional investment (purchase of stock) of existing owners. These funds belong to the owners and are available for either reinvestment in the business or for payment to the owners as dividends (withdrawals).

External financing represents debt or equity capital raised outside the firm. External debt financing may take the form of negotiated loans from creditors such as banks or commercial finance companies or debt obligations such as bonds which are sold in the open market. External equity capital is ownership financing raised through the sale of some portion of the ownership interest in the business to an outside investor.

Types of Financing

Seed money is the financing needed to develop and refine the business concept. The development stage of a business firm may be as involved as designing and producing a prototype product or as simple as having enough capital to marshal the resources needed to reach the start-up stage. The amount of seed money needed depends on the complexity of the development stage and can range from nominal sums to millions of dollars. Unfortunately, seed money must usually be furnished by the entrepreneur. Finding outside investors willing to take the large-scale risk that exists when the firm is nothing more than an embryo is difficult at best.

Start-up capital is the money needed to get the business going. It usually consists of the short-term working capital needed to finance initial operations and the long-term capital needed to obtain physical and human resources. While it may be somewhat easier to find start-up capital than seed money, sparking the interest of an outside investor at this stage is difficult as well. Normally, banks and other lending institutions will not make start-up loans. The degree of risk involved is too high for the limited-return loans they make. Some private investors and possibly a few venture capitalists may furnish start-up capital if (a) there is solid evidence of market acceptance of the concept, (b) there is the likelihood of exceptional commercial success, (c) there is the promise of large-scale returns on the money invested, and (d) the entrepreneur and other management are deemed to be capable administrators.

Working capital is the short-term financing needed to support recurring build-ups in current assets (inventory, accounts receivable, and cash). These assets play a large role in the firm's normal operating cycle and are expected to turn themselves into free cash flow at the end of that period. The major suppliers of working capital are typically commercial banks and trade creditors. The latter entities do not supply money per se but extend credit in the form of delayed payment under specified credit terms. Commercial banks and other lending institutions make working-capital loans to qualified businesses. In general, this type of financing is the easiest for a viable firm to obtain.

Long-term financing and/or *growth capital* is used to finance the firm's fixed (plant) asset base. These are the more permanent or long-lived assets used by the firm, such as buildings and equipment. The financing for fixed assets usually consists of some combination of long-term debt and owner's equity capital. The ability to borrow on a long-term basis requires an adequate base of owner's equity capital, an acceptable credit standing, adequate collateral, and a profitable track record.

GUIDELINE QUESTIONS

The preceding discussions provide potential sources for the information needed to prepare the firm's financial plan and an overview of forms of financing. By answering the following questions, the entrepreneur will have guidelines for identifying what information is needed and when enough information has been gathered to complete the effort.

■ Given the current stage of the firm's development, what category of financing should be used?

■ In what form, debt or equity capital, will this financing be raised?

■ Given the degree of risk to which the business is exposed, what is the maximum percentage of debt financing that should be used?

■ If debt financing is contemplated, would the proportion of debt existing after the financing violate the maximum?

■ Who can realistically be approached to provide the needed financing?

■ If the firm is an existing business, what has been its financial performance for the past three years as measured by the trend in key ratio values such as return on investments or sales growth?

■ If the firm is an existing business, what is its current financial position as measured by key indicators such as cash flow from operations, profit margins, and the debt ratio?

■ If the financial plan is prepared for a new venture, what key balance sheet and income statement relationships exist for the representative business in the firm's industry?

■ What attainable financial goals have been established for the upcoming planning period?

■ What control mechanism has been established to monitor the firm's progress toward meeting established financial goals?

■ What monthly sales are forecast for the next twelve months, and what annual sales are forecast for the next three years?

■ What is the expected percentage breakdown of monthly sales between cash and credit?

■ What is the expected accounts receivable collection pattern?

■ Given the sales forecast, what is the average level of inventory purchases each period?

■ How many days are expected to elapse between the time inventory is purchased and the time payment is made to the supplier?

■ What cash expenses, including taxes and loan repayments, are expected to be incurred and paid each month?

■ What is the minimum cash balance the firm should keep as a precaution against unforeseen emergencies?

■ As shown by the "Cumulative Financing" figure on the cash budget, what amount of seasonal working-capital financing is needed during this planning period?

■ Which financing sources can be realistically expected to provide this financing?

■ What are the historical percent-of-sales relationships between those asset and liability accounts that are directly related to sales?

■ What adjustments, if any, to the historical percent-of-sales relationships should be made to reflect expected changes during the planning period?

■ What dividend payouts (owner's withdrawals) are anticipated during the planning period?

■ As shown by the pro forma balance sheet, how much external financing must be raised to support anticipated growth during the planning period?

■ In what form should the required external financing be raised?

■ Which financing sources can be realistically expected to provide this financing?

WHEN TO INCLUDE A FINANCIAL PLAN WITH THE BUSINESS PLAN

As is true of the marketing plan, information from the financial plan is a critical component of any convincing business plan. This is true whether a complete business plan is prepared for outside presentation, whether the presentation package is limited to selected business plan information, or whether the financial plan is used internally. A well-prepared financial game plan is important to the effective management of the firm, and it is also affirmation of the entrepreneur's understanding of the financial side of the business.

STEPS TO PREPARING A FINANCIAL PLAN

The seven steps discussed below offer a logical sequence for gathering information and preparing the financial plan.

1. **Financial plan summary.** This optional section *may* be used when the financial plan is prepared for outside presentation. The summary is a convenience for the reader and should be no longer than what is needed for him or her to gain an understanding of the plan's major thrust. This can usually be accomplished in a paragraph that identifies the amount(s) and type(s) of financing needed to meet identified uses.

2. **The situational review.** If the firm is a going concern, this section should contain a review of the firm's financial performance for the past three to five years. The review should be sufficiently detailed to provide the reader with an understanding of where the firm has been, the progress (hopefully) it has made, and the current financial position from which the business plan departs.

In order to support the narrative for this section, key financial indicators should be presented in supporting tables or graphs. The historical financial statements (balance sheets, income statements, and cash-flow statements) from which these data are taken should be included in an appendix to the business plan. Their existence and location can be appropriately referenced in the review. The historical financial statements for A&D Sales and Service, the hypothetical firm used in the sample financial plan (Figure 10-1), are shown as

Tables 10-3, 10-4, and 10-5. A list of key financial indicators calculated from these statements is shown as Table 10-2 in the plan. Also, a short tutorial on the basics of ratio analysis and calculating a breakeven point are contained in the Appendix to this chapter.

If the financial plan is prepared for a new venture, the entrepreneur may wish to use this section to present the financial profile of the representative firm in the industry. As used in this context, a *financial profile* is a common-size balance sheet and income statement. These statements show the dollar amounts as percentages of sales or of a specific category total. As noted earlier, this information is readily available from published sources such as the *Annual Statement Studies* and *The Almanac of Business and Industrial Financial Ratios*.

The presentation of a representative financial profile in this section serves three important purposes. First, it provides the entrepreneur with guidelines for making the estimates needed for the venture's pro forma statements. Second, it provides the reader with a benchmark for evaluating the new venture. Third, it is additional evidence of the quality and depth of the research effort that has gone into preparation of the financial plan.

3. **Financial goals.** Financial goals are the benchmarks used to guide and measure the firm's progress. If a business does not enjoy financial success, it cannot remain viable. This means generating cash flow sufficient to:

- Meet out-of-pocket expenses as they come due.
- Service debt obligations.
- Replace assets as they wear out or become technologically obsolete.
- Implement and carry out planned activities.
- Earn a compensatory rate of return for the owner(s).

The financial goals set by the entrepreneur must reflect these fundamental needs. They should be clearly stated, realistic, measurable, and expressed in terms such as the following:

- **Financial ratio values:** For example, "It is our goal to achieve a return on investment (ROI) of 20% and to increase inventory turnover to five times per year."
- **Percentage growth rates:** For example, "An annual growth in sales, assets, cash flow, and profits of 10% is expected over the three-year planning horizon."
- **Percent profit margins:** For example, "It is management's intention to increase gross profit margin on the major product line to 48%."
- **Cost and expense relationships:** For example, "The investment in new equipment is expected to reduce labor cost by

25%, or the cost-control program that has been implemented is expected to reduce operating cost by 10%."

4. **Cash-flow planning—the cash budget.** Cash-flow planning is the process of estimating the financial resources (money and credit) needed to carry out planned operations and to keep the firm financially viable. Planning horizons are usually divided into short- and long-term time frames. *Long-term cash planning* covers three to five years, and pro forma (projected) statements are used to make the necessary estimates. *Short-term cash plans* are typically prepared for one year, and these detailed projections are made through a cash budget.

A *cash budget* is a period-by-period estimate of the amount and timing of the cash inflows (receipts) and outflows (disbursements) associated with planned operations. The budget is usually prepared for one year, which is divided into either monthly or weekly budget intervals. The estimates of cash inflows consist of:

- The cash receipts produced by normal operations. This includes the receipts from cash sales plus the collection of accounts receivable (credit sales).
- The cash receipts arising from nonoperating sources, such as the sale of a fixed asset or a tax refund.

Cash outflows consist of:

- The cash disbursements associated with normal operations, including the payments for purchases (accounts payable), payments for cash operating expenses such as wages and salaries, and tax payments.
- The cash disbursements associated with fixed asset purchases, repayment of debt obligations, and the payment of dividends (owner's withdrawals).

A typical format for the cash budget is shown as Table 10-6 in the Appendix to the sample financial plan at the end of this chapter. We now turn our focus to preparation of the cash budget.

While the cash budgeting process begins with a sales forecast, forecast sales are not a part of the actual budget. Rather, forecast sales values serve as reference numbers used in the estimation of the cash inflows that sales produce. For most businesses, some portion of sales are cash sales. These estimates are included in the budget as cash inflows. However, most business sales are made on credit, and a credit sale does not become a cash inflow until the outstanding account is actually collected. Projecting the cash inflows from this source requires an estimate of the percentage of outstanding accounts that are collected in a given period. These percentages are referred to as the *receivables collection pattern*.

If the firm is a going concern, the cash sales and the receivables-collection-pattern percentages can be estimated using the firm's past sales and collection experience, adjusted, if necessary, for changes the entrepreneur expects to occur. The estimated cash-sales percentage for a going concern can be established using the following approach:

- First, select a representative sample of historical sales figures for periods that correspond to the periods in the cash budget. For example, if the budget is prepared in monthly intervals, compile monthly historical sales figures.
- Next, identify the dollar amount of sales in each period that were made for cash. Convert these amounts to percentages by dividing the dollar amount of cash sales for each period by total sales for that period. Here is the formula:

Cash Sales Percentage = Cash Sales/Total Sales

- Then, apply the cash-sales percentage for each month to forecast sales for that month to obtain the estimate of cash inflow from cash sales.

The estimated cash inflow from the collection of receivables is determined by applying collection-pattern percentages to the forecast sales values for each period. These percentages represent the proportion of credit sales from a given budget period that is expected to be collected in the current or subsequent budget periods.

For the going concern, collection-pattern percentages can be established using information from the firm's historical sales and receivables records, and a technique known as the *payments pattern approach*. The payments pattern approach uses customer payments data to determine the percentage of a given month's credit sales that have been collected in that month and subsequent months. The following steps outline the approach used to establish collection-pattern percentages. A more detailed discussion of this technique can be found in most business finance textbooks.

- First, select a representative sample of historical credit-sales figures for periods that correspond to those used in the cash budget. For example, the percentages used to estimate collections for June, the first quarter, or the fall holiday season should be derived from their historical counterparts.
- Next, the sample of historical credit sales for each period should be separated into sales by individual customer or by groups of customers of the same size. Sales must be isolated by customer in order to identify when that customer pays the outstanding account.

- Then trace a given customer's receivable payment in a given month back to the month in which the sale was made. These payments would then be converted to percentages by dividing the receivable payment in a given month by the amount of the sale in the month the sale was made.
- Next, average the collection percentages in a given month and identify them in terms of the lag time between the month of sale and the month of collection. For example, the collection-pattern percentages may indicate that 50% of the credit sales made in January are collected one month later (in February), 40% are collected two months later (in March), and 10% are collected three months later (in April).
- Finally, apply the historical collection-pattern percentages to forecast sales to obtain the monthly estimates of cash inflow from receivables collections used in the cash budget.

Assume that the management of the XYZ Company, after examining historical credit sales and customer payments on accounts receivable, has decided that June is a representative month. The historical data for the most recent June indicate the following breakdown of credit sales by major customer. The Alex Shop, Avanti, Sunbloc, and Dosta Sports are XYZ's major customers, and credit sales to its remaining small customers are lumped together.

Credit Sales for Major Customers During June

Customer	June Sales
Alex Shop	$15
Avanti	10
Sunbloc	10
Dosta Sports	8
All Other Credit Sales	7
Total Credit Sales for October	$50

Analysis of the accounts receivable ledger on p. 183 indicated that these customers paid their accounts according to the pattern shown. Since the goal here is to associate payments received in a given month with the month in which the associated sale was made, these dollar amounts represent collections on sales originating in June. The collection pattern for June sales is indicated by the percentages in the last row of the table. The 40% figure under the July column ($20/$50) represents the proportion of June credit sales collected one month after the month of sale. Likewise, the 60% figure for August ($30/$50)

represents the percentage of credit sales in June collected two months
after the month of sale.

Receivables Collection Pattern for June Sales

Customer	July		August
Alex Shop	$ –		$15
Sunbloc	10		–
Avanti	10		–
Dosta Sports			8
All Other Credit Sales			7
Total Payments	$20		$30
Total Credit Sales During June		$50	
Percentage of June Sales			
Collected In:	40%		60%

To make certain that June was a representative month, XYZ's
management performed the same analysis for several other sample
periods. The collection pattern for these samples was about the same as
that for June, so the 40% and 60% estimates were used in cash budget.

If the financial plan is prepared for a new venture, initial cash sales
and collection estimates must be derived from the firm's intended sales
and credit policies and the information garnered from the entrepreneur's research. For example, the research done on the firm's industry,
market, and competitors should produce sufficient information to estimate sales and credit norms for the firm's industry or its competitors.
Also, if credit is to be extended to customers, then the adopted credit
terms provide some indication of the receivables-collection pattern.

A convenient device for making the calculations associated with
cash inflow estimates is the *cash budget worksheet*. A worksheet covering the first four months of the cash budget period for A&D Sales
and Service is shown as Table 10-1. Note from the table that while the
budget period starts with January, 19X4, historical sales for the previous November and December are shown. These months are
included because of the lag between the time when a credit sale is
made and the time the outstanding receivable is collected.

A&D's cash sales and collection pattern appears in the section of
Table 10-1 labeled Collections. The Cash Sales figure indicates that
10% of forecast sales in a given month are expected to be cash sales.
For example, the forecast sales figure for January is $54,000 and cash
sales for that month are estimated to be $5,400 (.10 × $54,000).

TABLE 10-1
The Cash Budget Worksheet
A&D Sales and Service
for the Pro Forma Period January to April, 19X4

Nov	Dec			Jan	Feb	Mar	Apr
$57,000	$55,000	Projected Sales		$54,000	$56,200	$93,400	$116,700
		Collections:					
		Cash Sales	10%	$ 5,400	$ 5,620	$ 9,340	$ 11,670
		1-Month Lag	60%	33,000	32,400	33,720	56,040
		2-Month Lag	30%	17,100	16,500	16,200	16,860
		Total Cash Inflows		$55,500	$54,520	$59,260	$ 84,570

The 1-Month Lag figure indicates that 60% of the sales in a given month are expected to be collected in the next month. Thus, the $33,000 figure for January represents 60% of credit sales from the previous December ($55,000). Likewise, the 2-Month Lag figure indicates that 30% of the sales in a given month are expected to be collected two months after the month of sales. For example, the March amount of $16,200 represents 30% of the forecast sales figure for January of $54,000.

The total of operating and nonoperating cash inflows for each period are transferred from the worksheet to the cash budget. By transferring only Total Cash Inflows, the cash budget is free of any possible confusion caused by numerical clutter.

Estimating cash outflows is the easier part of the cash budgeting process. Given the short-term nature of the cash budget, most cash outflows are the result of predetermined events and the firm's planned operations. For example, cash outflows for salaries and lease payments are fixed in amount over the short run. Likewise, other cash outflows such as labor costs or advertising expenditures are predetermined by management through plans and budgets. The remaining outflows can usually be estimated from historical patterns or established operating policies.

For example, payments for inventory purchases are a function of the firm's purchases or production policy and the credit terms extended by suppliers. Purchasing and production policies, which are normally based on estimated sales in a subsequent month, determine the cost that will be incurred. The credit terms, if any, extended by suppliers determine when the payment should be made for purchases. Other cost items such as telephone and utility expenses, vehicle expenses, and office supplies can be extrapolated from historical trends if the firm is a going concern, or estimated using research information gathered by the entrepreneur if the firm is a new venture. Estimated cash inflows and outflows for A&D Sales and Service are shown on the firm's 19X4 cash budget (see Table 10-6 at the end of this chapter).

The final cash budget issue to be resolved is the size of the *cash contingency balance* (i.e., the minimum cash balance that should be maintained to protect against unforeseen adverse developments and forecasting error). One major purpose served by the cash budget is identifying the funds needed to support anticipated business activity. The entrepreneur must decide how much additional cash to maintain over and above this amount.

In general, the size of this contingency balance should be sufficient to allow the entrepreneur to sleep worry-free, but yet not so large that the firm is needlessly foregoing earnings on idle funds that could have been put to work. While there is no precise answer to the question of what amount is appropriate, the size of the contingency balance should be determined by the stability of the business and its cash-flow pattern. If operations and cash flows are relatively stable and reasonably predictable, only minimal contingency balances are required. If operations and cash flows fluctuate dramatically from period to period, larger balances must be maintained.

Regardless of how proficient the entrepreneur's forecasting skills, cash projections are rarely precise. The firm operates in an uncertain world and forecasts are subject to error regardless of how well they are prepared. The entrepreneur can, however, deal with uncertainty by allowing for it in the planning and budgeting process. One widely used method for doing so is scenario analysis.

As applied to cash budgeting, *scenario analysis* means preparing multiple cash budgets for a given planning period. Each budget reflects a different set of assumptions. Usually, three sets of assumptions are used: the best-case scenario, the worst-case scenario, and the most likely scenario. For example, the worst-case scenario might reflect the entrepreneur's estimate of the least amount of sales, the slowest receivables-collection pattern, and the highest cash outflows that could reasonably be expected to occur. On the other hand, the most likely and best-case scenarios would reflect more optimistic assumptions for key forecast variables.

The *what if* focus of scenario analysis provides an estimate of the range of possible outcomes for key decision variables such as net cash flow and required financing. This information allows the entrepreneur to prepare one set of plans based on the most likely conditions and an alternate set of contingency plans reflecting the extreme cases.

5. **Cash-flow planning—pro forma financial statements.** *Pro forma* as used in the context of cash planning means projected or "as if" forecast conditions and planned activity had actually occurred. For example, the pro forma income statement or balance sheet is prepared in the same format as its historical counterpart, but the numbers reflect the assumption that planned events had actually occurred. Annual pro forma statements are typically used as part of the firm's long-term cash planning process and often cover a planning horizon of three to five years.

The *pro forma income statement* depicts the effect of planned operations on sales, expenses, and profits. The key variables used in its preparation are forecast sales values for each year in the planning horizon as well as an estimate of the expenses associated with these sales. The most commonly used technique for estimating starting values for expense items is the *percent-of-sales method.* This technique is based on the idea that expenses vary with sales and the relationship between the two can be expressed as a percentage of that key variable.

For example, the Cost of Sales account that appears on the pro forma income statements for A&D Sales and Service was assumed to be 51% of sales (see Table 10-7). Since forecast sales for 19X4 are $1,203,600, the dollar amount for Cost of Sales is estimated to be $613,836 ($1,203,600 × .51). The remaining expense items shown on the pro forma income statements for A&D's three planning periods were calculated in the same manner. For instance, the Wages & Salaries expense figure of $81,250 is 11.2% of the 19X1 Sales figure of $725,000 ($81,250/$725,000) and the Utilities expense figure of $12,805 is 1.77% of Sales ($12,805/$725,000). These percentages were applied to the pro forma 19X4 sales estimate of $1,203,600 to obtain the Wage & Salaries expense estimate of $134,886 ($1,203,600 × .112) and $21,258 ($1,203,600 × .0177) respectively.

In order to obtain the three profit levels, Gross Profit, Net Operating Income, and Net Income, the appropriate expense amounts are subtracted from Sales or the preceding profit level. A&D's pro forma income statements appear as Table 10-7 in the Appendix to the sample financial plan.

The next task is to determine *percent-of-sales values*. If the financial plan is prepared for an existing business, the percent-of-sales values used to make the initial expense estimates are usually determined from historical financial statement relationships. These percentages can be calculated from the most current income statement, from a statement for a year considered typical, or as averages of statement values for several years. If the initial percentages are not appropriate indicators of expected future conditions, they should be adjusted to reflect the entrepreneur's expectations.

To illustrate percent-of-sales calculations, assume the management of A&D Sales and Service anticipates a 20% annual growth in sales for the planning period 19X4 through 19X6. This translates to projected sales levels of $1,203,600 ($1,003,000 × 1.2), $1,444,320 ($1,003,000 × 1.2), and $1,733,184 ($1,444,320 × 1.2) respectively. Because the cost-control problems that caused profit margins to deteriorate during 19X2 and 19X3 have been corrected, A&D's management feels that the percent-of-sales figures from those statement years are not accurate indicators for the future. As indicated by the historical income statements shown on Table 10-3, the Gross Profit of $355,000 in 19X1 is 49% of sales ($355,000/$275,000). The Gross Profit figures for 19X2 and 19X3 are 43% ($363,750/$850,000) and 41% ($411,230/$1,003,000), respectively.

Upon investigation, it was determined that the percentage relationships from the 19X1 income statement were representative of what could be accomplished over the planning horizon. These percentages were calculated by dividing each expense category on the 19X1 income statement by the sales figure for that year. The resulting percentages were applied to forecast sales to obtain the expense estimates for A&D's pro forma income statements (see Table 10-7).

If the financial plan is prepared for a new venture, percent-of-sales values for the typical firm in the same industry may be used as either starting values or indicators for the venture's pro forma statements. These percentages would be adjusted, where appropriate, to fit the entrepreneur's expectations. Common-size income statements and balance sheets are available from a number of published sources. The most widely used among these are *Annual Statement Studies*, *The Almanac of Business and Industrial Financial Ratios*, and various industry and trade association publications.

The next financial statement to be prepared is the *pro forma balance sheet*. A pro forma balance sheet translates the effects of planned operations into projected levels of assets, liabilities, and owner's equity. By so doing, it provides a rough estimate of the financing that will be required to support long-term plans. The logic behind this key estimate is straightforward. If sales are to grow, then the firm's asset base must grow to accommodate the increase in sales, and these assets must be financed.

For example, sales growth normally requires the purchase of additional inventory, gives rise to more accounts receivable, and often requires additional fixed assets such as buildings, machinery, or equipment. The investment in additional assets requires financing. Some of this financing comes from the cash flow generated by the firm's operations, some from the normal time lag in routine payments such as wages and taxes (accrued liabilities) and, if the firm has established credit with suppliers, some from the credit extended by the firm's suppliers (accounts payable). If these *spontaneous sources*, as they are referred to in finance, are insufficient to finance the growth in sales and assets, then additional debt and/or equity financing beyond spontaneous sources will also be required. This *external financing required (plug figure)* is the focal point of the pro forma balance sheet.

As is true of the pro forma income statement, a pro forma balance sheet can be prepared using assumed relationships between balance sheet items and projected sales. Over long-term planning horizons, most asset, liability, and equity items vary with sales, and the percent-of-sales method provides reasonable approximations for these amounts. Where necessary, historical percent-of-sales relationships can be adjusted to reflect anticipated conditions.

The percent-of-sales method was used to prepare the pro forma balance sheets for A&D's three-year planning horizon. These statements appear as Table 10-8 in the Appendix to the sample financial plan. The historical percentages were calculated by dividing applicable balance sheet values for 19X1 by the 19X1 sales figure. These values, as well as the dollar amounts that are carried forward from the 19X3 balance sheet, are shown below. The values for the asset accounts Vehicles and Equipment shown or the pro forma balance sheets are supplied by management. These amounts reflect management's estimates of the firm's long-range needs. A step-by-step illustration of the preparation of A&D's 19X4 pro forma balance sheet is included on pages 190–193.

Statement Item	Percent-of-Sales or Specified Dollar Amount
Cash	4.5%
Accounts Receivable	8.9%
Inventory	8.3%
Prepaid Expense	0.0%
Accounts Payable	4.2%
Accruals Payable	.8%

Actual 19X3 Account Values	
Land	$ 75,000
Buildings	$375,000
Notes Payable	$112,100
Term Loan Payable	$ 60,000
Mortgage Payable	$260,921
Capital Stock	$ 75,000

The reasons specific dollar amounts are transferred from the most recent balance sheet to the pro forma statements are the following. First, A&D's management feels that no additional land will be needed to accommodate the anticipated growth. Consequently, the $75,000 in this account is carried forward to all three pro forma balance sheets. Second, the combination of the Notes Payable (typically short-term loans from a bank or commercial finance company), Term Loan Payable (installment debt from a financial institution), Mortgage Payable, and Capital Stock accounts represents external financing that was used to finance the firm's 19X3 asset base. Since these assets are essentially carried forward into 19X4, so is the financing that funded them.

The question resolved by the pro forma balance sheet, therefore, is how much additional external financing will be needed to support the additional assets that growth creates. That is, if sales growth creates a need for financing beyond what spontaneous sources are able to provide, the shortfall should be raised through some combination of additional notes payable, long-term debt, or owner's equity capital. The external financing required figure or plug figure shown on the pro forma balance sheet indicates this amount.

A balance sheet contains an important owner's equity account labeled *retained earnings*. In accounting parlance, this account represents that portion of net income earned in a fiscal period that has been retained and reinvested in the business rather than paid out as dividends (owner's withdrawals). The retained earnings value is calculated as (a) the retained earnings from the previous year, plus (b) net income earned in the current year, minus (c) dividends paid (owner's withdrawals).

For example, the Retained Earnings value shown on A&D's 19X5 pro forma balance sheet of $601,937 (see Table 10-8), is calculated as the 19X4 Retained Earnings of $455,840 plus pro forma net income for 19X5 of $146,097 (see Table 10-7). In this case, the full amount of net income was added to the previous retained earnings figure because dividend payments are not anticipated during the planning period.

The *external financing required* figure shown on the pro forma balance sheet is an adjustment value that balances any difference between total assets and the sum of total liabilities and owner's equity. Accounting systems are based on the principle of *double entry bookkeeping*. As applied to the balance sheet, this means the balance sheet must balance. In other words, total sources of funds (total liabilities and owner's equity) must equal total uses (total assets). Note, for example that the value of Total Assets equals the value of Total Liabilities & Owner's Equity on A&D's historical balance sheets.

On a pro forma balance, however, the growth in sales can result in an increase in total assets that exceeds total liabilities and owner's equity. This occurs when the growth rate is higher than what can be financed by:

- Spontaneous sources: cash flow generated by normal operations as indicated by the increase in the retained earnings account, and the increases in accounts payable and accrued liabilities.
- The value of negotiated, external financing represented by notes payable, long-term debt, and owner's equity that has been carried forward from the last actual balance sheet.

When projected total assets exceeds these sources of financing, the plug figure not only brings the balance sheet into balance, but it also represents the estimated additional financing needed in that period.

The *pro forma balance sheet plug figure* should be interpreted as follows:

- A negative value (minus figure) indicates that total assets exceed total liabilities and owner's equity. In this case, required financing should come from some combination of external sources (additional notes payable, long-term debt, or owner's equity).
- A zero value indicates that total assets and total liabilities and owner's equity are equal. In this case, spontaneous financing is just sufficient to accommodate the planned increase in sales and assets, and no additional financing is needed.
- A positive value indicates that total liabilities & owner's equity are greater than total assets. In this case, surplus funds exist, because spontaneous financing is more than sufficient to meet planned growth.

Understanding the rationale behind the plug figure is the key to understanding how the pro forma balance sheet is used for long-term cash planning. A&D's pro forma balance sheets illustrate this point. In 19X4, the anticipated 20% growth in sales causes Total Assets to increase to $1,114,842. Total Liabilities & Owner's Equity, however, increase to only $1,024,041 creating a shortfall or Plug Figure of ($90,801). Presumably, this amount would be financed with either additional notes payable, long-term debt, owner's equity, or some combination of these sources. As shown on the 19X5 balance sheet, an additional $11,175 must be raised in the form of external financing. By 19X6, however, the firm's ability to generate spontaneous financing is more than sufficient to meet the expected increases in assets. As shown by the positive Plug Figure, A&D should anticipate a $86,401 funds surplus in that year.

Preparing The Pro Forma Balance Sheet: An Illustration

The steps involved in preparing a pro forma balance sheet can be illustrated using the 19X4 data for A&D Sales and Service.

- **First, gather the appropriate data.** The required data include percent-of-sales values and, if the statement is prepared for an existing business, those account values that are carried forward. These data for A&D are shown on page 188. As indicated, the percent-of-sales values were calculated using 19X1 data. For example, the Cash percentage, 4.5%, was calculated as Cash from the 19X1 balance sheet of $32,500 divided by Sales from the 19X1 income statement of $725,000. The remaining percent-of-sales values were calculated in the same manner. The account values to be carried forward were, as suggested on page 188, a combination of management judgment and percent-of-sales procedure.

- **Next, calculate and enter asset values.** These amounts represent the addition to the firm's asset base; that is, the assets required to accommodate forecast sales and the financing required to obtain any these assets. For A&D, the asset values consist of both percent-of-sales calculations and management estimates. The percent-of-sales calculations involve applying the appropriate percentages to the forecast sales figure. For example, Cash as shown on A&D's 19X4 pro forma balance sheet of $53,594 was calculated as $1,203,600 (forecast sales) × .045. Next, enter management's estimated values. In this case, these include the Land, Buildings, Vehicles, Equipment, and Accumulated Depreciation figures. After the asset values have been entered, the 19X4 pro forma balance sheet would appear as follows:

Assets

Current Assets:	
Cash	$ 54,162
Accounts Receivable	107,120
Inventory	99,899
Prepaid Expenses	0
Total Current Assets	$ 261,181
Fixed (Plant) Assets:	
Land	$ 75,000
Buildings	650,000
Vehicles	132,811
Equipment	83,007
Accumulated Depreciation	(87,157)
Total Fixed Assets	$ 853,660
Total Assets	$1,114,842

- **Then, calculate current liabilities.** For A&D, current liabilities consist of notes payable (which figure is carried forward from the most recent historical balance sheet), the percent-of-sales or spontaneous liability items, accounts payable, and accrued liabilities. The 19X4 Accounts Payable and Accrued Liabilities values, $50,551 and $9,629, are calculated by multiplying the Forecast Sales figure, $1,203,600, by .042 and .008 respectively.
- **Next, enter the remaining carry-forward values.** These items include the Term Loan, Mortgage Payable, and Capital Stock accounts. After entering these values and those for the current liabilities as calculated above, the pro forma balance sheet would appear as shown below.

Assets

Current Assets:	
Cash	$ 54,162
Accounts Receivable	107,120
Inventory	99,899
Prepaid Expenses	0
Total Current Assets	$ 261,181
Fixed (Plant) Assets:	
Land	$ 75,000
Buildings	650,000
Vehicles	132,811
Equipment	83,007
Accumulated Depreciation	(87,157)
Total Fixed Assets	$ 853,660
Total Assets	$1,114,842

Liabilities & Owner's Equity

Current Liabilities:	
Notes Payable	$ 112,100
Accounts Payable	50,551
Accrued Liabilities	9,629
Total Current Liabilities	$ 172,280
Long-Term Liabilities:	
Term Loan Payable	$ 60,000
Mortgage Payable	260,921
Total Long-Term Liabilities	$ 320,921
Total Liabilities	$ 493,201
Owner's Equity:	
Capital Stock	$ 75,000

- **Finally, calculate retained earnings and plug figure.** The retained earnings value for the current year is the Retained Earnings value for the previous year, plus the net income for the current year, minus dividend payments. Thus, the retained earnings figure for the 19X4 pro forma balance sheet, $455,840, is calculated as 19X3 Retained Earnings of $334,692 plus 19X4 Projected Net Income of $121,148. After this value is entered on the pro forma balance sheet, Total Owner's Equity equals $530,840 and Total Liabilities and Owner's Equity equals $1,024,041. Note, however, the Total Asset value is $1,114,842. That is, Total Assets are $90,801 ($1,114,842 − $1,024,041) larger than Total Liabilities and Owner's Equity, and the balance sheet does not balance. The Plug Figure of ($90,801) as shown on Table 10-8 serves as the balancing amount and, as such, is the amount of external financing that is required.

6. **Capital structure planning.** The term *capital structure* refers to the firm's financing mix. This refers to the proportions of debt and owner's equity capital that are used to finance assets. The larger the proportion of debt financing used relative to equity capital, the greater the degree of financial risk to which the firm is exposed. Conversely, the larger the equity capital base, the lower the degree of financial risk and the more secure are the firm's creditors and owners. The base of equity capital is a cushion of protection for the firm's creditors, and it also serves as the foundation from which the firm develops and grows. An adequate equity base is also a necessary pre-condition for raising debt capital.

As previously discussed, debt financing represents borrowed funds and a legal obligation for the timely repayment of interest and principal. Failure to meet these payments gives the creditor the right to exercise his or her claim on the firm's assets. What's more, if the borrower has personally signed for or endorsed the promissory note evidencing the obligation, the lender also has a claim on the borrower's personal assets. In short, default on a loan could mean losing the business and, possibly, a good deal more. The message for the entrepreneur then, is clear: Debt financing means assuming a serious obligation and it must be used judiciously. This means striking an appropriate balance between the firm's debt- and equity-capital mix.

The appropriate goal for the firm's capital structure mix is to maximize the benefits that debt financing provides while, at the same time, minimizing the risk and cost involved. To do so, the entrepreneur must understand and carefully consider the factors that determine how much debt financing the firm can use. These factors are the *ability to borrow, the ability to repay, the business risk, and the quality of assets.* Each is discussed below.

Regardless of the entrepreneur's willingness to assume the obligations and risk of debt financing, borrowing limits are determined by the creditor's willingness to lend. It is important, therefore, that the entrepreneur understand what a given lending institution can and cannot do before approaching it with a financing request. For example, banks and commercial finance institutions are not venture capitalists. The returns from the loans they make are limited to the rate of interest charged. Consequently, these institutions must limit the risk they can assume when making a loan. In general, lenders expect these qualifications to be present before a loan is made:

- **An adequate base of equity capital.** In general, creditors will not make loans when they are supplying more capital to the business, and implicitly assuming more financial risk, than the owner(s). While rules of thumb are usually not reliable gauges for making decisions, banks and other lending institutions often use the 50% debt and 50% equity capital structure rule as a rough guideline for the maximum proportion of debt financing they will supply.
- **A favorable earnings record and good prospects for continued success.** The firm's ability to meet loan obligations depends on the continuing ability to generate positive cash flows.
- **Evidence of good management.** Experienced lenders know that all businesses experience difficult periods, and it is usually good management that separates the survivors from the failures.
- **Adequate collateral where needed.** When the firm's future is uncertain or its earnings record questionable or unproven, the lender will demand adequate collateral to reduce the loss in the event of default. In general, good collateral for a loan is characterized as assets that are legally and physically controllable, are easily liquidated, and can be sold in a market that has relatively stable prices. Examples of assets that meet these criteria are financial securities such as bonds, stocks, and savings certificates; land and buildings; and selected equipment, accounts receivable, and inventory.

The primary consideration for both the prospective lender and the entrepreneur is the firm's ability to service its debt obligations. Normally, this is not a problem when the economy is booming and businesses are doing well. The major concern is the firm's ability to generate free cash flow during business downturns. The amount of cash flow that is expected to be available for servicing debt during business downturns should determine the maximum amount of debt the firm can safely carry.

Business risk refers to the uncertainty surrounding the firm's ability to generate net operating income and positive cash flows. Some businesses are, by their very nature, more risky than others. In general, business risk is high when:

- **Sales and earnings are subject to wide fluctuation.** For example, industries characterized by widely fluctuating product demand due to rapid technological change, consumer whims and fads, or changes in general economic conditions have high business risk.
- **The firm's cost structure has a high proportion of fixed costs.** Fixed costs are inflexible and cannot be reduced when the firm experiences a sales downturn.
- **The firm has little or no control over the selling price of its product/service or the cost of the resources it uses.** In these cases, the firm's profit margins are heavily influenced by external factors rather than management control.

If business risk is high, lenders are more cautious about making loans. They expect the firm to have a higher proportion of equity capital in the financing mix and also demand more collateral to support the loan.

The last factor to be examined here is quality of assets. If all else fails, the creditor first looks to the firm's asset base to satisfy unpaid obligations. In general, the easier it is to liquidate an asset and the greater its liquidation value, the greater its collateral value, and the more likely the lender is to make the loan. All things being equal, firms with tangible assets such as real property or financial securities are able to borrow more than those whose assets consist primarily of intangibles such as copyrights, patents, or growth prospects. Likewise, firms with assets that are highly marketable and free from existing creditor claims are able to borrow more than those having assets that are not.

With regard to collateral, it is important to note that rarely, if ever, will a lender consider good collateral as a substitute for good credit standing and the ability to repay. To the lender, collateral serves as a safety net. It reduces the risk of loss in the event that plans and expectations for future cash flow do not materialize and the borrower defaults. A lender will not, however, make a loan when the likelihood is high that the asset will eventually have to be seized and liquidated. The limited return on a loan does not compensate for the risk, cost, and headaches involved with such a loan.

7. **Financial controls.** Financial controls are an essential component of the entrepreneur's arsenal of management control tools.

The budgets that evolve from the firm's operating plans are expressed in numerical terms, and these numbers serve as standards for evaluating actual operations. *Budgeted financial goals* may be expressed as:

- Percentage growth measures, such as a goal of 20% growth in sales, cash flows, and profits.
- Financial ratios, such as a goal to increase the inventory turnover rate to five times per year, or to increase the firm's ROI to 15%.
- Cost measures, such as a goal to reduce operating costs by 10%.
- Cash flows or profits, such as a goal of generating a given dollar amount of free cash flow each year.

Since monitoring actual operations is the basis of managerial control, it is important that the firm's financial information system provide the data needed to so. It is not enough to have an accounting system that produces basic financial statements. The firm must have a system that has the flexibility to output data in the form needed for control. It is up to the entrepreneur to define what data are needed and in what form they should be produced.

TIPS FOR PREPARING A FINANCIAL PLAN

■ **Cash planning is necessary.** The cash plan is an important part of both the business plan and of the entrepreneur's day-to-day management of operations. First, cash planning puts the entrepreneur in touch with the realities of a financing request. This understanding is needed to clearly identify the amount of financing needed, the purpose for which the funds are needed, the length of time for which the funds are needed, and how the financing will be repaid. These issues are of key concern to the prospective financier. Second, a sound cash plan increases the entrepreneur's credibility. Financiers are acutely aware of the small-firm manager stereotype: overburdened and administratively deficient. This image is substantiated when a financing request is poorly prepared or undocumented. On the other hand, the financier's confidence is bolstered when a sound, well-documented cash plan accompanies the proposal.

■ **Practice by doing.** Quality of financial planning and the effectiveness of the cash budget and pro forma statements increase as the entrepreneur gains experience. Financial planning on a regular basis should be a top priority item, and the financial plan should clearly indicate to the intended reader the entrepreneur's intention of making it that.

■ **Document underlying assumptions.** Improving the art of financial planning requires an after-the-fact understanding of which underlying assumptions were valid and which were not. With this understanding, the entrepreneur knows what to repeat and what to correct. In order to make after-the-fact comparisons between actual and assumed, underlying assumptions should be carefully documented at the time plans are prepared. It is also important to note that a financial plan lacking documentation will be considered a pipe dream by the intended reader.

■ **Expert assistance may be necessary.** Given the importance of this component of the business plan, it *may* be in the entrepreneur's best interest to seek expert assistance, if needed, with either preparing the financial plan or checking the validity of a completed plan. Such assistance can be obtained on a fee basis from a financial consultant or a professional accountant, or possibly at no cost through a consultant from the U.S. Small Business Administration or the local small business development center.

■ **Be a financial manager.** The firm's financial performance and financial condition do not manage themselves. The entrepreneur must understand the financial side of the business, and this understanding must be conveyed to the intended reader of the business plan. A financier is not going to provide financing if there is doubt about the entrepreneur's ability to effectively manage it.

■ **Use debt financing judiciously.** While financiers are naturally cautious about extending too much debt, the entrepreneur should be even more cautious about overuse. He or she has much more to lose. It is important that the financial plan convey this understanding. The most effective method for doing so is a well-documented cash-flow analysis indicating the firm's ability to service its debt.

■ **Save for a rainy day.** Cash flows retained in the business increase owner's equity and provide a margin of safety against periods of adversity. It is, therefore, important that the entrepreneur resist the temptation to take extravagant bonuses and dividends when times are good. A reasonable, clearly stated retention policy improves the firm's liquidity position, provides the financial strength necessary to weather the inevitable business downturn, and sends a strong message to the reader about the entrepreneur's financial judgment.

■ **Closely monitor accounts receivables and inventory.** The entrepreneur's control efforts should focus on the critical areas of the business. For most firms, the level of accounts receivable and inventory are two of the most critical. Experienced businesspeople and financiers are aware of the serious problems that are created by the liberal extension of credit and sloppy or nonexistent inventory control. If credit is to be extended, sound credit standards and the procedure for monitoring receivables should be established and clearly stated in the financial plan. The same holds true if the business will have raw materials and/or finished goods inventory.

A SAMPLE FINANCIAL PLAN

A&D Sales and Service sells and services medium-sized equipment such as forklifts and backhoes. The firm is incorporated, but 100% of its shares are held by the owner, Alex Duke, and other family members. A&D has been in business for three and one-half years. The company has had an exclusive distributorship for its main product line for a well-known equipment manufacturer for the past two years. The financial statements for the firm's first three years of operation are shown as Tables 10-3, 10-4, and 10-5.

A&D has experienced rapid growth over the past two years, and Mr. Duke is even more optimistic about the next three years. He estimates that sales will grow by 20% per year over this planning horizon. However, as noted in the Situation Review section of the Plan, growth has been a mixed blessing. The benefits from increases in sales and earnings have been offset by the consequences of poor financial management practices.

Alex Duke has recognized these problems and has developed a financial strategy for dealing with them. This strategy is detailed in the firm's business plan [*not shown*], which will be presented to a bank as part of a financing proposal. The major points from A&D's Financial Plan are highlighted below.

FIGURE 10-1 *The Financial Plan for A&D Sales and Service*

Financial Plan Summary

This Financial Plan outlines the financial strategy that will be used to effectively manage the firm's anticipated 20% annual growth in sales, cash flows, and earnings over the next three years. As discussed in the Cash Planning sections of this Plan, total financing of $173,850 will be needed. Of this amount, $72,000 (rounded) is needed in the form of a line of credit to support seasonal working-capital needs. The cash budget indicates that the line of credit, if granted, should be repaid in full by July. The remainder of A&D's financing needs, $103,000 (rounded), are long-term. The management of A&D feel that if the firm's existing term loan is restructured to provide the needed financing, both the existing balance on the term loan and the additional debt will be repaid in full by 19X6.

Situational Review

The annual financial statements for the first three full years of
the company's operation are shown as Tables 10-3, 10-4, and
10-5. The key financial indicator values for this three-year
period appear below in Table 10-2.

TABLE 10-2
Key Financial Ratios for the A&D Sales and Service
19X1 Through 19X3

	19X1	19X2	19X3
Sales Growth	—	17%	18%
Net Profit Growth	—	3.7%	0.6%
Net Cash Flow	—	($67,225)	($20,125)
Average Collection Period (in days)	32	59	59
Inventory Turnover (times per year)	6.1	3.4	3.6
Cash Cycle in Days	61.8	136.3	130.5
Total Asset Turnover	1.25	1.02	1.11
Times Interest Earned	18.3	16.4	13.3
Total Debt to Total Assets	53.0%	57.0%	55.0%
Gross Profit Margin	49.0%	42.8%	41.0%
Operating Profit Margin	17.7%	15.9%	13.8%
Net Profit Margin	10.0%	8.9%	7.6%
Return on Investment	18.7%	15.7%	15.3%
Return on Owner's Equity	22.6%	21.0%	18.5%

The data from Table 10-2 evidence the rapid growth A&D
has enjoyed since gaining exclusive distributorship rights for its
primary equipment line in 19X2. Sales increased by 17% in
19X2 and 18% in 19X3 and, as indicated by the historical balance sheets, Table 10-4, total assets grew by 21.9% and 8.3%
respectively. These gains have not, however, been free of problems commonly associated with rapid growth. The absence of
effective controls has, as indicated by the Average Collection
Period, Inventory Turnover, and Profit Margin ratios, resulted
in an unwarranted buildup in accounts receivable and inventory
and a deterioration in profit margins. These problems also
caused the large cash drain indicated by the 19X2 and 19X3
Net Cash Flow figures. These figures appear on the Statement
Of Changes In Cash Position (Table 10-5) for those years.

Management recognizes these problems and has implemented strong corrective measures. As indicated by the firm's

FIGURE 10-1 *(continued)*

financial goals and shown on the pro forma statements for 19X4 through 19X6, the corrective measures taken should return profit margins, cash flow, inventory, and accounts receivable to a level of efficiency equivalent to that experienced in 19X1.

Financial Goals

The management of A&D has instituted control measures designed to accommodate the anticipated 20% growth in sales and assets and, at the same time, produce a sound liquidity position and acceptable profit margins. Specifically, management expects to meet the following financial goals over the next three years.

- To enjoy a 20% growth rate in sales, assets, profits, and cash flows.
- To retire short-term working-capital loans by midyear of the year in which the line of credit is granted.
- To retire both the existing balance on the outstanding term loan and the additional funds extended on this loan by the end of 19X6.
- To reduce the average collection period on accounts receivable to 40 days or less.
- To increase inventory turnover to six times per year.
- To restore the gross profit margin and net profit margin to 51% and 10% respectively.
- To reduce the total debt ratio to 40% or less by 19X6.

Cash Flow Planning—The Cash Budget

A&D's 19X4 short-term cash plan was prepared using the cash budget contained in the Appendix to this Plan. The cash-flow data clearly indicate the highly seasonal nature of A&D's business. Operations are at a peak during spring and summer months and slow down dramatically during fall and winter months. As indicated by the largest Cumulative Financing figure on the cash budget, peak activity months create the need for temporary working-capital financing in the amount of $71,733.

The effects of A&D's inventory and receivables control measures are best reflected in the pattern of Net Cash Flow figures on the cash budget. As shown by these values, A&D should be in position to repay the full amount of temporary working capital financing by July 1994. Management proposes, therefore, that the Bank grant A&D a Line Of Credit in the amount of $75,000.

Cash Flow Planning—Pro Forma Financial Statements

A&D's long-term financing needs for the planning period 19X4 through 19X6 were estimated using pro forma financial statements. These statements, which are shown as Tables 10-7 and 10-8 in the Appendix to this Plan, were prepared using the percent-of-sales method. The data from these statements reflect the following key assumptions:

- An annual sales growth rate of 20%.
- Cost-to-sales and profit-to-sales relationships equivalent to those experienced in 19X1.
- Asset-to-sales and spontaneous-liabilities-to-sales relationships equivalent to those experienced in 19X1.

The decision to use 19X1 financial relationships reflects management's belief that the cost and current asset control measures that have been implemented to correct the cash-flow and profit-margin problems of 19X2 and 19X3 will return operations to the level of efficiency experienced in 19X1. The benefits of this program are reflected on the pro forma statements for 19X4 through 19X6. The income statements reflect the substantial increases in gross profit, operating income, and net profit that should occur as a result of expected sales growth and tighter cost control; and the balance sheets reflect the effects of the reduced average collection period and improved inventory turnover relationships.

In order to increase the equity capital proportion of the firm's anticipated financing needs, A&D's owners have elected to forgo dividend payments during this period. This decision allows 100% of earnings to be retained in the business and ensures that growth will be financed with a prudent mix of internally generated owner's capital and debt.

As indicated by the plug figures for 19X4 and 19X5, the anticipated growth will create the need for $103,000 ($91,305 + $10,811) of external financing. Management proposes that this amount be borrowed through a restructuring of the existing term loan. This restructuring would require the Bank to add the new financing to the existing principal and extend the maturity of the loan for two more years. As indicated by the 19X6 plug figure, the Bank can anticipate that A&D will

FIGURE 10-1 *(continued)*

generate surplus funds in an amount sufficient to retire the full amount of the term loan by the end of that year.

Capital Structure Planning

A&D is currently using more debt in its capital structure than the 40% target debt ratio deemed appropriate by management. While the debt ratio will temporarily rise to 52.4% in 19X4 [($493,201 + $90,801)/$1,114,842] if the proposed loan restructuring is done, this condition will be corrected by the end of 19X6. At that time, the combination of a retired term loan, anticipated growth in profits over the planning period, and dividend omissions will produce an equity capital base that will comfortably accommodate the firm's expected growth beyond 19X6.

Financial Controls

Operating costs and inventory and accounts receivable levels will be monitored on a monthly basis to ensure that adopted control measures remain effective. The data necessary to do so are produced monthly by the firm's accountant. Included in these data are:

- Common-size income statements.
- A summary report on order quantities and item costs.
- Inventory turnover ratio results, and data from a physical inventory taken each quarter.
- Average collection period ratio results and an accounts receivable aging report.

TABLE 10-3
A&D Sales and Service
Annual Income Statements
for the Periods 19X1 Through 19X3

	19X1	19X2	19X3
Net Sales	$725,000	$850,000	$1,003,000
Cost of Sales	370,000	486,250	591,770
Gross Profit	$355,000	$363,750	$ 411,230
Operating Expenses:			
Wages & Salaries	$ 81,250	$ 82,600	$ 98,707
Payroll Taxes	11,250	17,400	20,793
Rent & Lease Expense	13,500	9,000	10,755
Utilities	12,805	13,045	15,589
Insurance	31,750	31,750	37,941
Advertising	15,000	13,750	16,431
Vehicle Expense	50,945	49,790	59,499
Accounting & Legal	6,000	6,000	7,170
Depreciation Expense	4,500	5,000	5,975
Total Operating Expenses	$227,000	$228,335	$ 272,860
Net Operating Income	$128,000	$135,415	$ 138,370
Less: Interest Expense	7,000	8,250	10,400
Net Income Before Taxes	$121,000	$127,165	$ 127,970
Less: Income Taxes	48,373	51,833	52,160
Net Income	$ 72,628	$ 75,333	$ 75,809

TABLE 10-4
A&D Sales and Service
Annual Balance Sheets
for the Periods 19X1 Through 19X3

Assets	19X1	19X2	19X3
Current Assets:			
Cash	$ 32,500	$ 7,500	$ 8,850
Accounts Receivable	64,445	136,500	161,070
Inventory	60,418	140,313	165,569
Prepaid Expenses	0	12,500	14,750
Total Current Assets	$157,363	$296,813	$350,239
Fixed (Plant) Assets:			
Land	$ 75,000	$ 75,000	$ 75,000
Buildings	375,000	375,000	375,000
Vehicles	80,000	96,500	125,100
Equipment	50,000	48,500	46,000
Accumulated Depreciation	(52,500)	(57,500)	(67,850)
Total Fixed Assets	$527,500	$537,500	$553,250
Total Assets	$684,863	$834,313	$903,489

Liabilities & Owner's Equity

	19X1	19X2	19X3
Current Liabilities:			
Notes Payable	$ 52,775	$ 95,000	$112,100
Accounts Payable	30,500	42,280	49,890
Accrued Liabilities	5,700	9,225	10,886
Total Current Liabilities	$ 88,975	$146,505	$172,876
Long-Term Liabilities:			
Term Loan Payable	$ 0	$ 64,170	$ 60,000
Mortgage Payable	275,000	265,000	260,921
Total Long-Term Liabilities	$275,000	$329,170	$320,921
Total Liabilities	$363,975	$475,675	$493,797
Owner's Equity:			
Capital Stock	$ 75,000	$ 75,000	$ 75,000
Retained Earnings	245,888	283,638	334,692
Total Owner's Equity	$320,888	$358,638	$409,692
Total Liabilities & Owner's Equity	$684,863	$834,313	$903,489

TABLE 10-5
A&D Sales and Service
Statement of Changes in Cash Position
for the Periods 19X2 and 19X3

	19X2	19X3
Cash Flow From Operating Activities:		
Net Income	$75,333	$75,809
Plus: Depreciation Expense	5,000	5,975
Less: Increase in Receivables	(72,055)	(24,570)
Less: Increase in Inventory	(79,895)	(25,256)
Less: Increase in Prepaids	(12,500)	(2,250)
Plus: Increase in Payables	11,780	7,610
Plus: Increase in Accruals	3,525	1,661
Total Cash Flow From Operating Activities	($68,813)	$38,979
Cash Flow From Investing Activities:		
Less: Increase in Fixed Assets	($15,000)	($26,100)
Cash Flow From Financing Activities:		
Plus: Increase in Term Loan Payable	$64,170	($ 4,170)
Less: Decrease in Mortgage Payable	(10,000)	(4,079)
Less: Dividends Paid	(37,583)	(24,754)
Total Cash Flows From Financing Activities	$16,588	($33,003)
Net Cash Flow	($67,225)	($20,125)

TABLE 10-6

A&D Sales and Service
The Cash Budget
for Pro Forma 19X4

	Jan	Feb	Mar	Apr	May
Total Cash Inflows	$ 55,500	$54,520	$59,260	$ 84,570	$110,570
Cash Outflows:					
Payment for					
Purchases	$ 49,890	$30,525	$29,986	$ 32,593	$ 46,514
Wages & Salaries	11,239	11,239	11,239	11,239	11,239
Payroll Taxes	1,556	1,556	1,556	1,556	1,556
Rent & Leases	1,868	1,868	1,868	1,868	1,868
Utilities	1,772	1,772	1,772	1,772	1,772
Insurance	13,177	0	0	13,177	0
Advertising	6,226	0	0	6,226	0
Vehicle Expense	7,048	7,048	7,048	7,048	7,048
Accounting & Legal	830	830	830	830	830
Income Taxes	20,191	0	0	20,191	0
Total Cash Outflows	$113,797	$54,838	$54,299	$ 96,500	$ 70,826
Net Cash Flow	$ (58,297)	$ (318)	$ 4,961	$(11,930)	$ 39,744
Plus: Beg. Cash Balance	8,850	15,000	15,000	15,000	15,000
Total Cash This Month	(49,447)	14,682	19,961	3,071	54,744
Less: Minimum Balance	15,000	15,000	15,000	15,000	15,000
Financing Needed					
(Repaid)	64,447	318	(4,961)	11,929	(39,744)
Cumulative Financing	64,447	64,765	59,804	71,733	31,989
Excess Cash	0	0	0	0	0
Ending Cash Balance	$ 15,000	$15,000	$15,000	$15,000	$ 15,000

June	July	Aug	Sept	Oct	Nov	Dec
$125,490	$145,390	$155,400	$141,100	$120,200	$84,900	$63,100
$ 60,814	$ 69,020	$ 79,965	$ 85,470	$ 77,605	$66,110	$46,695
11,239	11,239	11,239	11,239	11,239	11,239	11,239
1,556	1,556	1,556	1,556	1,556	1,556	1,556
1,868	1,868	1,868	1,868	1,868	1,868	1,868
1,772	1,772	1,772	1,772	1,772	1,772	1,772
0	13,177	0	0	13,177	0	0
0	6,226	0	0	6,226	0	0
7,048	7,048	7,048	7,048	7,048	7,048	7,048
830	830	830	830	830	830	830
0	20,191	0	0	20,191	0	0
$ 85,126	$132,926	$104,277	$109,783	$141,512	$90,423	$71,008
$ 40,364	$ 12,464	$ 51,123	$ 31,318	$ (21,312)	$ (5,523)	$ (7,908)
15,000	23,375	35,989	87,112	118,430	97,119	91,597
55,364	35,839	87,112	118,430	97,119	91,597	83,690
15,000	15,000	15,000	15,000	15,000	15,000	15,000
(31,989)	0	0	0	0	0	0
0	0	0	0	0	0	0
8,375	20,839	72,112	103,430	82,119	76,597	68,690
$ 23,375	$ 35,989	$ 87,112	$118,430	$ 97,119	$91,597	$83,690

TABLE 10-7
A&D Sales and Service
Pro Forma Income Statements
for the Planning Periods 19X4 Through 19X6

	19X4	19X5	19X6
Net Sales	$1,203,600	$1,444,320	$1,733,184
Cost of Sales	613,836	736,603	883,924
Gross Profit	$ 589,764	$ 707,717	$ 849,260
Operating Expenses:			
Wages & Salaries	$ 134,886	$ 161,863	$ 194,236
Payroll Taxes	18,677	22,412	26,894
Rent & Lease Expense	22,412	26,894	32,273
Utilities	21,258	25,510	30,612
Insurance	52,709	63,251	75,902
Advertising	24,902	29,882	35,859
Vehicle Expense	84,576	101,491	121,789
Accounting & Legal	9,961	11,953	14,344
Depreciation Expense	7,471	8,965	10,758
Total Operating Expenses	$ 376,851	$ 452,222	$ 542,666
Net Operating Income	$ 212,913	$ 255,495	$ 306,594
Less: Interest Expense	11,000	12,000	13,000
Net Income Before Taxes	$ 201,913	$ 243,495	$ 293,594
Less: Income Taxes	80,765	97,398	117,438
Net Income	$ 121,148	$ 146,097	$ 176,157

TABLE 10-8
A&D Sales and Service
Pro Forma Balance Sheets
for the Planning Periods 19X4 Through 19X6

Assets	19X4	19X5	19X6
Current Assets:			
Cash	$ 54,162	$ 64,994	$ 77,993
Accounts Receivable	107,120	128,544	154,253
Inventory	99,899	119,879	143,854
Prepaid Expenses	0	0	0
Total Current Assets	$ 261,181	$ 313,417	$ 376,101
Fixed (Plant) Assets:			
Land	$ 75,000	$ 75,000	$ 75,000
Buildings	650,000	650,000	650,000
Vehicles	132,811	159,373	191,248
Equipment	83,007	99,608	119,530
Accumulated Depreciation	(87,157)	(104,589)	(125,506)
Total Fixed Assets	$ 853,660	$ 879,392	$ 910,272
Total Assets	$1,114,842	$1,192,809	$1,286,373

Liabilities & Owner's Equity			
Current Liabilities:			
Notes Payable	$ 112,100	$ 112,100	$ 112,100
Accounts Payable	50,551	60,661	72,794
Accrued Liabilities	9,629	11,555	13,626
Total Current Liabilities	$ 172,280	$ 184,316	$ 198,759
Long-Term Liabilities:			
Term Loan Payable	$ 60,000	$ 60,000	$ 60,000
Mortgage Payable	260,921	260,921	260,921
Total Long-Term Liabilities	$ 320,921	$ 320,921	$ 320,921
Total Liabilities	$ 493,201	$ 505,237	$ 519,680
Owner's Equity:			
Capital Stock	$ 75,000	$ 75,000	$ 75,000
Retained Earnings	455,840	601,937	778,094
Total Owner's Equity	$ 530,840	$ 676,937	$ 853,094
Total Liabiabilities & Owner's Equity	$1,024,041	$1,181,634	$1,372,774
External Financing Required (Plug Figure)	$ (90,801)	$ (11,175)	$ 86,401

CHAPTER PERSPECTIVE

The financial plan is the vehicle through which estimates are made of the types and amounts of financing that are needed to carry out the firm's strategic and operating plans. The components of the financial plan are the summary and situational review, financial goals, cash-flow planning, capital structure planning, and financial controls. The primary tools of financial planning are the cash budget and pro forma financial statements. Financial ratios are tools used to analyze the firm's financial statments in order to evaluate its financial position and performance.

Appendix to Chapter 10
What Is Financial Ratio
Analysis?

INTRODUCTION

Balance sheets and income statements can offer insight into a firm's financial condition and financial performance. The trick is knowing how to extract the appropriate information from them. Financial ratio analysis is, when properly used, the tool that provides this information. This Appendix offers a brief tutorial on ratio analysis.

A *financial ratio* is simply a fraction that compares a balance sheet or income statement numerator value to a balance sheet or income statement denominator value. The result is an index number or percentage that, when compared to some meaningful standard, can provide insights into some aspect of the firm's financial performance. The keys to effective ratio analysis are:

■ Choosing financial relationships that provide useful information about the important facets of a firm's financial operations.
■ Focusing on trends of ratio values rather than single-period measures.

The following discussion uses data from the A&D Sales and Service financial statements for 19X1, 19X2, and 19X3 to illustrate how several of the more common ratios are calculated and interpreted. The ratio results are shown on Table 10-2. (See page 199.)

WIDELY USED FINANCIAL RATIOS

Average Collection Period (ACP)

This ratio, which is also known as the *average days credit sales outstanding*, is calculated as (accounts receivable × 365)/net sales. It measures the average number of days that credit sales are uncollected. In general, the shorter the time period (the lower the number of days) that credit sales remain outstanding, the shorter the time period that the firm's scarce cash is tied up. A rising trend of ACP values signals a red flag. Failure to control credit and the investment in accounts receivable has caused the demise of many firms, both small and large. Note from Table 10-1 (see page 184) that the ACPs for A&D are sending ominous danger signals. This ratio almost doubled from 32 days [($64,445 × 365)/$725,000] in 19X1 to 59 days in 19X3.

Inventory Turnover

This ratio is calculated as (cost of sales/inventory) and represents the average number of times per year that inventory is purchased (or produced) and converted to sales. All other things being equal, the higher the turnover figure the more liquid and more profitable the firm. Table 10-1 indicates that A&D's inventory turnover rate slowed dramatically from 6.1 ($370,000/$60,418) in 19X1, to 3.6 ($194,500/$165,569) in 19X3. This is a signal that inventory is building to excessive levels and severely straining the firm's liquidity.

Total Asset Turnover

This ratio measures the productivity of the firm's asset base. *Productivity* in this case means the dollars of sales that the firm is able to generate for each dollar invested in assets. All other things being equal, the greater the number of sales dollars generated per dollar of assets, the more productive the asset base, and the greater the firm's earning power. The ratio is calculated as (sales/total assets). Table 10-1 indicates a slight decline in A&D's asset turnover from 1.25 in 19X1 ($725,000/$684,863) to 1.11 in 19X3.

Times Interest Earned

This ratio is most often calculated as (net operating income/interest expense). The calculation represents the dollars of operating income that are generated to meet interest obligations. The more dollars of earnings a firm generates relative to its interest charges, the bigger the financial cushion and the lower the financial risk. A declining trend is a sign of increasing financial risk and a clear danger signal. The decline in A&D's ratio to 13.3 in 19X3 ($138,370/$10,400), while a matter of concern, is not as yet so low as to be alarming.

Debt Ratio

This ratio is calculated as (total debt/total liabilities and owner's equity) (or total assets). It measures the percentage of the firm's total financing (assets) that has been provided by creditors relative to the percentage invested by the owners. When the firm's asset base is financed with increasing amounts of debt (higher debt-ratio values), mandatory payment obligations are increased and the degree of financial risk to which the firm is exposed increases. The slight increase in A&D's debt ratio to 55% in 19X3 ($493,797/$903,489) is not as yet alarming.

Gross Profit Margin

This ratio is calculated as (gross profit/net sales). The resulting percentage indicates the proportion of each sales dollar remaining after cost of sales has been deducted. For example, A&D's gross profit margin of 41.0% in 19X3 ($411,230/$1,003,000) means that $.41 out of each dollar of sales remained after $.59 was deducted as cost of sales. This was an alarming decline from the 49% figure for 19X1.

Net Operating Profit Margin

This ratio is calculated as net operating income divided by net sales and reflects the amount of each sales dollar remaining after all normal costs of operations have been deducted. A&D experienced a decline in the operating profit margin from 17.7% in 19X1 ($128,000/$725,000) to 13.8% in 19X3. As suggested by the gross profit margin results, the decline in net operating income margin is attributed to increasing cost of sales.

Net Profit Margin

This ratio is calculated as net income divided by sales. It measures the percentage of each sales dollar remaining after all costs of operations, including taxes, have been deducted from sales. On a continuing basis, the net profit margin on sales represents the long-run capacity of the firm to generate dividends for the owner (owner's withdrawals) and produce satisfactory returns on the owner's investment. For A&D, the decline in net profit margin to 7.6% ($75,809/$1,003,000) in 19X3 is further evidence of the alarming increase in the overall cost of operations.

Return On Investment (ROI)

This ratio is most often calculated as net operating income divided by total assets. The resulting percentage reflects the dollars of income earned per dollar invested in assets. The larger the ROI, the more efficiently operations and assets (as well as the capital used to finance them) have been utilized, and the more profitable the firm. The decline in A&D's ratio to 15.3% in 19X3 ($138,370/$903,489) reflects the deterioration of profit margins and the excessive buildup of accounts receivable and inventory.

Return on Owner's Equity (ROE)

This ratio is calculated as net income divided by owner's equity. It measures the dollars of net income earned per dollar of owner's investment. The result of this calculation reflects the efficiency with which the owner's invested capital has been employed. Generating a satisfactory return is the reason an entrepreneur risks time, effort, and capital. If the firm does not generate a fair rate of return for the owners, then there is no economic justification for its existence. The decline in A&D's ROE to 18.5% in 19X3 ($75,809/$409,692) is additional evidence of the deterioration in profitability.

A Note on Ratios, the Cash Cycle, and Working Capital

Working capital refers to the investment (dollars tied up) in cash, accounts receivable, and inventory that is required to conduct normal operations, as well as the financing that is used to support operations. Many businesses experience seasonal increases in operations (production or purchasing and sales) and, as a result, a temporary buildup in cash, accounts receivable, and inventory. This buildup creates the need for temporary financing.

The length of time required for the asset buildup to be converted into cash is referred to as the firm's *working-capital cycle* or *cash cycle*. It is determined by the average number of days required to turn over its inventory, plus the average number of days required to collect its receivables (ACP) (see page 211), minus the average number of days the firm is able to defer payment for its purchases and operating expenses (average payment period, or APP). Assuming A&D's suppliers offer 30-day credit terms, the number of days in its cash cycle in 19X3 is determined as follows:

$$\text{Cash Cycle} = (\text{Inventory Turnover in Days} + \text{ACP}) - \text{APP}$$
$$= (365/3.6 + 59) - 30$$
$$= 130 \text{ days}$$

The number of days in the cash cycle, along with an estimate of the firm's average expenditures per day, can be used to make a rough estimate of the amount of financing needed to support seasonal working capital. To obtain this estimate, first calculate the firm's average cash expenditures per day by dividing cash operating expenses (operating expenses – depreciation expense) by 365. For A&D, average cash expenditures per day in 19X3 is determined as follows:

$$\text{Average Expenditures per Day} = \text{Cash Operating Expenses}/365$$
$$= \$266,885/365$$
$$= \$731$$

Second, calculate the amount of working-capital financing required as the number of days in the cash cycle times the average cash expenditure per day. For A&D, this is:

$$\text{Required Financing} = \text{Cash Cycle} \times \text{Average Expenditure per Day}$$
$$= 130 \times \$731$$
$$= \$95,030$$

BREAKEVEN ANALYSIS

As used in business, the term *breakeven* most often refers to the level of operations at which sales revenue and total cost are equal. That is, the level of operations that produces net operating income of zero. The breakeven point can be calculated in terms of either units or sales revenue, and it can be calculated for a single product, a product line, or for overall operations.

To make the breakeven calculation, the firm's cost structure as shown on its income statement must be reclassified into variable and fixed costs. *Variable costs* are those that vary directly and proportionately with changes in sales. For example, assume XYZ Company manufactures bicycles, and one of the parts it uses has a variable cost of $10. If one bicycle is produced and sold, one part is used and total variable cost is $10. If sales double (increase by 100%), the cost of the component also doubles, to $20. If 100 units are produced and sold, total variable cost is $1,000.

Fixed costs are those that remain the same when sales vary. For example, the rent on the building XYZ uses to make bicycles is fixed regardless of the number of units produced and sold. Given the firm's variable and fixed costs, the breakeven point is calculated as follows:

$$\text{Breakeven (Units)} = \frac{\text{Fixed Cost}}{\text{Selling Price per Unit} - \text{Variable Cost per Unit}}$$

$$\text{Breakeven (Sales)} = \frac{\text{Fixed Cost}}{(\text{Sales} - \text{Variable Cost})/\text{Sales}}$$

These simple calculations can be illustrated using the abbreviated, hypothetical income statement for the XYZ Company shown below. Assume the firm's financial officer has analyzed the cost data and indicated variable and fixed cost with a (V) or (F).

Sales (30,000 units @ $300/unit)	$3,000,000
Cost of Sales (V)	1,500,000
Gross Profit	$1,500,000
Operating Expenses:	
Wages & Payroll Taxes (V)	$ 380,000
Salaries & Payroll Taxes (F)	190,000
Rent (F)	100,000
Utilities (V)	40,000
Maintenance & Repairs (V)	50,000
Advertising (V)	30,000
Depreciation (F)	20,000
Total Operating Expenses	$ 810,000
Net Operating Income	$ 690,000

These expenses can be reclassified using an alternative format known as the *contribution format income statement*. This format is useful for a wide range of decisions, including the breakeven calculations. As shown below, sales minus variable cost, the denominator of the breakeven calculation, is referred to as *contribution margin*. It is the amount remaining from sales after deducting those costs that vary directly with sales.

	Total	Per Unit
Sales (10,000 units @ $300/unit)	$3,000,000	$300
Less: Variable Costs		
Cost of Sales	$1,500,000	
Wages & Payroll Taxes	380,000	
Utilities (V)	40,000	
Maintenance & Repairs (V)	50,000	
Advertising (V)	30,000	
Total Variable Cost	$2,000,000	$200
Contribution Margin	$1,000,000	$100
Less: Fixed Costs		
Salaries & Payroll Taxes (F)	190,000	
Rent (F)	100,000	
Depreciation (F)	20,000	
Total Fixed Cost	$ 310,000	
Net Operating Income	$ 690,000	

Given these data and calculating the contribution margin ratio of 33.333% (contribution margin of $1,000,000/sales of $3,000,000), the unit and sales breakeven points can be calculated as follows:

$$\text{Breakeven (Units)} = \frac{\text{Fixed Costs}}{\text{Selling Price per Unit} - \text{Variable Cost per Unit}}$$

$$= \frac{\$310}{\$300 - 200}$$

$$= 3,100 \text{ units}$$

$$\text{Breakeven (Sales)} = \frac{\$310,000}{.33333} = \$930,000$$

Financing Fundamentals and Financing Sources

CHAPTER

11

INTRODUCTION

A continuous supply of internally generated funds and externally raised financing is the lifeblood of any business. All too often, however, the entrepreneur finds financiers apathetic to the needs of the firm. This can even occur when the firm is an acceptable candidate for a loan or investment. While it is virtually impossible to improve the financing opportunities for an unqualified business, the odds of doing so for the qualified and nearly qualified firm can be improved by approaching the appropriate financier with the proper information.

After studying the material in this chapter, you will:

■■ Understand the fundamentals of risk and return.

■■ Know what information is needed before approaching a financier.

■■ Understand the basic differences between the major types of financial institutions.

■■ Know which financier to approach for a particular type of financing.

INFORMATION NEEDS

Before approaching a prospective financier, the entrepreneur should be knowledgeable in three areas. He or she should have:

■■ A clear understanding of the firm's financing needs and repayment capabilities.

■■ A clear understanding of the risk/return trade-off the financing request represents for the prospective financier.

■■ A basic understanding of the nature of the prospective financier's business.

As stressed in previous chapters, the quest for financing begins with a sound financial plan and financing proposal. The proposal should effectively summarize the important supporting information from the financial plan. It should identify:

■■ The specific amount, type, and maturity of the financing needed.

■■ How the financing will be used.

▬ When and how it will be repaid.

▬ What collateral is available, if needed, to secure a loan.

An effective financing proposal must also convince the financier that the transaction will be successful. This means a financing arrangement that is equally beneficial to both the firm and the financier. Success to the firm means financing that will be profitably invested and will generate compensatory cash flows. To the financier, success means the funds will be in the hands of a competent, scrupulous entrepreneur, and the level of risk to which the funds will be exposed is acceptable.

An effective financing proposal must also be presented to the appropriate financier. Financial institutions are not monolithic. They differ in such fundamentals as basic purpose, the types of loans or investments made, lending and investing policies, and attitude toward risk. Given these differences, it is important for the entrepreneur to approach the financier who provides the type of financing needed and who is in a position to accept the degree of risk exposure the financing represents. Selecting an appropriate financier sends an important message: The entrepreneur understands the financier's business and major concerns about the financing request.

THE FUNDAMENTALS OF RISK AND RETURN

Both creditors and equity investors have an important stake in any business they finance. They can avoid loss and earn a compensatory rate of return only if the firm is successful. This means financiers are exposed to the same risks as the firm and the entrepreneur. If the financing proposal is to convince the prospective financier that his or her risk exposure will be minimized, the entrepreneur must first understand the risk/return trade-off the firm represents.

What Is Risk?

Risk can be defined as uncertainty about the occurrence of some future event or, alternatively, the possibility that a less than desirable outcome can occur. Risk is present whenever future events, such as the amount of sales or cash flow the firm will generate, are not completely predictable. The risks faced by the typical business firm fall into two basic categories: business risk and financial risk.

Business risk. Business risk is the underlying uncertainty to which any business firm is exposed regardless of how it is financed. It consists of the unpredictable fluctuations in sales and operating cash flows that result from changes in the general level of business and economic activity (such as a recession or rapidly escalating interest rates), from changing conditions within the firm's particular market (such as demographic changes or a competitor's development of a superior product), and from changes in the degree of competition faced by the firm. The more sensitive the firm's sales, costs, and prices are to these influences, the greater the degree of business risk to which it is exposed. As business risk increases, there is greater uncertainty over the firm's ability to generate a level of sales and cash flows that will fully compensate creditors and owners.

Financial risk. Financial risk arises through debt financing. Borrowing creates a legal obligation to repay the creditor and to meet the terms and stipulations of the underlying debt contract. If the firm defaults on its debt obligations, creditors can bring suit and, if necessary, put the firm into bankruptcy. Bankruptcy generally means that all parties with a vested interest in the firm lose. The entrepreneur and other equity investors, however, will lose the most. In the typical bankruptcy proceeding, creditors end up with less than the amount of their claims and the owner(s) end up with nothing. What's more, if the entrepreneur or other owners have personally endorsed the note, their personal assets are also at risk.

While debt obligations are certain, there is no guarantee that the firm will generate sufficient cash flow to meet them. This uncertainty is known as financial risk. The greater the amount of debt financing used by the firm, the greater the financial risk and the greater the risk exposure of creditors, equity investors, and the entrepreneur.

For the entrepreneur seeking financing, three important points on risk should be kept in mind. First, there is no financial risk associated with equity financing. As opposed to debt, equity financing does not involve mandatory payments and poses no threat of insolvency. It provides a financial cushion for creditors and reduces some of the impact of the firm's business risk.

Second, firms with a high degree of business risk should avoid using large amounts of debt financing. Heaping financial risk on business risk magnifies the firm's overall risk exposure and endangers the position of all parties with a vested interest in the firm. Substantial business risk means large fluctuations in sales and cash flow and an increased likelihood that fixed financial obligations cannot be paid.

Third, the major concerns of any financier are loss of the amount loaned or invested and failure to earn a rate of return that is consistent with the risk assumed. The creditor wants assurances that cash flows will be sufficient to repay principal and make the required interest payments. The equity investor wants assurances that the firm will generate the earning power to pay dividends and provide capital appreciation. In order to make a convincing case for the firm's ability to do so, the entrepreneur must provide credible cash-flow projections. The financier must be convinced that the numbers from the cash budget and pro forma statements will materialize.

Rate of Return

A fundamental financial principle governing the dealings of all rational financial decision-makers is the existence of a positive relationship between risk and return. That is, the greater the degree of risk associated with a financial venture, the greater the rate of return the rational individual would require as compensation. Financiers rigidly adhere to this principle. Lending institutions such as commercial banks earn returns that are limited to the amount of interest charged on loans. The reality of limited returns forces banks to assume limited risk in their lending and investing activities. On the other hand, the venture capitalist making an equity investment in a firm knowingly assumes a large degree of calculated risk. This risk is accepted when the firm offers the promise of large-scale returns.

In order to send the correct message to the financier, the entrepreneur must do his or her homework. He or she must identify the appropriate financier to approach given the firm's particular needs and circumstances.

MAJOR SOURCES OF FINANCING

Credit Extended by Suppliers

The credit extended on inventory purchases by a firm's suppliers is an important form of financing for virtually all businesses. Known as *trade credit*, this form of financing does not involve the direct loan of funds. Rather, trade credit involves delayed payment for goods or services received. The time period for which payment can be delayed depends on the credit terms offered by the supplier. Normally, this will be at least 30 days, and there may be the additional advantage of a discount from the invoice price for early payment.

Trade credit is also an important form of financing because it is spontaneous or self-generating. Once the firm establishes a creditworthy relationship with its supplier, the amount of credit used automatically rises and falls with changes in the volume of operations. No negotiation or conscious decision on the part of management is necessary. Accounts payable swells automatically when purchases are made and shrinks when payment is made. During the interim credit period, the firm is receiving an interest-free loan of the goods or services purchased.

The most important determinants of the entrepreneur's ability to obtain trade credit are integrity and the practice of sound business and financial management. If the firm is not overextended, if obligations are met on time, and if the firm is prudently managed, suppliers are usually eager to establish an ongoing, profitable credit relationship. Given the importance of trade credit to most businesses, it is in the firm's best interest to jealously safeguard this source of financing.

Commercial Banks

The next most important source of financing for businesses is borrowing from commercial banks. Since the business practices of banks are typical of many lending institutions, the entrepreneur should understand the mechanics of banking.

Essentially, a bank is a privately owned dealer in debt. The primary reason for a bank's existence is accepting deposits and lending. The majority of the funds used to make loans comes from deposits to checking accounts and savings accounts. To a much lesser extent, banks also receive working capital through occasional borrowing from other lenders, borrowing through the sale of debt securities in public markets, or from the proceeds of the sale of common stock.

Commercial banks receive the right to operate as a regulated, depository institution through a charter granted by either the state or federal government. With the charter goes the responsibility to help service the financial needs of the community in which it operates. Equally important, the charter obligates the bank to submit to supervision of its lending and investing activities and to abide by banking regulations.

Factors influencing loans. A banker's choice of which loans and investments to make is influenced by three primary considerations:
- The type of deposits held by the bank.
- The expectations of bank examiners
- The risk/return perspective of its officers.

A bank, like other businesses, attempts to synchronize its cash inflows and outflows. It does this by confining the maturity of its loans and investments to a time period that is roughly equivalent to the deposits it holds. If the bulk of a bank's depositors hold checking accounts, it must guard against the instability and sudden cash drains that are characteristics of these short-term balances. It does so by concentrating on short-term loans and investments. On the other hand, savings deposits tend to be more stable, thereby allowing the bank to make longer-term loans and investments.

The types of loans and investments banks make are also influenced by the possible adverse reaction of examiners to its dealings.

As a regulated institution, a bank's portfolio of loans and investments is subject to periodic scrutiny by examiners from the various bank regulatory agencies. If deviations from regulations or acceptable policy are found, the bank is subject to penalties that can range from reprimands to the loss of its charter. The intimidation caused by the jaundiced eye of a bank examiner goes a long way toward explaining the conservative attitude of bankers.

A banker's attitude toward risk is also tempered by a realistic view of the risk/return trade-off inherent in the choice between lending versus investing in low-risk securities. When the typical bank officer considers making a business loan, he or she naturally compares this use of funds to the return that could be earned on a low-risk investment such as U.S. Treasury bills, notes, or bonds. The comparison is made by estimating the degree of default risk inherent in the loan relative to that of the low-risk investment alternative. To compensate for the higher degree of risk associated with the loan, the banker charges an interest rate higher than what could be earned on the low-risk investment.

Theoretically, a bank could make loans with any degree of risk by simply charging a sufficiently high interest rate. In the real world, this is not possible. There are state usury laws that set upper limits on the rate of interest that can be charged. In the case of high-risk loans, a bank could not legally charge a compensatory interest rate. Since interest returns are limited, a bank is not in position to suffer the potential loss on high-risk loans. The bank carefully screens borrowers and requires loans to be fully collateralized by all but their most credit-worthy borrowers.

Types of bank loans. Although banks today make a greater variety of loans and are more aggressive lenders than in the past, their most important loans are still short-term working-capital loans and intermediate-term installment loans to businesses. To a lesser extent, most banks make mortgage loans and asset-backed loans, and larger banks often have industrial leasing departments.

▬ **Working-capital loans:** Working-capital or self-liquidating loans are typically made for less than one year, may be either unsecured or secured depending on the borrower's credit capability, and are used to finance temporary increases in working capital (inventory, accounts receivable, and liquid cash balances). These loans take two basic forms: a secured or unsecured transaction loan or a secured or unsecured line of credit. The *transaction loan* is a single-payment financing arrangement that is evidenced by a promissory note. The single payment covers either the loan principal if the interest has been deducted from the original proceeds of the loan (a discounted loan), or principal and interest if it has not. When banks require collateral to support a working-capital loan, accounts receivable or inventory are often used.

The maturity on a transaction loan is usually between one and six months but can range up to slightly less than one year. While it is possible for a good customer of the bank to pay the interest at maturity and renegotiate (roll over) the loan for another maturity period, commercial banks generally require short-term business borrowers to "clean up" loans for a 30-day to 60-day period each year. This simply means that the borrower must be free from short-term bank debt for that period. The purpose of this requirement is to ensure that the borrower is not attempting to meet long-term financing needs by manipulating lower-cost, short-term bank credit.

A *line of credit* is a commitment from a bank to provide a creditworthy business customer with a specified maximum amount (credit line) of short-term financing for a specified time period. This time period, which is intended to coincide with the firm's working-capital cycle, may extend to as long as 11 months. As is true of the transaction loan, the bank expects the credit line to be cleaned up once per year. The firm can draw down or borrow against its credit line as needed, and the borrowing can be paid back at any time during the credit period. Interest is paid only on the funds actually used and only for the time period they were used. Banks may require a fee for granting the credit line and will typically impose a compensating balance requirement on both transaction loans and lines of credit. A *compensating balance provision* requires the borrowing firm to maintain a minimum average monthly balance in its checking account that is equal to a specified percentage of the loan amount.

▬ **Accounts receivable financing:** When receivables are used as collateral for a bank loan, the agreement has four important components: (a) the specific receivables that will be accepted as collateral, (b) the percentage of the face value of accepted receivables that will be advanced, (c) the notification system that will be used, and (d) the interest rate that will be charged.

The collateral value of a receivable depends on its quality. The quality of a receivable is a function of the credit standing of the borrowing firm's customers, the borrowing firm's returns and allowances record, the credit standing of the borrowing firm, and the integrity of the borrowing firm's management. In general, the higher the overall quality of the receivables pledged, the lower the firm's sales-returns-and-allowances experience, and the higher the firm's standing as a customer of the lending institution, the larger the percentage of the face value of the receivables that will be advanced.

If the borrowing firm is perceived as an acceptable credit risk, the loan against pledged receivables will normally be made on a non-notification basis. This means the borrowing firm's customers are not notified of the firm's financing arrangement, and payment of the outstanding receivable is made to the firm in the normal manner. Under the non-notification arrangement, the lender must either trust that the borrower will remit customer payments as they are received or conduct periodic audits of the borrower's books to ensure that loan payments are being properly made. Under a notification arrangement, the customers whose accounts have been used as collateral are instructed to make payments directly to the lender.

The interest rate charged depends on the borrower's credit standing and the quality of the receivables pledged as collateral. In addition to the interest rate, the bank will add an administrative charge of from 1% to 3% of the face value of the loan.

■ **Inventory financing:** The process surrounding inventory financing is, in principle, the same as that of pledging receivables. The bank may use a general lien to secure all of the borrower's inventory holdings or a lien pinpointing the specific items of inventory that will be used as collateral. A common method for the bank to maintain physical and legal control over finished goods inventory is to have the items stored in a bonded warehouse. In this case, the bank retains the warehouse receipt and releases goods only when sales are made or the loan is repaid.

In order for inventory to qualify as collateral, it must have characteristics that allow the bank to easily maintain legal and physical control and to repossess and liquidate in the event of borrower default. For example, nonperishable raw materials sold in active markets at reasonably stable prices, such as grain, crude oil, or integrated electronic circuits, are desirable collateral. Finished goods that are easily identified, readily sold if the borrower defaults, and easily monitored or controlled by the lender, such as automobiles or major appliances, are also considered suitable collateral. On the other hand, work-in-process inventory in various stages of completion does not make suitable collateral.

As is true of loans on accounts receivable, the interest rate charged on inventory loans depends on the borrower's credit standing and the value of the inventory. Also, if the inventory loan takes the form of warehouse receipt financing, there will be warehouse and administrative fees added to the interest rate. This latter cost can range from 1% to 3% of the amount of the loan.

■ **Term loans:** A term loan is the title given by lenders to traditional business installment debt. It is defined as amortized, intermediate-term financing covering a period of from one to ten years. As its name implies, the typical term loan is repayable in equal installments over the life of the contract. Occasionally, one of three alternative repayment arrangements may be negotiated: a balloon payment, a recapture clause, or an equity sweetener.

A *balloon payment* is a large, lump-sum payment made at the end of the loan period. The payment compensates the bank for payments that are either smaller than normal or limited in number during the loan period. A *recapture clause* is an agreement that requires the borrower to repay the loan more quickly if the firm's sales and cash flows, or some other performance measure, exceed expectations. An *equity sweetener* is a stock option that grants the lender, in addition to the fixed interest charges on the loan, the right to purchase a specified number of shares of common stock in the borrower's firm at an attractive price. The sweetener is designed to compensate the lender for higher risk exposure by raising the potential return above that provided by the fixed interest charges. Equity sweeteners are not, however, normally used by commercial banks.

Term loans are usually secured with a lien on the asset(s) purchased with the loan proceeds, with other fixed assets of the firm, or with personal assets of the owner. The maturity of the term loan is usually tied to the expected service life of the purchased asset. The assets most commonly financed through term loans are equipment, real property, and the permanent component of working capital.

The interest charged on term loans depends on the borrowing firm's credit standing and the asset(s) pledged as collateral. Because a term loan has a longer maturity than a working-capital loan, the interest rate will be scaled up from the bank's prime rate. In addition to the interest cost, the borrower may also be required to maintain a compensating balance and to pay service charges to cover the costs of credit analysis, loan origination fees, or legal fees.

■■ **Revolving credit loans:** An offshoot of the standard term loan is a revolving credit loan. This arrangement combines the features of a term loan with those of a line of credit. Under a revolving credit agreement, the lender makes a legally binding commitment to (a) loan the firm a specified amount of funds over an extended time period (usually up to five years), and (b) to continue lending up to the stated amount until the end of the agreement period. As is the case with a line of credit, a revolving credit loan provides the flexibility to use financing only at the time it is needed. In addition, as the original principal is reduced through repayment, the firm can re-borrow up to the stated maximum. For this privilege, the firm pays a commitment fee on the unused portion of the loan in addition to the established interest rate on the financing.

■ **Mortgage loans:** Mortgage lending is financing provided by a security interest in real property (land and buildings). Mortgage loans are virtually identical in character to term loans. They are amortized over the life of the agreement, but because of the nature of the asset involved, usually have longer maturities than term loans. Mortgage loans made to businesses are similar to those made for residential financing except for slightly shorter maturities and the use of quarterly rather than monthly installments.

The rate of interest charged on commercial mortgage financing depends on the characteristics of the secured property and the credit standing of the borrower. If the borrowing firm has acceptable credit and the property has multiple uses, is high in resale value, and is easily liquidated, interest rates will be competitive with the general level of mortgage rates. Conversely, the weaker the borrowing firm's credit standing and the more specialized the asset, the greater the risk to the bank and the higher the interest rate demanded.

■ **Asset-backed loans:** Equipment that is owned free of any liens and is in good operating order may serve as collateral for *extended-term financing*. The financing arrangement used is normally a term loan with a maturity tied to the remaining service life of the asset. As is true of all secured financing, the bank takes a security interest in the pledged asset and limits the amount of the loan to some percentage of its estimated liquidation value. The liquidation value is often established by a qualified appraiser who must be hired and paid by the borrowing firm. The term *asset-backed loan* is also used at times to refer to a receivables- or inventory-backed business loan.

Loan policies on asset-backed loans vary among lenders. While some commercial finance companies rely solely on the value of the pledged asset to judge the merits of the loan, commercial banks require the borrower to have acceptable credit standing and the ability to generate adequate cash flow. The interest rate charged by banks on asset-backed loans is normally equivalent to that charged on term loans. In addition to the interest cost, the borrower may also be required to maintain a compensating balance and to pay service charges to cover the costs of credit analysis, loan origination fees, or legal fees.

■ **Leasing:** Leasing business assets is simply a specialized, alternative form of debt financing in which the lessee (the firm) enters into a binding contract to rent the services of the asset in question from the lessor (the financial institution). The usual procedure is for the lessor to buy the asset required by the lessee and lease its services according to the terms of the lease agreement. This arrangement allows virtually any business asset, including specialized plant or equipment items, to be leased. The lessor remains the legal owner of the asset and is entitled to depreciation and any other tax benefits that ownership provides. If the lease agreement meets IRS guidelines, the lease payments made by the lessee are tax deductible.

Business leases fall into two basic categories, operating leases and financial leases. An *operating lease* is a short-term transaction akin to that involving property rental. In contrast, the *financial lease* has a longer maturity and is equivalent in principle to a secured term loan. The financial lease may not be canceled without full payment of all amortized costs to the lessor bank. The lease amortization process provides the bank with the return of principal and the expected interest yield (rate of return) on that principal.

■ **Consider a simplified bank loan package.** Small businesses *may* have the opportunity to use a simplified, low-cost, loan application package when applying for bank financing. This loan package, known as the Business Credit Information Package (BCIP), was developed by an association of bank lending officers known as Robert Morris Associates (RMA) in conjunction with the American Institute of Certified Public Accountants (AICPA). It is designed to provide the lender with minimum accounting, financial, and business information through a questionnaire the borrower completes and an accountant's Compilation Report. The latter item summarizes and compares key financial statement data for the last two years. These data are used in place of the requirement that the borrower supply costly CPA-audited financial statements. In order to use the BCIP, two conditions must be met:

1. The bank must agree in writing through a Request Letter issued to the borrower to accept the financial data prepared in the BCIP format along with the accountant's Compilation Report in lieu of audited financial statements.
2. The borrower must agree in advance to complete the RMA Business Borrower Questionnaire.

Commercial Finance Companies

Commercial finance companies are the business-world counterpart to consumer finance companies. They are lending institutions that make secured working-capital and plant and equipment loans to businesses. Like commercial banks, typical commercial finance companies also engage in industrial leasing. Unlike banks, finance companies are not permitted to hold checking account and savings account deposits. They are strictly lending institutions that raise loan funds through the sale of debt securities in the open market. Because commercial finance companies must cover the cost of the funds raised and because they lend to higher-risk borrowers, the interest rates charged on loans are generally higher than those charged by banks.

Factors

Factors are specialized financial institutions that provide receivables-backed financing to businesses through a process known as *factoring*. As opposed to pledging accounts receivable to secure a loan, factoring involves the outright sale of the firm's accounts to the factor. That is, the title to the receivables passes from the firm to the factor. The procedures, conditions, and charges associated with factoring are detailed in a contract known as the factoring agreement.

A factor performs three important functions for the borrowing firm. These are financing, credit analysis and collection, and risk bearing.

■ **Financing:** The factor provides funds for the firm through either of two methods: maturity factoring or advance (discount) factoring. Under *maturity factoring*, the firm receives payment for receivables sold to the factor on either the date the customer's payment is received or on the last day of the credit period, whichever comes first. When *advance factoring* is used, the factor advances funds to the firm when the customer is invoiced for the purchase.

■ **Credit analysis and collection:** As a normal part of the factoring arrangement, the factor evaluates the credit standing of each of the firm's customers. The receivables of customers not meeting the factor's credit standards are not accepted for purchase. In contrast, the factor takes full responsibility for collecting all amounts due and for any bad-debt loss on all accepted receivables. By performing the credit and collection functions, the factor relieves the firm of the cost and responsibility of each.

■ **Risk bearing:** Most factoring arrangements call for the purchase of receivables on a *nonrecourse* basis. This means that the factor must absorb the loss of a default on the accepted receivable. The nonrecourse arrangement passes title as well as default risk to the factor and also relieves the firm of bad-debt expense.

Equipment Manufacturers

Often manufacturers of business equipment make secured financing available to customers either directly or through a financing subsidiary known as a captive financing company. The financing may take the form of a standard term loan or an operating or financial lease. Providing financing for its customers has important advantages for a manufacturer and for its buyers.

First, by offering financing, the manufacturer increases product sales. Second, since financing a sale produces both the profit margin on the sale and the interest return on the financing, the manufacturer can sell and extend credit to higher-risk customers. This may allow for marginally qualified firms to obtain financing that would otherwise not be available from a traditional financial institution. Also, dealing directly with a manufacturer makes it convenient for the buyer to combine the purchasing and financing functions in one transaction. Last, this type of financing usually requires a smaller down payment and the debt or lease contract will have less stringent covenants than a bank loan.

Savings and Loan Associations

A savings and loan (S&L) is a depository or thrift institution that raises funds by offering savings deposits and certificates to the public. Prior to the deregulation of commercial banks and S&Ls in the 1980s, S&L lending was limited to residential mortgages and to temporary financing for the initial stages of residential and commercial construction. While these loans still make up the bulk of the typical S&L's portfolio, most S&Ls have expanded their lending to include extended-term mortgage financing to businesses.

Life Insurance Companies

The typical life insurance company has sizable amounts of premium dollars that must be invested on a regular basis. For the most part, these dollars are in marketable, fixed-income securities (such as corporate bonds), industrial leases, and fixed-rate term and mortgage loans to businesses.

Both term loans and commercial mortgage loans made by insurance companies differ in two important respects from those of commercial banks. First, insurance companies are willing to offer longer maturities than typically offered by banks. Second, the loan agreement for both loans either prohibit prepayments or the early retirement of principal, or impose a stiff penalty for the right to do so.

A recent trend in insurance company lending has been the addition of an *equity sweetener* or *equity kicker* on riskier business loans. This provision justifies assuming higher risk by allowing the lender to share in the earnings success of the firm as well as to enjoy the interest yield on the loan. The sweetener may take several different forms. Common among these are a share of the earnings from the commercial real estate that has been financed; warrants that allow the lender to buy stock in the borrowing firm at an attractive price; or, in the case of bond financing, a conversion privilege that allows the lender to exchange the bond for a specified number of shares of common stock in the borrowing firm.

Independent Leasing Companies

The largest volume of business lease financing is provided by specialized financial institutions known as independent or industrial leasing companies. These firms tend to specialize in operating leases or financial leases. The former group of lessors concentrates on leases of standardized, short-lived business assets such as computers and commercial vehicles. The latter group writes financial leases for the specialized asset needs of the lessee.

Industrial Development Financing

Virtually all state and local governments have economic development agencies charged with the responsibility to promote business and economic growth in their jurisdictions. The incentives offered by these agencies to qualifying businesses take a variety of forms, including financing assistance at attractive rates. Most often, this financing comes in the form of packaged loans in which the agency, local lenders such as commercial banks, and possibly the U.S. Small Business Administration participate.

The purpose of the financing is to create jobs by inducing businesses to locate in the area and to encourage local businesses to make job-creating investments in new plants and equipment. Some agencies also offer leases on land, buildings, or other plant assets on attractive terms. While the bulk of the financing made available has an intermediate-term or long-term maturity, some agencies also provide working-capital financing.

U.S. Small Business Administration

The U.S. Small Business Administration (SBA) is an independent government agency created by Congress in 1953 to provide assistance to small businesses. This assistance takes a variety of forms, including such activities as:

- Providing free business and technical counseling for small-firm entrepreneurs.
- Providing educational services to small firm entrepreneurs through workshops, seminars, and a variety of topical literature on small business management.
- Ensuring that small firms receive an equitable proportion of government purchases, contracts, and subcontracts.
- Licensing, regulating, and lending to small business investment companies (SBICs).
- Helping qualified small business entrepreneurs obtain financing.

To be eligible for financing assistance, a business firm must first meet the criteria set by the SBA's definition of "small firm."

SBA loan activity takes a variety of forms, including disaster loans, economic injury loans, surety bond guarantees, loans to economic development agencies, loans to SBICs, and direct and participating small business loans. Since its inception, the SBA has maintained, to varying degrees, a direct business loan program. The purpose of the program is to fulfill its intended role as "lender of last resort" for qualified firms unable to raise funds in the private sector. Financing for this program comes directly from Congress through budget appropriations. The amount of these appropriations has declined steadily since 1980, however, and the SBA has increasingly removed itself from direct lending.

In recent years, the SBA/bank loan participation program has been the primary focus of the agency's financing activity. Under this program, the small firm entrepreneur applies directly to and negotiates with a local commercial bank interested in making such loans. If the applicant is deemed an acceptable credit risk by both the bank and the SBA, the bank makes the loan and the SBA guarantees up to 90% of the outstanding principal for the lending bank. Participating loans made to finance permanent working capital and equipment are in the form of standard term loans with maturities of up to approximately seven years. Principal and interest on these loans are amortized through monthly or quarterly installments. Guaranteed loans for the purchase or construction of real property may have maturities of up to 20 years.

Venture Capitalists

For businesses offering attractive growth potential or the start-up firm with an innovation that has large-scale profit potential, debt or equity financing may be available from a venture capitalist. Venture capitalists fall into two broad categories: (a) those licensed and regulated by the federal government through the U.S. Small Business Administration and (b) nonregulated firms. The former group consists of small business investment companies (SBICs) and the latter are venture-capital companies or simply venture capitalists.

Venture-capital companies have a wide variety of operating philosophies and investment interests. They do, however, share a common trait: The firms are made up of professional business investors who are attracted to higher-risk business opportunities offering potentially large-scale sales and profits. To obtain returns sufficient to compensate for both the inevitable losses associated with high-risk investment and the extended time period over which financing is committed, the venture capitalist must share in the earnings success of a highly promising firm through an equity interest. This financing will usually have the following characteristics. It will be:

■ The first equity financing for the firm outside that of the original owners. While venture capital will cost the firm a substantial share of its common stock, the amount will usually be less than 50% of the ownership of the firm.

■ Provided in the form of intermediate or gap financing that fills the firm's needs until the firm is taken public.

■ Accompanied by the expectation of (a) providing management assistance to the target firm in those areas of identified administrative weakness, and (b) taking an active voice in the firm's policy- and decision-making process.

■ Provided with the expectation of earning large returns. Depending on the financing stage at which funds are provided the firm, the typical venture capitalist limits investments to opportunities that provide expected returns of from 25% to better than 50% per annum on invested funds.

■ Expected to require a lengthy investment period. Successful venture-capital investments often take five to seven years to come to fruition.

■ Accompanied by an agreement specifying a clearly defined opportunity for the venture capitalist to exit the target firm. Normally a venture capitalist expects to liquidate his or her investment through an agreement to repurchase his or her shares at a specified date, to go public with a common stock offering, or to seek a suitable merger partner interested in buying the target firm.

SBICs fall into two broad categories: captive firms whose management and operating policies are dictated by a parent organization, which is often a bank or insurance company; and privately owned and operated non-captive firms. As is true with venture capitalists in general, SBICs have divergent philosophies and operating policies. Some specialize in equity financing, while others provide debt financing in several different forms. This latter group of SBICs is the richest source of debt financing for small businesses outside commercial banks.

In general, SBICs do not confine their financing to specific industries or business types. Rather, an SBIC tends to focus on businesses whose opportunities are consistent with its particular investment policy. SBICs specializing in equity or equity-participation financing lean toward small firms with extraordinary growth potential. Those specializing in debt financing favor stable firms with a history of profitability. To qualify for SBIC consideration, the target firm must meet the SBA's definition of a "small business". Beyond meeting these standards, the individual SBIC has total discretion over whether financing is extended and over the specific terms and features of the financing agreement.

TIPS FOR NEGOTIATING FINANCING

■ **Be realistic.** Seed money and start-up money is difficult if not impossible to find. Rarely if ever will a traditional lending institution provide this type of financing. The risk is too great for the limited return received. Convincing a lender to make a loan for these purposes normally requires pledging virtually risk-free collateral such as government bonds or bank savings certificates in an amount greater than the amount of the loan. Venture capitalists do make seed money or start-up financing available, but only when the opportunity promises large-scale returns.

■ **Be cautious.** The decision to enter into a debt agreement must not be taken lightly, nor should it be made in haste. Entering into a debt contract places the firm's assets at risk and, most likely, risks the personal assets of the entrepreneur as well. Also, the entrepreneur not only suffers the constant pressure of the possibility of loss from loan default, but he or she must also live with the terms and covenants of the loan contract. Before making the decision, the entrepreneur must objectively evaluate and cost-justify every detail of the debt contract.

■ **Be prepared for the negotiation process.** In order to effectively and convincingly discuss the firm's financing needs with a financier, the entrepreneur must be certain what these needs are. If he or she has not personally justified the risk/return trade-off associated with the financing, the financing request cannot be articulated and justified in a manner that will satisfy the prospective financier.

■ **Consider all relevant factors.** While cost is an important consideration in any financing decision, nonfinancial factors should also be carefully evaluated. In order to remain viable, the firm must be sufficiently flexible to alter operations or change directions as the need arises. The entrepreneur must be certain, therefore, that restrictive provisions in a financial contract do not eliminate this advantage. Also, a strong relationship with a financial institution that serves the firm's financing needs may be more important in the long run than minor cost savings from another institution.

■ **Shop carefully.** Financial institutions vary in their operating philosophy and policies. It is in the entrepreneur's best interest to shop for financing. This is especially true if a financing request is rejected. A financing proposal that one financier finds unsuitable may be acceptable to another.

■ **Learn from rejection.** The rejection of a financing proposal can often be a valuable educational experience for the entrepreneur. As is often said in athletics, the important lessons are learned from losing, not from winning. A rejection should be carefully evaluated to identify the underlying reasons and to determine whether the problem can be remedied. Often, the financier with whom the negotiation has been conducted is willing to discuss the reasons for the rejection. This knowledge may make the difference between success or failure on the next attempt and may provide valuable insight into operational weaknesses that require the entrepreneur's attention.

CHAPTER PERSPECTIVE

This chapter stressed the importance of approaching the right financier for the type of financing needed. In addition to having a convincing business plan and financing proposal, the entreprencur should have an understanding of the nature of the prospective financier's business, the type of financing normally provided, and his or her attitude toward risk. The major sources of financing available to businesses range from the highly conservative financiers such as commercial banks to the risk-seekers such as venture capitalists.

Glossary

Accounts receivable the money owed to a firm for goods or services sold on credit. Accounts receivable are shown on the firm's balance sheet as a current asset.

Advertising any paid form of nonpersonal persuasive message delivered through mass media.

Amortization when applied to a debt financing, amortization means making a scheduled series of periodic payments over the life of the loan that cover interest for the period and provide for the gradual retirement of principal.

Articles of partnership a legal agreement between partners that specifies the role, involvement, duties, and responsibilities of each partner.

Asset something that is owned by and is of value to the business.

Asset-backed (based) loan a loan made with business assets, such as machinery or equipment, used as collateral. Occasionally, the term is also used to refer to a loan made with accounts receivable or inventory used as collateral.

Bonded warehouse an insured, independent, public warehouse that will not release stored items without presentation of the issued warehouse receipt. This vehicle is popular with lenders who must maintain close physical or legal control over finished goods inventory that the borrower has pledged as collateral for the loan.

Breakeven point that level of operations where sales revenue is just equal to operating expenses; that is, the volume of sales that results in a net operating income of zero.

Budget a plan expressed in quantitative terms such as units of a product in a production budget, revenues and expenses in a marketing budget, or cash inflows and outflows in a cash budget.

Business concept as used in the business plan, the business concept is a statement summarizing what the business is, how it will meet the needs of its customers, why it can do this better than its competitors, and what resources are required to do so.

Business description the component of the business plan that provides the reader with a summary of the plan's important points and conclusions.

Business plan a detailed study of what the business or business concept is, where and to whom the business will market its product or service, and how it will conduct its operations.

Business risk the uncertainty and fluctuation surrounding the firm's ability to generate sales, cash flows, and earnings.

Capital structure the mix or proportion of long-term debt and owner's equity capital used to finance the firm's fixed assets.

Cash budget a financial planning tool showing the period-by-period estimates of the amount and timing of expected cash inflows and out-flows.

Cash discount a reduction from the invoice price of purchased goods for early payment. For example, the credit terms "2/10, in 30" mean the buyer can deduct 2% of the invoice price if payment is made within 10 days. Otherwise, the full invoice price is due in 30 days.

Channels of distribution the interconnected series of marketing middlemen used to get a product from the producer to the ultimate consumer.

Collateral assets that have been pledged to secure a loan. The creditor (lender) holds a lien on the assets and can claim them in the event the borrower defaults.

Commercial bank a state or federally chartered financial institution that accepts demand deposits (checking accounts) and makes loans to businesses.

Commercial finance company a non-depository financial institution that loans and leases to businesses.

Commercial success (feasibility) a volume of sales sufficient to provide a satisfactory level of cash flow and profits.

Commitment fee the fee charged by the bank for granting the loan and committing to the maximum amount that can be borrowed against the line of credit or rendering credit agreement and also the fee charged against the amount of the credit line not used by the borrower during the time period of the agreement.

Consumer goods the four major product classes that identify the goods consumers buy. These include convenience, shopping, specialty, and unsought products.

Contribution format income statement an alternative format income statement that classifies costs, variable and fixed, by their relationship to sales.

Control a basic management function that involves comparing actual events to planned expectations to determine whether remedial action is required.

Compensating balance a bank loan provision requiring the borrowing firm to maintain a minimum average balance in its checking account that is equal to a specified percentage of the loan amount.

Corporation a legal and taxable entity that has a life, existence, duties, and responsibilities separate and distinct from its stockholders (owners).

Cover letter the introductory letter accompanying a business plan that identifies the entrepreneur, the firm, and the reason the business plan has been presented.

Credit policy the combination of the firm's credit standards used to gauge customer credit-worthiness, the credit terms offered its customers, and its collection policy.

Current assets the assets of the firm consisting of cash and the assets expected to turn over or be converted into cash in less than one year. Typically, these latter assets are accounts receivable and inventory.

Customer profile the distinguishing geographic, demographic, psychographic, and behavioral characteristics that define a specific group of consumers.

Cyclical business pattern recurring swings in general business activity that move production, sales, cash flows, profits, and employment through a recession phase to the peak of an upswing.

Debt capital funds borrowed under a legally binding contract that requires, among other possible enforceable provisions, the payment of interest and repayment of principal.

Dividends distributions of profits to stockholders.

Entrepreneur the term comes from the French language and literally translated means go-between or between-taker: one positioned between the financier of a venture and the ultimate consumer but who does not risk financial capital. In this book, we use the term entrepreneur to mean an individual who recognizes a market opportunity that promises a suitable return; is willing to accept the risk associated with acquiring and organizing resources (land, buildings, money, people, etc.) to take advantage of this opportunity; and has the initiative, drive, tenacity, and skills to start the venture and see it through to completion.

Equity capital ownership funds which represent a proportionate claim on the firm's cash flows and profits and a proportionate right to a voice in operating the business.

External environment that set of aggregate variables, such as the economic, industry, market, and competitive environment, that affect the firm's performance but are outside management's direct control.

Factoring the sale of the firm's accounts receivable to a specialized financial institution known as a factor in order to raise funds.

Feasibility study a detailed study of how and why a business or business concept is expected to succeed. Justifiable rationale and evidence for how and why a business will succeed should be the central theme for each component of a business plan.

Financial lease a lease contract used in the leasing of business assets that has the characteristics of a debt contract.

Financial plan the plan that reflects the amount of financing needed to make operating plans feasible, when and in what form the financing is needed, who will be approached for the needed funds.

Financial risk the uncertainty surrounding the firm's ability to generate the cash flows needed to meet its contractual financial obligations.

Financial success (feasibility) a business firm able to generate a level of cash flow and profit sufficient to compensate its owner(s) for the time, effort, investment, and risk assumed is a financial success.

Financing proposal a supporting document to the business plan that details the nature and purpose of the financing request.

Fixed (plant) assets these are the firm's long-term assets such as land, buildings, and equipment.

Free cash flow the cash flow remaining after meeting operating needs, debt service, the replacement of assets, and dividend payments.

General partnership an association of two or more persons to conduct business as co-owners. Each general partner has management equality and unlimited personal liability for the debts of the partnership.

Gross domestic product (GDP) a measure of the value of all goods and services produced in an economy in a given time period. Formerly known as gross national product (GNP), GDP is the most widely quoted indicator of the health of an economy.

Growth capital the long-term financing needed to finance additions to the firm's fixed asset base.

Industry that group of businesses supplying related products or services and the complementary businesses that support them.

Industry analysis a study of the set of characteristics that define and influence a group of primary and secondary businesses supplying a related product or service. The industry analysis is a major component of the business plan.

Industry classification the various segments (retailing, wholesaling, etc.) into which the primary businesses (merchandising, manufacturing, etc.) of the industry are divided.

Internal environment those facets of the business, such as basic operations or its marketing and financial strategies, that are under management's direct control.

Inventory those current assets that will be converted into salable products or services, those that have been partially converted into salable products or services, or those finished products available for resale. Inventory is shown on the firm's balance sheet as raw materials, work-in-process, or finished goods.

Job analysis a study of the job-qualifications needed to effectively perform the duties and responsibilities of a job.

Job description a written description of the duties, responsibilities, and job qualifications associated with a given job.

Just-in-time inventory system an inventory management system designed to reduce inventory costs by pressuring suppliers to ship parts just as they are needed.

Lien a lender's legal claim on the borrower's assets that have been pledged as collateral for a loan.

Life-cycle concept in business, *life cycle* refers to the various stages of existence for a product, firm, or industry. These periods are usually identified as the development stage, the growth stage, the maturity stage, and the decline stage.

Limited partner a co-owner of a partnership whose liability is limited to his or her investment in the firm and who typically has no voice in management.

Market the geographical boundaries within which a product or service is offered for sale, the customers for that product or service, and firms competing for the customers' business.

Market analysis a study of the basic factors that define the market for the firm's product or service and how the firm must be positioned in order to reach this market.

Marketing budget the estimate of sales revenues and marketing expenses that are expected to result from planned marketing activities.

Marketing mix the combination of product/service, price, distribution, and promotion that has been determined as best suited to meet the needs and expectations of the firm's target market.

Market niche a specific segment of a larger consumer or business market that the firm can profitably exploit.

Marketing plan a coordinated action program for reaching the firm's target market and for motivating this customer group to purchase the firm's product/service.

Metropolitan category system the method used by the U.S. Bureau of Census to classify market segments. Market segments are divided into three metropolitan categories: Standard Metropolitan Statistical Areas (SMSAs), Primary Metropolitan Statistical Areas (PMSAs), and Consolidated Metropolitan Statistical Areas (CMSAs).

Net operating income the amount of profit that is generated by operations that are normal to the firm. As reflected on an income, net operating income is the amount of profit remaining after cost of sales and normal operation expensed are deducted from sales revenue.

Operating plan the plan that identifies the intended set of activities and procedures that create value for the firm's customers.

Operations the set of activities that converts resource inputs into valuable outputs for the firm's customers.

Organization a structured group of human, physical, informational, and financial resources combined to accomplish specific goals.

Organization plan the blueprint of the firm's organization structure. This plan identifies the key positions in the organization, the authority/responsibility relationships between them, the flow of information and communication between them, and the job qualifications needed to fill them.

Percent-of-sales method a technique for estimating the value of a given variable by expressing it as a percentage of estimated sales.

Planning the art and science of deciding what future course of action the firm will take to meet established objectives.

Primary Task the activity or set of activities that form the reason for the firm's existence.

Primary information source the information gathered through the research of original data sources.

Prime rate the interest rate a bank charges its most credit-worthy customers on short-term loans.

Producers goods the six major product classes that identify the goods that businesses and organizations buy. These include installations, accessory equipment, raw materials, components, supplies, and professional services.

Pro forma balance sheet a projected balance sheet used in financial planning.

Pro forma income statement a projected income statement used in financial planning.

Promissory note the legal document evidencing the borrower's debt obligation to the lender.

Promotion the strategy and techniques used to communicate information about the product or service between seller and potential buyer.

Receivables-collection pattern the estimated percentages of the credit sales from a given month that are expected to be collected in that month or subsequent months.

Resources those tangible and intangible assets that are used in the business to create value. They include physical assets such as equipment and buildings; human resources; monetary assets including cash, investments, and credit capability; and intangible assets such as goodwill or technical know-how.

Return on investment (ROI) a financial ratio that indicates the percentage of income generated per dollar invested in assets.

Risk the uncertainty surrounding the occurrence of some future event.

Sales forecast an estimate based on assumptions about the future sales during specific time periods.

S corporation a corporation that has elected under subchapter S of the Internal Revenue Code to be treated for tax purposes as a sole proprietorship or partnership. This status avoids double taxation and provides other benefits as well.

Savings and loan association a financial institution which raises its funds by offering savings deposits and makes residential and commercial mortgage loans.

Seasonal business patterns these are pronounced changes in business activity within a calendar year.

Seed money the financing needed to develop and refine the business concept.

Secondary information source information gathered from published sources.

Secret partner a co-owner of a partnership who is active in management and has unlimited liability, but is unknown to the public as a partner.

Scenario (what if) analysis a method for treating the uncertainty inherent in planning by preparing multiple sets of plans using different sets of assumptions.

Silent partner a co-owner of a partnership who has unlimited liability but does not have an active voice in management.

Sole proprietorship a business firm established, owned, and usually operated by one person.

Small business investment company (SBIC) a venture capital firm licensed by the U.S. Small Business Administration.

Spontaneous sources of financing the temporary sources of financing, typically accounts payable and accrued liabilities, that rise and fall automatically with changes in the level of business activity.

Standard Industrial Classification (SIC) system the SIC system is a uniform number-coding and verbal-description system created by the federal government to classify business firms according to the specific business activity in which they engage.

Start-up capital the financing needed to initiate business operations.

Stockholders the owners of a corporation. The proportionate ownership interest of a stockholder is evidenced by the number of shares of common stock held.

Table of contents the document which identifies the content of the presentation package and the components of the business plan by name and page location.

Target market the group of potential customers identified by the entrepreneur as having characteristics to which the firm's product/service should appeal and toward which the marketing effort is directed.

Time-series analysis the mathematical tools used to identify the basic trend, cyclical movements, and seasonal patterns in time-series data.

Title page the cover sheet for the business plan.

Unlimited liability with the sole proprietorship and general partnership forms of ownership, the assets of the business as well as the personal assets of the owner(s) are subject to the claims of the firm's creditors.

U.S. Small Business Administration an independent agency of the U.S. Government created by Congress to provide assistance to small businesses.

Venture capitalist typically a high-risk financier who provides equity financing to ventures that promise supernormal growth in sales and profits and a high rate of return on invested capital.

Working capital in finance the term is most often used to refer to those temporary current assets, primarily accounts receivable and inventory, that are expected to turnover or release funds within a short time.

Working-capital financing short-term debt financing used to carry the temporary buildup in working capital.

INDEX